DECOLONISING the human

DECOLONISING the human

Reflections from Africa on difference and oppression

Edited by
MELISSA STEYN AND WILLIAM MPOFU

Published in South Africa by:
Wits University Press
1 Jan Smuts Avenue
Johannesburg 2001

www.witspress.co.za

First published 2021

http://dx.doi.org.10.18772/22021036512

978-1-77614-651-2 (Paperback)
978-1-77614-655-0 (Hardback)
978-1-77614-652-9 (Web PDF)
978-1-77614-653-6 (EPUB)
978-1-77614-654-3 (Mobi)
978-1-77614-678-9 (Open Access PDF)

Project manager: Elaine Williams
Copyeditor: Karen Press
Proofreader: Inga Norenius
Indexer: Rita Sephton
Cover design: Hybrid Creative
Typeset in 10 point Garamond Pro

CONTENTS

ACRONYMS AND ABBREVIATIONS

Aids	acquired immune deficiency syndrome
AMCU	Association of Mineworkers and Construction Union
DEIC	Dutch East India Company
EEIC	English East India Company
EIC	East India Company
HIV	human immunodeficiency virus
IDP	Integrated Development Plan
LGBT	lesbian, gay, bisexual and transgender
LGBTIQ+	lesbian, gay, bisexual, transgender, intersex or questioning
NASA	National Aeronautics and Space Administration
NUM	National Union of Mineworkers
RDP	Reconstruction and Development Programme
TB	tuberculosis
UN	United Nations
US	United States
USA	United States of America

THE TROUBLE WITH THE HUMAN

WILLIAM MPOFU AND MELISSA STEYN

All communities create notions of their place within the array of sentient and non-sentient beings with whom they share their worlds. The principal trouble with the grand construction of *the human* of Euro-modernity, however, is that it was founded on unhappy circumstances and for tragic purposes. *Man*, as a performative idea, created inequalities and hierarchies usable for the exclusion and oppression of the other. The status of the *human* was self-attributed to dominant people powerful enough to name themselves and define others. That which was categorised as non-human became things, reduced to resources, usable and disposable by the unapologetic *humans*. The attribute *human,* in other words, is not self-evident or assured. It can be wielded; given and taken away. The threat of its withdrawal from, or permanent denial to, weaker peoples in peripheralised spaces continues to define life within a climate of fear that makes being human a fragile condition and an uncertain reality (Soyinka 2004). These dispensable others and objects of power are found everywhere as black people, women, the poor and homeless, refugees and foreigners, gay, lesbian, queer and trans people, the old and vulnerable, people living with disabilities and other others.

The prevailing constructs of 'man' and 'human' began with the durable handiwork of (male) European humanists of the fifteenth and sixteenth centuries who needed convenient and powerful tools for classifying themselves and categorising others (Mignolo 2015, 158). The male Westerner, as the Christian and paradigmatic *human*, entered into relationships on grossly unequal terms. Conquerors in the shape of patriarchs, empire builders, merchants and missionaries employed different approaches in disciplining the bodies of the conquered through violence, arresting the appetites and desires of the natives with goods and services, and dominating the minds and hearts of the subjects with gospels and hymns. Conquest was designed to make the conquered docile and obedient, subject to exploitation and ownership.

Mahmood Mamdani (2013) elucidates this political principle as 'define and rule', where power is able to name and by so doing dominate its subjects as inadequate people with deficits and lacks, whose oppression may therefore not be so morally wrong. Power has distributive privilege and enjoys the resources of classifying and categorising the objects and subjects around itself. Human differences, in that scheme of constructions, classifications and hierarchisations, are not expressions of human diversity, but excuses for the oppression and exploitation of the other. Power, without naming itself, is able to name, define, judge and place others as weaker. It enjoys the privilege of presenting itself in salvationist, protective, developmentalist, democratic and humanitarian terms that hide the domination it exercises and the often deadly consequences of this for those who have lost their equality and full membership of the human category.

The paradox of Western modernity, therefore, is that its grand rhetoric which announces freedom, happiness, progress and development has marched hand in hand with the logic of coloniality. The coloniality of Western modernity has participated in the appropriation of natural resources, exploitation of labour, legal control of 'undesirables', imposition of the interests and world view inherent in a capitalist economy, and denial of the full humanity of the disempowered and the impoverished (Mignolo 2015, 164). The condition of the oppressed is not a condition resulting from natural causes. Gendered violence and inequality are not the inevitable consequence of biology. Peripheralised countries are not undeveloped, their people are not powerless and poor; the countries have been underdeveloped, the people impoverished and also disempowered through displacement and dispossession.

The enslavement and colonisation of Africans was based on their removal from the category of the human. Those who were to be enslaved and colonised first had to lose their human equality and be characterised as inferior and incomplete beings. The work of decoloniality in Africa, therefore, becomes a search for completeness through the recovery, restoration and recognition of the equal belonging of black people to the world. Dani Wadada Nabudere

(2011, 1) correctly notes that 'Afrikology' as a philosophy is the search for human wholeness in a world that has been defined by loss of equality and denial of the full humanity of the conquered and oppressed. The fight for liberation as a form of social justice is also a struggle for the recovery of denied and lost humanity. Our book is positioned within this decolonial struggle.

THE PHILOSOPHICAL DILEMMA OF THE HUMAN IN THE GLOBAL SOUTH

'Where and when exactly did the rain begin to beat us?' is a philosophical question that is posed by Chinua Achebe (1989, 43) in his meditation on the African political and social condition. Achebe is one of the African thinkers who have demanded a return to historical sources and political genealogies and provenances in search of the time and place in which Africans lost their equality within the human family. Achebe ponders the 'hopes and impediments' that have defined attempts at understanding between the North and the South, and amongst people positioned differently within intersecting power relations.

Achebe's demand to know what happened to the common humanity of human beings reminds us of the unstable link between the *human* and the *humane*. How some humans use power to monopolise being human and expel others from the human family remains a haunting philosophical dilemma of inhumanity that has a long historical trajectory in the South and in the North. Socrates, a questioning mind, left the fourth century BCE with the haunting question of why everyone on earth seemed to believe in humanity 'but not in the existence of humans' (Plato 2010, 24). He was perplexed by the fact that everywhere, from religious pulpits to political podiums, beautiful things were being said about the love of humanity, and yet the majority of human beings were being oppressed everywhere. Multitudes were being thingified right in the centre of Athens, the city state celebrated as the cradle of reason and democracy, much as coloniality was born and bred right at the centre of what has been celebrated as liberty and progress.

In the same vein as Achebe (1989) pondering the beginnings of the dehumanisation of Africans, Jean-Jacques Rousseau ([1755] 2004, 1) in the eighteenth century agonised over the 'origins of inequality' among human beings, to the extent that he wished humans could have remained at the level of animals that show respect for life and mercy for the weak among themselves. Yearning for the ways of the animal kingdom was Rousseau's way of condemning the evil done by humans to other humans. To compare the human to the animal, and to favour the animal, becomes an expression of the deepest philosophical indictment of the evil perpetrated by humans. Human success in the arts and the sciences, Rousseau opined, only served to conceal the truth that humans were worse than beasts in their cruel and evil practices.

Friedrich Nietzsche ([1906] 1968, 1) called 'the will to power' an insatiable and unreasonable appetite for profit, power and domination. Oppression begins with an appetite and a passion. What allows war to be celebrated as necessary and natural (Machiavelli [1532] 2009) is the desire to, by any means necessary, conquer and dominate the other. The era of the Enlightenment itself, storied as the death of God and the birth of reason that would liberate humans and brighten the world with progress, became an era of the false promise. Steve Martinot (2011), for instance, notes that the epoch of the same Enlightenment that set alight development and advancement in the West darkened the South with human suffering, disasters and pain. The year in which the conquest of the Americas was consolidated, 1492, when modernity is supposed to have begun to infiltrate the Global South, when the idea of the nation state was born, is the year that Enrique Dussel (1996, 1) describes as the beginning of 'the invention' and also 'eclipse' of the 'inferior' other by the conquering and 'superior' big Other on the planet. The conquered peoples of the New World were judged to have no souls and no religion, and they therefore became legitimate subjects of conquest, domination, enslavement and expulsion from their lands, from the world and from life itself. God and religion became political capital, a resource that was used to include some and exclude others from the human family. People were divided into the categories of the godly and the godless, and thus were they separated, and the weaker amongst them condemned.

The always already gendered (Kitch 2009; Oyěwùmí 1997; Trinh 1989) classification of human beings according to race began, and was spread as an accompaniment of modernity and coloniality to the regions of Latin America, Asia and Africa (Quijano 2000). From slavery in the Americas through colonialism in Africa to apartheid in South Africa, 'race' was used in political systems where darker-skinned people across the globe found themselves dehumanised (Magubane 2007). Defiantly defending 'the souls of black folk' in reaction to the gravity of the removal of black slaves from the human family on American plantations, and the enduring domination and marginalisation of African Americans, W.E.B. Du Bois ([1859] 1969, xi) identified 'the problem of the Twentieth Century' as 'the problem of the colour line', where humanity was tragically torn asunder between the black- and the white-skinned peoples. Some philosophers have noted that the 'social contract' governing and organising the present world system is in fact a 'racial contract' (Mills 1997, 1–3). According to Charles Mills, white supremacy is 'the unnamed political system that has made the modern world what it is today', where 'racism is itself a political system, a particular power structure of informal or formal rule, socioeconomic privilege, and norms for the differential distribution of material wealth and opportunities, benefits and burdens, rights and duties' (1997, 3). In other words, racism is the powerful but largely concealed governing system and logic of the present Euro-North American world system. Racist maps, borders, fences and boundaries that were constructed in the course of conquest still exist physically and metaphysically, governing imaginaries and political practices. Upsurges of xenophobia and attacks on refugees, immigrants, women and lesbian, gay, bisexual, transgender, intersex or questioning (LGBTIQ+) people are connected to colonial demarcations of who is human and who is not. The contract that governs the world is not the social contract of the bond, implicit in the all-encompassing expression 'we the people', that is imagined to have moved humans from their state of nature to become members of civil society and subjects of modern government. It is, instead, the bond of the humans who count and matter, the humans of consequence: 'we the white people', in Mills's telling observation (1997, 30).

Sufferings and calamities that humans have encountered in the world have not come along expected and linear paths. The religious and racially defined human inequalities that eventually became political and economic inequalities led to a worldwide human struggle for power and domination. What Hannah Arendt (1968) called 'the origins of totalitarianism' privileged domination and hegemony in absolutist terms. Violent and absolutist forms of power and the appetite for domination produced both the Nazism that led to the Holocaust – the mass persecution and slaughter of Jews and others in Hitler's Germany – and the Zionism that has seen Israel develop policies of apartheid enacted against Palestinians. The victims of anti-Semitism and the Holocaust, within a few decades of the formation of the State of Israel in

1948, had morphed into the oppressors and managers of the debility (Puar 2017) of the Arabs and Muslims in Palestine, in a historical and political paradox that Mamdani (2001) has described as the scenario in which victims of power and domination systematically become oppressors and killers of others. There are, it seems, no permanent oppressors and permanent oppressed. Frantz Fanon (1963) noted how the ambition of the oppressed, the colonised and dominated may become the spirited drive to be an oppressor and a coloniser. Liberation movements of the Global South, after the decolonisation of their countries, became the new colonisers and oppressors of the people. The difference between a Robert Mugabe in Zimbabwe and an Ian Smith in Rhodesia became a difference of skin colour only, because of the way in which the supposed liberator reproduced the uses of power of the coloniser. At its most successful and powerful, coloniality, as an assault on the human, reproduces itself through the victims and turns them into its practitioners, defenders and multipliers.

The crooked, unstable and uncertain line of persecution of the human can be concealed even under the many representations and discourses of decolonisation, the struggle for human rights and liberation. Much in the same ways that slavery, colonialism, apartheid and imperialism came enveloped in promises of civilisation, modernisation, development and democratisation, forms of human domination, violence and oppression may be dressed in the languages of human rights, decolonisation and liberation. The very vocabularies and grammars of the fight for human rights may conceal assaults and negations of human rights. Those that have claimed God and championship of the human have betrayed humanity to the extent that Carl Schmitt (1996, 3), himself a Nazi ideologue, could warn that 'whoever speaks for the human wants to cheat', by using a grand narrative and ideal to conceal criminal tendencies such as the love of power and tyranny. Many years after Schmitt wrote in 1932, the observation can be made that inside the very institutions and organisations that claim to represent the human and human rights, human beings are negated and violated. In spite of the bold Universal Declaration of Human Rights in 1948 (UN 1948), the human itself has not been universalised, and rights and freedoms have not been equally distributed. The historical paradox is that this declaration took place at a time when the rights of the colonised and of those who were to live under apartheid in Africa were still being trampled upon by these same champions of the rights of Man. This has compelled Walter Mignolo (2009, 7) to ask the question 'who speaks for the human in human rights?' Speaking from what is often constructed as the world's most mature democracy, the USA, Donald Trump frequently scares the world with expressions of bigotry towards and hate for those who have been produced as foreigners, refugees, migrants and blacks from Africa, a continent of countries that he has referred to as 'shitholes'. The metaphor of shit signifies how the weakened are easily made abject, contemptible, waste matter.

White supremacism and heteropatriachy have contributed to a scramble for belonging to the human race that has excluded people on more grounds of difference than skin colour alone. Giorgio Agamben (2005, 26) describes a powerful 'anthropological machine' by means of which those in powerful and dominant social and political positions process, give and take humanness from others. It is a hierarchising social technology that distributes humanness by classifying and declassifying people according to markers such as race, culture, sexuality, religion, age, ability of body and even geographic location and origins. In her concept of the 'Kyriarchy', Elisabeth Schüssler Fiorenza (2001) has helpfully coined a word for the interacting, interlocking systems of domination and subordination that inform the modern world. As a pyramidal system, the Kyriarchy includes not only sexism, racism and heteronormativity, but also, among other things, militarism and anthropocentrism. The vaunted human has endangered the climate and sparked an ecological crisis that threatens the very existence of the human species, the animal kingdom, plant life, water and air. The trouble of the human is therefore not only an internal human 'family' matter, but also an external ecological crisis that has disturbed and provoked nature, making the world a dangerous place for the human and for other life forms.

THE HUMAN AND WAR IN THE MODERN WORLD

Threats and implementation of violence are principal factors in disciplining humans and human subjectivities into dominant and oppressed groups. In the present world order, war and violence have given time and place their identity. At the end of the twentieth century, Mamdani (2004, 3) could argue that 'we have just ended a century of violence, one possibly more violent than any other in recorded history' for its 'civil wars, revolutions and counter-revolutions'. Staggering violence should not surprise us in a modernity where 'violence has become the midwife of history' (Mamdani 2004, 3). Perhaps the normalisation of violence in the modern colonial world has not found a more perfect expression than in the representation of war as a natural accompaniment of the human condition. For instance, it was with the force of argument and refined erudition that Nietzsche preached of war as part of life in the modern world: 'Life is a consequence of war, society itself a means to war' ([1906] 1968, 33).

For Nietzsche, and an entire tradition of other philosophers and influential thinkers, peace was something to be dismissed as decadence, and a disturbance of the normal and natural state of war. For a philosopher who boasted of his rare intelligence, it was a canonical observation of the epoch to note that humanity 'should love peace as a means to new wars – and the short peace more than the long' (Nietzsche [1885] 1969, 74–75). Nietzsche's celebrations of war could be dismissed as the musings of a bored philosopher ranting from his closet and meaning no harm to the world, if such leaders of the world as former US President George Bush had not waged wars in Nietzschean ways. Wars have given meaning to nihilism and relevance to brute force, in that claims of democracy and freedom have been accompanied by new wars and productions of unfreedom. More recently Azar Gat (2008, xi) has stated that '[with] war being connected to everything else and everything else being connected to war, explaining war and tracing its development in relation to human development in general almost amount to a theory and history of everything'.

War, in spite of its punishments and costs to humans, has become accepted as part of the very identity of life. For the Global North, the political power of states and their economic prosperity, the wealth of nations, has been connected to wars and genocides of conquest that led to the exploitation of slave labour and the extraction of resources from the colonies in the Global South. Fanon (1963) and Eric Williams (1964) differently but with equal force describe how the power and opulence of the West was founded on the proceeds of slave-based, imperial and colonial crimes against the humanity of Latin Americans, Asians and Africans. In this sense, 'to understand war is thus to understand ourselves' (Gelven 1994, 8). Writing as a Westerner, Daniel Hallin (2008) could say 'you have to understand war in order to understand our culture'. A hegemonic culture of war (Maldonado-Torres 2008) pervades world political thinking amongst the ruling regimes of powerful nations, failing and failed states, and so-called terrorist and dissident organisations. Albert Camus (1953, 1) understood the war and violence of the present world as that which has been not only naturalised and normalised, but philosophised and decorated. As far as war is concerned, Camus notes that criminals have been elevated to the position of judges. Powerful states that claim to be peacemakers of the world occupy the front seat in propelling wars. For leaders of superpowers who declare war on their enemies and those of dissident organisations that valorise violence and war, war is no longer 'unique like a cry; now it is universal like science, yesterday it was put on trial, today it is the law' (Camus 1953, 1). The powerful use their power to give permission and respectability to violence.

Based on a reading of the human as 'Economic Man', economics, a privileged social science whose claim is that it has the duty to calculate, measure and help in the creation of wealth and happiness, has also been weaponised. World economics, through such international financial organisations as the World Bank and the International Monetary Fund, has itself not just failed to escape but has participated in causing and promoting violence and wars. In the same way that the genocides of conquest and their fruits of slavery, colonialism, imperialism and apartheid had both hidden and overt economic objectives of dispossessing and displacing the other, and of exploiting labour and other resources, world economics from Adam Smith to the present has been implicated in violence and war. Yash Tandon (2015) describes the present systems of world economics, trade and accounting as the 'West's war' against the rest in the way asymmetrical power and economic relations are sustained and promoted, poverty is globalised and the poor are kept fixed in their poverty. Capitalist economics ensures the production of poverty and misery as much as it guarantees the wealth of a minority of states, and of global corporations that have become richer and more powerful than some countries of the Global South.

In political and economic relations with 'the rest', the West has presented its political power and economic leadership as violent, warlike impositions and forms of domination. Refusal and resistance are met with cruel punishments. In observing this, Ramón Grosfoguel (2007, 217) notes that as the Global South we have received '[no] respect and no recognition for Indigenous, African, Islamic or other non-European forms of democracy. The liberal form of democracy is the only one accepted and legitimated. Forms of democratic alterity are rejected.'

On pain of war the Euro-American Empire has forced itself upon the world. For the reason that the paradigm of clashes and war rules the world in theory and in practice, Samuel Huntington (1996) advances a political proposal to the USA, disguised as an intellectual observation, that civilisations of the world, mainly the Islamic and the Western ones, are inevitably headed for a 'clash of civilisations': a cultural, political and military war that the USA and the West at large must win. Huntington does not condemn or discourage war, but uses his powerful position as a trusted political advisor to the world's most powerful and warlike nation to implicitly encourage it. Achille Mbembe (2001, 25) is correct in his argument that conquest, with its enforced rules and regulations, founds itself, legitimates itself and eventually maintains itself through physical and symbolic rituals and ceremonies of violence that remain fixed in the imaginary of the conquered, who are domesticated through fear and guilt. The brutality of the event of conquest, and the actions that accompany domination, remain silently but forcefully lodged, like any other trauma, in the psyche of the conquered, creating a 'past that is not past' (Sharpe 2016, 23).

What has effectively been put paid to is Francis Fukuyama's optimistic but violently Euro-North American-centric prediction of the end of history and the total victory of neoliberal democracy and capitalism in the world, where the 'end of history' would mean the end of wars and bloody revolutions. In Fukuyama's thesis, given their agreement on goals and intentions men would no longer have any large causes for which to fight in the neoliberal paradise. They would satisfy their needs through economic activity, and would no longer have to risk their lives in battle (Fukuyama 1992, 311). Contra-Fukuyama, the West's own wars of invasion of such countries as Iraq in 2003, Libya in 2011, the present stalemate in Syria, and such events as the attacks of 9/11 on New York and Washington DC and other so-called terrorist attacks in different parts of the world, have created conditions in which human beings, especially the poor and the weak, endure rather than enjoy life. In sum, modern politics has indeed been corrupted by a 'fetishism of power' (Dussel 2008, 3) that is violently opposed to the 'will to live' (2008, 13) espoused by the decolonial philosophy of liberation, which holds power to be peace and liberation itself.

VIOLENCE AND KNOWING THE HUMAN

Huntington and Fukuyama are two spokespersons of empire, that is, of the present world system led by the Euro-North American regime: one celebrating illusory peace based on the neoliberal triumphalism of the West, and the other implicitly advocating for a war of civilisations based on the rapacious expansionism of empire. The two also exemplify the uses and abuses of knowledge in defence of the violence that has become an organising idea of the present world system. In the world academy that includes the Westernised university in Africa and Asia, privileged academics and intellectuals use their professorial and expert authority to defend and promote empire. It is in that, and other ways, that empire has co-opted, usurped and colonised knowledge and the academy.

Knowledge, in the shape of science and philosophy, has been constructed and mobilised to lend respectability, acceptability and normality to war, social inequalities and dehumanisation of the lesser other. The colonisation of the Global South and the enslavement of black people were scientifically planned and defended. Celebrated Western rationality and enlightenment became complicit in the irrational and dark oppression of black people, whose humanity was carefully doubted and opportunistically dismissed. It was with some of the finest scientific and philosophical erudition that Carl von Clausewitz published a treatise in 1812 on 'principles of war' that characterised violence and war as midwives of history, as the other form of politics that should be the rule rather than the exception (Von Clausewitz [1812] 1942). It was, too, with some political and intellectual triumphalism that, on the eve of American independence in 1776, Adam Smith presented his thesis holding that through the exploitation of the labour of the defeated, the wealth of nations would be created (Smith [1776] 2001). The wealth and prosperity of nations that Smith described were to be based on the colonisation and enslavement of others.

Biological sciences were deployed in overdrive in attempts to provide a scientific justification for the perceived inferiority and animal nature of black people (Magubane 2007). Trusted scientists of empire such as Charles Darwin ([1859] 2011), who investigated the 'origin of species', had their works used to deduce that some human beings were naturally unfit, and therefore less human, in a world whose logic of life was the survival of the fittest. Theology, too, was mobilised to project the enslaved and the colonised as people without souls who must be grateful to their conquerors for bringing them closer to God. Science and religion were married, and deployed together in separating human beings into those who were normatively human and those who were expelled from the privileged human family.

The production of knowledge that circulated ideas about the lesser humanity of the colonised and enslaved was accompanied by epistemicides, the systematic destruction of the sciences, philosophies and histories of the conquered (Grosfoguel 2013). That the colonised and the enslaved were humans who had sciences, religions and histories of their own was a truth that empire could not and cannot live with. It is for this reason that Boaventura De Sousa Santos (2014), in his forceful philosophical plea for 'justice against epistemicide' in the world, advances an argument that the Western understanding of life, the human and the world is not the only understanding. Santos pleads for the fight for social justice in the world to be necessarily accompanied by the struggle for 'cognitive justice' (Santos 2014: 42). One may add hermeneutic justice, such that other interpretations of the human, life and the world besides the Western one can also be taken seriously. The first freedom, in the observation of Sabelo Ndlovu-Gatsheni (2018), is epistemic freedom, which is the freedom of people to think and to know who they are and where they are, without fear and encumbrance of the Eurocentric standard. Without the guilt of being second-comers or even visitors to thought and knowledge, he argues, marginal peoples should dare to invent and recover life and the world from the abyss of hegemonic constructions.

The question 'can non-Europeans think?' is asked satirically by Iranian scholar Hamid Dabashi (2015). The question is asked because of the prevalent assumption in Western thought that non-Europeans are naturally not gifted with thought and rationality. In effectively and violently imposing its model of power, the Euro-North American empire became a pretender to universalism, and used force and persuasion to make its culture a world culture (Mazrui 2001). In the attempt to homogenise global culture and to hegemonise its power and control of the world, the patriarchal West crushed human diversity and narrowed the world according to its imaginary.

Enslaved and colonised peoples have been rendered through a distorted mirror, forcing them to see and understand themselves in a way that gives their conquest and domination some sense, if not justification: 'In this way, we continue being what we are not. And as a result we can never identify our true problems, much less resolve them, except in a partial and distorted way' (Quijano 2000, 556). The victims of empire are given a false and distorted sense of themselves and their condition. The experiences of coloniality and domination are mirrored and reflected in falsified and misleading terms that favour the coloniser. The reflected image 'occupies an important place in dialectics exalting the coloniser and humbling the colonised. Further it is economically fruitful' (Memmi 1974, 123). This is government through stereotyping. Images of the oppressed are produced that justify their oppression and present it as salvation. In more and more emphatic ways, the oppressed are given understandings of themselves as deserving of their dehumanisation. Du Bois ([1859] 1969) captured well the way in which the oppressed are refused their positionality as people who have a problem, and are fraudulently treated as people who are a problem. Oppression and domination are presented as a consequence, rather than a cause, of the dehumanisation of the marginalised and inferiorised other.

Critical humanists, among them decolonial thinkers, critical diversity scholars and activists of both the Global South and the Global North in search of the liberation of the human from coloniality, are increasingly unmasking and resisting the coloniality of knowledge that stereotypes and simplifies the oppressed. Achebe (1989, 40), as noted above, is one of the African novelists who have written in critical ways that lament how African thinkers and writers have reproduced coloniality by looking, thinking and writing on Africa and African peoples in frames and terms that are defined in the Eurocentric paradigm of knowledge. Achebe exhorts African thinkers and writers, including himself, to resist the Eurocentric colonial sensibility. In other words, the march of the coloniality of power and the coloniality of knowledge in the Global South should not, Achebe argues, go unchallenged. The project of critical diversity literacy (Steyn 2015), specifically, and decoloniality more generally, should not only be to unmask and describe the coloniality of power and the coloniality of knowledge, but also to cultivate among the oppressed and dominated a critical consciousness and resistance to colonial ways of understanding the human and its condition. Power, and the multiple privileges that it produces and protects, should, in intellectual and social justice terms, be rendered vulnerable and open. To Dabashi's satirical question 'can non-Europeans think?' Mignolo (2015) replies, 'yes we can!', insisting that non-Europeans and all other inferiorised, marginalised and oppressed peoples of the world can think and produce knowledge, among the full range of human attributes. That there is no one model of the human, and that others, all marginalised people, are humans too, and have the capacity to know, is a truth to be defended. Coloniality of knowledge must be met with decoloniality of thinking and knowing. Being human, rational and knowledgeable should be liberated from being hostage to the Eurocentric world view, and established as a quality of all people, with all our differences. One of the baptismal statements of the decolonial moment is that all people are produced by, and come from, legitimate histories and knowledges.

BEING HUMAN IN THE MODERN COLONIAL WORLD ORDER

The modern world that Jean-Paul Sartre encounters and describes phenomenologically (Sartre ([1943] 2003) is a world where the powerful and the privileged have 'being', and the powerless and oppressed have 'nothingness' and emptiness. For the racialised former slaves in the Americas, blacks in apartheid and post-apartheid South Africa, and the poor at large, the combination of the coloniality of power and the coloniality of knowledge produced in them senses of deficit and inadequacy as human beings. The lack of the wholeness that Fanon describes (Fanon 2008, 3) refers to the emptiness that is created in the oppressed by dehumanising oppression and exploitation such as they encountered in the experience of slavery and its aftermaths. The oppressed develop a 'double consciousness' (Du Bois [1859] 1969, 45) whereby they judge themselves by the standards of their oppressors. Those whose full humanity has been doubted may develop self-doubt and self-hate. A veil of invisibility masks the oppressed by silencing and erasing their human agency, rendering their lives, as Judith Butler (2009, xix) argues, 'ungrievable', disposable and dispensable.

The formal end of slavery, colonialism and apartheid in South Africa, however, did not evaporate coloniality: its oppressions and exploitations remain stubbornly durable and haunting to its victims. Power and privilege are at their most forceful when they are concealed and invisible. It is in its invisibility and its power that Nelson Maldonado-Torres (2008) notes coloniality to be a metaphysical catastrophe that overwhelms former slaves and the former colonised of the Global South. Oppression, in the arguments of Maldonado-Torres and Dussel (1985), is a kind of war upon the being of all the dominated and oppressed. What Maldonado-Torres (2007) defines as the coloniality of being refers to the forms of slavish and colonial power relations that remain and are reproduced even after administrative slavery and juridical colonialism have been abolished. Slavery and colonisation in their full application became systems that gave birth to other, more toxic forms of power relations and orders of the distribution of privilege and division of labour. Aimé Césaire (1972) describes colonisation as an all-enveloping system that left no relations unaffected and uninfected by its violence. For that reason, in talking about the colonised and former colonised, Césaire is talking about metaphysically compromised communities and beings. Colonialism, as he describes it, did not end with the physical dispossession and displacement of the colonised but extended into psychological, sociological and theological punishment of all its victims, who were left emptied of all the content of being. Such victims became so enmeshed in coloniality itself that they began to reproduce and magnify it in a multiplicity of ways, including becoming oppressors in their own right. Once the oppressed assimilate oppressor consciousness, Paulo Freire (1993) argues, they begin to be accessories and functionaries of oppression, which they begin to imagine as normal and natural; they begin to fear the prospects of freedom and resist their own liberation.

Struggles for liberation from oppression and for rehumanisation of the dehumanised, therefore, have to reckon with the resistance that comes even from among the oppressed, who would have navigated and negotiated oppressive positions of their own within the system of domination and do not imagine a world outside forms of dominance and oppression. Oppression is in its fullest flight when the oppressed seek out their own pockets of privilege within the system of dominance, and cannot imagine inclusive liberation. The human, as an idea and an experience in the world, has become so troubled within the contestations that pit power against justice, that the storied debate between Noam Chomsky and Michael Foucault in 1972 (Elders 1974) dwelt on whether there are any qualities and values any more that can be called properties of the human, in a world where humans themselves seem so passionately invested in the negation of liberation and of the human. In the paradigm of war, of nihilist political and economic competition, the human is assailed by forms of physical and metaphysical violence that have rendered being itself scarce and to be distributed in troublingly asymmetrical terms.

In complex and interlocking ways, these constructions and reconstructions have taken being human away from some and given others the monopoly of it. Maldonado-Torres (2007, 245) notes that at play is an 'imperial attitude' that he calls 'racist/imperial Manichean misanthropic scepticism'. Conquered and marginalised people become dehumanised through the characterisation and definition of certain deficits and lacks. Those whose histories and languages are denied importance and remain native and indigenous are, as of old, peripheralised as uncivilised rustics, bereft of reason and rationality. In such circumstances the task of liberation becomes an intellectual and political project of rehumanising the dehumanised. For Fanon (1963, 251), 'Europe undertook the leadership of the world with ardour, cynicism and violence' of power and knowledge that left the weak and dominated of the world 'wretched' and 'damned', in spite of the talk about man and humanity that European philosophy professes. A new model of the human is wanted. Fanon's decolonial resolution is not a simple one, but rather a proposition for creating another world in the same world where Europe made itself hegemonic and turned its values into common sense. Fanon proposes a radical departure from the Eurocentric paradigm of the human that loudly celebrated the human and human rights, but participated in genocides of conquest, enslavement and colonisation which killed human beings in their millions.

Power loses its legitimacy by indulging in the privilege of dehumanising the powerless. Oppression dehumanises both the oppressor and the oppressed, and one cannot ignore or suspend the humanity of the other without compromising one's own (Freire 1993). A need has arisen for humanity to depart from the European and Western colonial example of power and knowledge, to champion other human directions in pursuit of liberated futures. Liberation from oppression, therefore, demands the rehumanisation of both the oppressor and the oppressed.

ORGANISATION OF THE BOOK

This volume begins with the present chapter that demonstrates how, through social and political constructions, some human beings were disqualified and removed from the human family. Power and the privilege that accompanies it have worked to instrumentalise knowledge, including the scientific and the theological, to construct and produce the oppressed and the exploited. Their struggles for social justice and liberation start with defending their basic belonging to the human family. Life is experienced daily as a social and political war waged upon those who have lost their human equality. This chapter unfolds the canvas of a multivocal conversation that will take place in this book, one that is troubled by imaginations and constructions of the other while seeking to trouble dominant and hegemonic inventions of this oppressed and exploited other. William Mpofu and Melissa Steyn, in this chapter, provide a vocabulary, critical accent and tone that initiate an engaged exploration of the human in a dehumanising world.

In chapter two, Sabelo Ndlovu-Gatsheni and Patricia Pinky Ndlovu treat the issue of 'blackness' – which, just like that of 'whiteness', is a sociogenic question – as that which emerges from the invented modern Euro-North American-centric world system and its ever shifting global orders. This examination of blackness at a world scale makes possible the revelation of how blackness was constructed as the social, ideological and political inferiorisation and infantilisation of enslaved and colonised Africans. The authors use Maldonado-Torres's (2007) concept of the coloniality of being to unmask the dismemberment of the human at a world scale, and to gesture towards decolonial technologies of rehumanisation and re-membering as forms of liberation. In as much as blackness and whiteness are constructions of the modern colonial world system, this chapter argues for a decolonial re-membering and reconstruction of the human at a world scale, and suggests that decoloniality, as a deconstruction of the toxic constructions of coloniality, is a move towards human liberation.

Writing from a critical perspective that is sensitive to human bodies that have been disqualified from the human family because of their sexual orientation, and indeed their non-gender conformity, Olayinka Akanle, Gbenga S. Adejare and Jojolola Fasuyi ask the troubling question, 'to what extent are we all humans?' in chapter three. The case study of the chapter is Nigeria, where through expressions of hatred and violence, backed by state power and machinery, some human beings are discriminated against and persecuted, and thus expelled from the category of the human because of their sexual orientation. The ways in which the dehumanising structure of systematic heteronormativity in the Nigerian setting uses the cover of religion, law and morality to minimise the humanity of those that do not conform to its dictates are highlighted. Same-sex intimate relationships in Nigeria and in many other countries are banned by law, and penalties that range from social ostracisation to imprisonment are levied against offenders. Like the blackness examined in chapter two, homosexuality is used to exclude, marginalise and dehumanise the other, who is rendered punishable and dispensable. This chapter highlights exactly how social and mental constructions such as gender are weaponised against the human, especially against those people who have been constructed and produced as inferior, in the world.

In chapter four, Sibonokuhle Ndlovu delves into the important, but often neglected, question of how disability is socially constructed, and with critical insight illuminates how it can be deconstructed. This chapter forcefully insists on the humanity of people who live with disabilities in a world that erects prejudices and hatred against them, and uses bodily functions to deny dignity and human recognition to the differently abled. Normalcy itself is a construction and confabulation, used by those whom it empowers and privileges to suppress and exclude their others from mainstream and dignified life. This chapter contributes to the growing number of scholarly and critical voices that seek to dismantle hierarchies of ableism and to recover the denied humanity of people living with disabilities of the body and the mind. In its intellectually rigorous critical approach, the chapter contributes to a social justice vision for the recovery of the lost common humanity of all human beings.

Cary Burnett, in chapter five, engages with ageism as an othering tool. She artistically and critically explores the important question of what it means to be old, female, alone and out of step with the technological world around one. Using the narrative of her screenplay, *When Granny Went on the Internet,* Burnett seeks to creatively subvert hegemonic and normative expectations around age and the different phases of life in the world of rapidly changing knowledge and technology. The chapter critically recovers life stages as aspects of being human, and restores ageing as part of the normal journey of life. This chapter is novel not only in the way it weaves the analytical and the artistic together, but also in how it restores the long time people spend on earth to the sphere of opportunities for liberation.

Arguing from the point of view of black mineworkers in post-apartheid South Africa, in chapter six Robert Maseko examines how conditions of poverty and the endurance of racism beyond decolonisation infantilise these workers, who retain the status of 'minors' in spite of their experience and maturity, and the hard and exploitative labour they perform. Black mineworkers still bear a bleeding colonial wound, long after administrative colonialism and apartheid have been abolished in South Africa. Using a case study of the South African Platinum Belt, Maseko exposes the existential experiences of black South African labourers who continue to live out apartheid-era relations and conditions well after the political independence of the country was achieved, and well into what is supposed to be a democratic era. Through his study, Maseko demonstrates that democratic dispensations in Africa seem to have failed to evaporate the durable realities of coloniality.

In chapter seven, Tendayi Sithole addresses the gendered nature of exploitation, using the experiences detailed in a slave narrative. At stake here is the politics of the slave, the figure who is denied any form of being. The life and death of Aunt Hester, Frederick Douglass's aunt immortalised in his *Narrative of the Life of Frederick Douglass* ([1845] 1995), is dependent on the will of her master, Captain Anthony, who is human, after all, and has the prerogative to lord it over her existence because she is the slave, his possession, his property, his thing – that is, nothing human. In many ways, in its form and its content, this chapter performs the violence suffered by the dehumanised in a world where being human is not guaranteed.

Much like human cultures, customs and traditions at large, human languages do not walk on their own legs, separate from the human bodies that bear them. Brian Sibanda, in chapter eight, argues the case for language understood as part of being human. Using the literature of Ngũgĩ wa Thiong'o (1981), Sibanda presents a critical vindication of language as being, and as a central part of the human. The political activism of Wa Thiong'o, who in protest against the cultural imperialism of the English language resorted to writing in his Gikuyu mother tongue, is understood to be a gesture towards the recovery and restoration of pride and dignity in being a human being. Like Morgan Ndlovu in chapter eleven, Sibanda contributes to and expands the thinking on the decolonisation of knowledge and decolonisation of being. The linguicides (killing of languages) and linguifams (famines of language) that colonialism perpetrated in Africa are not all that removed from the genocides of conquest that systematically and en masse eliminated the bodies of the natives. Decolonisation of language is presented as another principal way of restoring being to the human, in Africa and elsewhere.

Nokuthula Hlabangane, in chapter nine, contributes to the exploding of the myth of the superiority, objectivity and neutrality of Western science.

The pretence of universality and rationality in Western knowledge and knowledge-making are not removed from the rhetoric of civilisation and modernisation that accompanied the enslaving and colonial missions in the Global South. In a powerful argument, Hlabangane, like many decolonial thinkers, insists on the provincialism and situatedness of Western thought. The gesture of this chapter is towards a decolonial delinking from Western thought for purposes of re-linking with it as one aspect of the thought that human beings have produced in the world, and not as the totality of world knowledge.

Paradoxically, some non-human entities such as commercial companies are increasingly being humanised and given personhood. In a modern capitalist world order corporations and non-human business entities have achieved the status of legal persons and corporate citizens. C.D. Samaradiwakera-Wijesundara contributes, in chapter ten, to a reassessment of the personhood of the juristic person in relation to 'other' people. Without either physical body or soul, the company in the modern world has hegemonically achieved a life and a kind of personhood of its own that frequently eclipses that of humans as we know them. This chapter explores the history and relationship of the company as a juristic person in a world where humanity and humanness are contested and cannot be taken for granted. The intersection of the power of money and that of law and politics in distributing humanness is a subject of interest in this important chapter.

Morgan Ndlovu, in chapter eleven, deploys a decolonial perspective to unmask the usurpation of traditional knowledges through the exoticisation and commercialisation of cultural villages. Ndlovu shows how the business of cultural tourism naturally depends on the idea of cultural differences, and how, in the non-Western world, it also serves as a ritual of denialism of the idea of co-humanness. In the tourism business of cultural villages, Ndlovu finds that the humanness and cultural being of poor, indigenous peoples are suppressed, and cultural differences manipulated, for purposes of profit by global corporations, in a form of theft and exploitation of indigenous knowledges that pits the powerful against the powerless. This chapter expands our understanding of coloniality of knowledge and coloniality of being, and contributes to the unmasking of invisible structures of power and privilege.

Fittingly, this volume concludes with a critical search for a decolonial humanism and a diversal global dialogue. In chapter twelve, Siphamandla

Zondi provides a critique of the ways in which humanity has been fragmented, and human communication reduced to a monologue in which power talks down to the powerless. The chapter philosophically bemoans the classification of human beings according to race that has impeded symmetrical dialogue between peoples with different access to power and privilege, in a world where human difference has been criminalised. The chapter is a critical plea for the decolonisation of being and restoration of communication, as a means of political and cultural translation aimed at achieving human understanding in human difference.

REFERENCES

Achebe, Chinua. 1989. *Hopes and Impediments: Selected Essays*. New York, NY: Anchor Books.

Agamben, Giorgio. 2005. *State of Exception*. Translated by Kevin Attell. London: University of Chicago Press.

Arendt, Hannah. 1968. *Imperialism: Part Two of The Origins of Totalitarianism*. London: Harvest Books.

Butler, Judith. 2009. *Frames of War: When is Life Grievable?* London: Verso.

Camus, Albert. 1953. *The Fastidious Assassins*. London: Penguin Books.

Césaire, Aimé. 1972. *Discourse on Colonialism*. Translated by Joan Pinkham. New York, NY: Monthly Review Press.

Dabashi, Hamid. 2015. *Can Non-Europeans Think?* London: Zed Books.

Darwin, Charles. [1859] 2011. *On the Origin of Species*. London: Collins Classics.

Douglass, Frederick. [1845] 1995. *Narrative of the Life of Frederick Douglass*. Mineola, NY: Dover Press.

Du Bois, W.E.B. [William Edward Burghardt]. [1859] 1969. *The Souls of Black Folk*. London: Penguin Books.

Dussel, Enrique. 1985. *Philosophy of Liberation*. Translated by Aquilina Martinez and Christine Morkovsky. New York, NY: Orbis Books.

Dussel, Enrique. 1996. *The Invention of the Americas: Eclipse of 'the Other' and the Myth of Modernity*. Translated by Michael D. Barber. New York, NY: Continuum.

Dussel, Enrique. 2008. *Twenty Theses on Politics*. Translated by George Ciccariello-Maher. Durham, NC: Duke University Press.

Elders, Fons, ed. 1974. *Human Nature: Justice versus Power*. London: Souvenir Press.

Fanon, Frantz. 1963. *The Wretched of the Earth*. Translated by Constance Farrington. New York, NY: Grove Press.

Fanon, Frantz. 2008. *Black Skin, White Masks*. Translated by Charles Lam Markmann. London: Pluto Press.

Freire, Paulo. 1993. *Pedagogy of the Oppressed*. Translated by Myra Bergman Ramos. London: Penguin Books.

Fukuyama, Francis. 1992. *The End of History and the Last Man*. London: Penguin Books.

Gat, Azar. 2008. *War in Human Civilisation*. Oxford: Oxford University Press.

Gelven, Michael. 1994. *War and Existence: A Philosophical Inquiry*. University Park, PA: Pennsylvania State University Press.

Grosfoguel, Ramón. 2007. 'The Epistemic Decolonial Turn: Beyond Political-Economy Paradigms'. *Cultural Studies* 21(2–3): 211–23.

Grosfoguel, Ramón. 2013. 'The Structure of Knowledge in Westernized Universities: Epistemic Racism/Sexism and the Four Genocides/Epistemicides of the Long 16th Century'. *Human Architecture: Journal of the Sociology of Self-Knowledge* 11(1): 73–90.

Hallin, Daniel C. 2008. 'You Have to Understand War to Understand our Culture'. Accessed 12 October 2019. vox publica: http://voxpublicano/2008/01.

Huntington, Samuel P. 1996. *The Clash of Civilisations and the Remaking of the World*. New York, NY: Simon and Schuster.

Kitch, Sally L. 2009. *The Spectre of Sex: Gendered Foundations of Racial Formation in the United States*. Albany, NY: State University of New York Press.

Machiavelli, Niccolò. [1532] 2009. *The Prince*. Translated by J.G. Nichols. London: Oneworld Classics.

Magubane, Bernard. 2007. *Race and the Construction of the Dispensable Other*. Pretoria: Unisa Press.

Maldonado-Torres, Nelson. 2007. 'On the Coloniality of Being: Contributions to the Development of a Concept'. *Cultural Studies* 21(2–3): 240–70.

Maldonado-Torres, Nelson. 2008. *Against War: Views from the Underside of Modernity*. Durham, NC: Duke University Press.

Mamdani, Mahmood. 2001. *When Victims Become Killers: Colonialism, Nativism and the Genocide in Rwanda*. Princeton, NJ: Princeton University Press.

Mamdani, Mahmood. 2004. *Good Muslim and Bad Muslim: America, the Cold War, and the Roots of Terror*. New York, NY: Pantheon Books.

Mamdani, Mahmood. 2013. *Define and Rule: Native as Political Identity*. Johannesburg: Wits University Press.

Martinot, Steve. 2011. 'The Coloniality of Power: Notes Toward Decolonization'. Unpublished paper. San Francisco State University. Accessed 15 May 2018. https://www.globaljusticecenter.org/papers/coloniality-power-notes-toward-de-colonization.

Mazrui, Ali A. 2001. 'Pretender to Universalism: Western Culture in a Globalizing Age'. *Journal of Muslim Minority Affairs* 21(1): 11–24.

Mbembe, Achille. 2001. *On the Postcolony*. Translated by A.M. Berrett, Janet Roitman, Murray Last and Steven Rendall. Berkeley, CA: University of California Press.

Memmi, Albert. 1974. *The Colonizer and the Colonized*. Translated by Howard Greenfeld. New York: Routledge.

Mignolo, Walter D. 2009. 'Dispensable and Bare Lives: Coloniality and the Hidden Political/Economic Agenda of Modernity'. *Human Architecture: Journal of the Sociology of Self-Knowledge* 7(2): 69–87.

Mignolo, Walter D. 2015. 'Yes We Can'. Foreword to *Can Non-Europeans Think?* by Hamid Dabashi, viii–xlii. London: Zed Books.

Mills, Charles W. 1997. *The Racial Contract*. Ithaca and London: Cornell University Press.

Nabudere, Dani W. 2011. *Afrikology: Philosophy and Wholeness*. Pretoria: Africa Institute of South Africa.

Ndlovu-Gatsheni, Sabelo J. 2018. *Epistemic Freedom in Africa: Deprovincialization and Decolonization*. London: Routledge.

Nietzsche, Friedrich. [1906] 1968. *The Will to Power*. Translated by Walter Kaufmann and R.J. Hollingdale. Edited by Walter Kaufmann. New York, NY: Vintage Books.

Nietzsche, Friedrich. [1885] 1969. *Thus Spoke Zarathustra: A Book for Everyone and No One*. Translated by R.J. Hollingdale. Harmondsworth: Penguin.

Oyěwùmí, Oyèrónkẹ́. 1997. *The Invention of Women: Making an African Sense of Western Gender Discourse*. Minneapolis, MN: University of Minnesota Press.

Plato. 2010. *Socrates' Defence*. Translated by Christopher Rowe. London: Penguin Books.

Puar, Jasbir K. 2017. *The Right to Maim: Debility, Capacity, Disability*. Durham, NC: Duke University Press.

Quijano, Anibal. 2000. 'Coloniality of Power and Eurocentrism in Latin America'. *International Sociology* 15(2): 215–32.

Rousseau, Jean-Jacques. [1755] 2004. *Discourse on the Origin of Inequality*. Edited by Greg Boronson. Mineola, NY: Dover Publications.

Santos, Boaventura de Sousa. 2014. *Epistemologies of the South: Justice against Epistemicide*. Boulder, CO: Paradigm Publishers.

Sartre, Jean-Paul. [1943] 2003. *Being and Nothingness*. Translated by Hazel Estella Barnes. London: Routledge Classics.

Schmitt, Carl. 1996. *The Concept of the Political*. Chicago, IL: University of Chicago Press.

Schüssler Fiorenza, Elisabeth. 2001. *Wisdom Ways: Introducing Feminist Biblical Interpretation*. New York, NY: Orbis Books.

Sharpe, Christina. 2016. *In the Wake: On Blackness and Being*. Durham, NC: Duke University Press.

Smith, Adam. [1776] 2001. *The Wealth of Nations*. Mineola, NY: Dover Publications.

Soyinka, Wole. 2004. *Climate of Fear*. London: Profile Books.

Steyn, Melissa E. 2015. 'Critical Diversity Literacy: Essentials for the 21st Century'. In *The Routledge International Handbook of Diversity Studies*, edited by Steven Vertovec, 379–89. London: Routledge.

Tandon, Yash. 2015. *Trade is War: The West's War against the World*. New York, NY: OR Books.

Trinh, T. Minh-ha. 1989. *Woman, Native, Other: Writing Postcoloniality and Feminism*. Bloomington, IN: Indiana University Press.

UN (United Nations). 1948. *Universal Declaration of Human Rights.* Adopted as Resolution 217 at the third session of the United Nations General Assembly, Palais de Chaillot, Paris, 10 December.

Von Clausewitz, Carl. [1812] 1942. *Principles of War*. Translated and edited by Hans W. Gatzke. Mineola, NY: Dover Publications.

Wa Thiong'o, Ngũgĩ. 1981. *Decolonising the Mind: The Politics of Language in African Literature*. Harare: Zimbabwe Publishing House.

Williams, Eric. 1964. *Capitalism and Slavery.* London: Andre Deutsch.

2 THE INVENTION OF BLACKNESS ON A WORLD SCALE

SABELO J. NDLOVU-GATSHENI AND PATRICIA PINKY NDLOVU

> *The medieval European world knew the Blackman chiefly as a legend or occasional curiosity, but still as fellow man – an Othello, a Prester John, or an Antar. The modern world, in contrast, knows the Negro chiefly as a bond slave in the West Indies and America … and we face today throughout the dominant world [the belief] that colour is a mark of inferiority.* – W.E.B. Du Bois, *The Negro*

> *Modern hierarchies of race appear to have emerged in the contradictions between humanism's aspirations to universality and the needs of modern colonial regimes to manage work, reproduction, and social organization of the colonized; the intimacies of four continents formed the political unconscious of modern racial classification.* – Lisa Lowe, 'The Intimacies of Four Continents'

Wole Soyinka's widely cited injunction against Négritude, 'a tiger does not proclaim its tigritude, it pounces' (Ischinger 1974, 23), suffers miserably from ahistoricity. If the tiger's essence or being as a tiger was questioned and renamed derogatively as an ant or something similar, it would definitely be forced to proclaim its tigritude (its essence or being) as part of its resistance and defensive self-constitution. At the very centre of 'doing human' is the politics of self-constitution and self-definition, particularly for a people whose humanity has been denied or degraded. Soyinka misses this point in his quick critique of Négritude, which emerged within a context of French colonialism, called 'assimilation', that was very aggressive towards and destructive of African culture, and indeed attacked the colonised people's essence, their being. At least he later corrected himself, and admitted that his earlier critique of Négritude had been mistaken. In May 2016, he delivered a lecture entitled 'Repositioning Négritude: The Dialogue Resumes' at the Department of Arts and Culture Africa Month Colloquia in South Africa, where he reappraised Négritude as an embodiment of relevant humanism. He posited that 'it is possible that the last service of Négritude to humanity will be to assist us in redefining humanity' (Soyinka 2016, 3). He concluded that 'Négritude therefore suffers from no negative baggage and should thus be unafraid to pronounce upon what others shy from' (2016, 4).

This chapter underscores the legitimacy and logics of all the African or black initiatives aimed at decolonial self-definition and self-reconstitution, such as Négritude, Ethiopianism, Garveyism, the Harlem Renaissance, African Personality, the Black Consciousness Movement, Afrocentricity, Pan-Africanism, the African Renaissance, Decoloniality and many others. These are discourses and initiatives of self-definition and self-reconstitution produced by people resisting and fighting racism, enslavement, colonialism and neocolonialism. Inevitably, these discourses will be problematic, limited and imperfect, as they have emerged from the battlefield of history and human struggles. The ambivalences, ambiguities and even contradictions of these discourses and initiatives are well covered in Kwame Anthony Appiah's *In My Father's House: Africa in the Philosophy of Culture* (1992). However, their inevitable ambivalences and imperfections do not justify the dismissal of African struggles for self-definition and self-reconstitution, otherwise known as self-determination. At the core of these discourses and initiatives has been the problem of dismemberment and dehumanisation.

Blackness emerges within the history of racism, enslavement and colonisation as a badge of sub-humanity and inferiority. Two concepts – dismemberment and re-membering – enable this chapter to empathetically make sense of the technologies of invention of 'blackness' as a marker of sub-human, if not deficient, identity, as well as to appreciate African and black people's struggles for self-reconstitution and resistance to dehumanising Eurocentrism. In *Critique of Black Reason* (2017), Achille Mbembe posits and examines the thesis of a modern, troubled world that was 'becoming black'. Blackness, in Mbembe's analysis, is a product of the racism that reduced human bodies and living beings 'to matters of appearance, skin and colour' (Mbembe 2017, 2). This is how he puts it:

> Across early capitalism, the term 'Black' referred only to the condition imposed on peoples of African origin (different forms of depredation, dispossession of all power of self-determination, and, most of all, dispossession of the future and of time, the two matrices of the possible). Now, for the first time in human history, the term 'Black' has been generalized. The new fungibility, this solubility, institutionalised as a new norm of existence and expanded to the entire planet, is what I call the *Becoming Black of the world*. (2017, 5–6)

However, in an earlier publication Mbembe (2001) was very critical of what he referred to as 'African modes of self-writing', which he associated with the politics of Afro-radicalism, nativism and narcissism of minor difference. The truth of the matter is that African modes of self-writing are part of the politics of and struggles for self-reconstitution. These modes of writing emerged within an anti-black white world. It was the anti-black white world that provoked Aimé Césaire to pose what he termed three 'tormenting questions': 'Who am I? Who are we? What are we in this white world?' (Césaire quoted in Thiam 2014, 2). This is how the complex theme of black subjectivity came to haunt history and philosophy. The question of 'blackism on a world scale' is at the very centre of what Lewis R. Gordon (2000, 2008) terms 'Africana philosophy' and 'Africana existential thought'. According to Gordon,

> Africana philosophy is a species of thought, which involves theoretical questions raised by critical engagements with ideas in Africana cultures and their hybrid, mixed, or creolized forms worldwide. Since there was no reason for the people of the African continent to have considered themselves African until that identity was imposed upon them through conquest and colonization in the modern era (the 16th Century onwards), this area of thought also refers to the unique set of questions raised by the emergence of 'Africans' and their diaspora here designated by the term 'Africana'. Such concerns include the convergence of most Africans with the racial term 'black' and its many connotations. Africana philosophy refers to the philosophical dimensions of this area of thought. (Gordon 2008, 1)

Somehow it is these legitimate concerns that Mbembe (2001, 6–7) seems to ridicule, caricature and dismiss as informed by three tragic acts (slavery, colonialism and apartheid), 'three spectres and their masks (race, geography, and tradition)', and 'three rituals so constantly repeated as to become inaudible' – refutation of Western definitions of Africa, denunciation of what the West has done and continues to do to Africa, and disqualification of the West's claims to monopoly of what it means to be human. This critique sounds like an apologia for what Euro-North American-centric modernity, enslavement and colonialism have done to Africa. With the coming of resurgent and insurgent decolonisation and decoloniality, spearheaded by student and youth movements under such banners as Rhodes Must Fall, Fees Must Fall and Black Lives Matter, the quest for African self-writing is once more being forcefully inserted into the public arena. However, in his return to the same subject of 'blackness' in *Critique of Black Reason*, Mbembe is somewhat more measured in his analysis of African struggles for self-reconstitution through self-writing, though still critical of what he terms 'black reason': 'Black reason consists of a collection of voices, pronouncements, discourses, forms of knowledge, commentary, and nonsense, whose object is things or people of "African origin". It is affirmed as their name and their truth (their attributes and qualities, their destiny and its significance as an empirical portion of the world) ... From the beginning, its primary activity was fantasizing' (Mbembe 2017, 27).

The reality is that the resurgent and insurgent decolonisation of the twenty-first century, as a planetary movement, has brought into the public arena what one of the authors of the present chapter (Ndlovu-Gatsheni 2018b) terms 'epistemic freedom' (the right to think, write, communicate, theorise, view the world and produce knowledge from an African locus of enunciation). The current resurgent and insurgent demands for decolonisation point to the structural, systemic and institutional reality of coloniality (Ndlovu-Gatsheni 2013a, 2013b; Quijano 2000). Grace Khunou and her colleagues, in *Black Academic Voices: The South African Experience* (2019), capture the personal accounts given by black academics of their lived experiences at South African universities in the context of the ongoing resurgent and insurgent decolonisation of higher education. The questions of black subjectivity and the paradigm of difference emerge poignantly as haunting products of apartheid colonialism, as well as making a strong case for African self-writing as a decolonial move.

In the rich decolonial scholarship, the planetary issue of 'blackness', just like that of 'whiteness', is approached as a sociogenic question rather than as an ontogenic question – that is, rooted in the paradigm of difference constitutive of an invented modern Euro-North American-centric world system whose ever shifting global orders are mediated by the paradigm of difference. Sociogenesis here names the racial materiality of Euromodernity which enabled the social classification of the human population and its racial hierarchisation. This is a different rendition from that offered by Mbembe (2001, 8), in which the problem of blackness on a world scale is viewed as propelled by 'constant repetition, a set of pious dogmas and empty dreams'. As a concept, 'blackism' enables a sociodiagnostic approach to both technologies of dehumanisation (dismemberment) and struggles for rehumanisation (re-membering). It speaks to an invented problematic human condition, and embodies the complex politics of invention of 'personhood' within the context of Euro-North American-centric bourgeois modernity. Since the time of colonial encounters, blackness has emerged and unfolded as an identitarian phenomenon and a form of consciousness (as can be seen in black power movements and black consciousness movements).

However, in the first epigraph to this chapter, W.E.B. Du Bois articulates two senses of blackness (Du Bois 2001, 6). The first is that of legendary curiosity among medieval Europeans about blackness as a state of being. That curiosity was not yet contaminated by the poison of race. The second is the sense of dismemberment, infantilisation, inferiorisation and enslavement that was constitutive of the unfolding of Euro-North American modernity. What emerges poignantly from this context is blackism on a world scale, as the outcome of 'coloniality of being' (Maldonado-Torres 2007). Coloniality of being names 'a certain skepticism regarding the humanity of the enslaved and colonised sub-others' (Maldonado-Torres 2007, 256). At the very centre of this coloniality of being are technologies such as dismemberment, dehumanisation and inferiorisation of some human species by other human species. Pigmentation is effectively used to render the lives of those deemed to be black as the dispensable other. This is why Mbembe (2017, 47) posits that 'the history of slavery and colonialism constituted the term "Black" as the name "of the slave: man-of-metal, man-merchandise, man-money"'.

Thus, the concept of dismemberment, which contributes to the framing of this chapter, speaks to how those who were 'othered' as black people were pushed out of the human family, and underscores the very denial of their humanity (their thingification) (Maldonado-Torres 2007; Ndlovu-Gatsheni 2015). Dismemberment is part of the unfolding and expansion of Euro-North American-centric modernity, which in practice involved submission of the modern world to European memory (Mudimbe 1994, xii). Exploration, surveying, 'discovering', mapping, conquest, colonisation, naming, dispossession and claims of ownership of everything in the modern world formed the core of dismemberment. Thus we posit that blackism on a world scale emerged at a time when the continents were being invented, not only through cartography but through the spread of the capitalist economic system across the human world, and through the nascent unfolding of a global division of labour.

C.L.R. James (1982) highlights the political economy within which blackness emerged. To him, the unfolding of modernity from the eighteenth century onwards not only resulted in the creation of slave societies like San Domingo (Haiti), but also established an exploitative set of connections whereby Europe, Africa and the Americas were linked through nexuses of mercantile and capitalist accumulation of wealth by Europe, laying the foundations of globalisation. For instance, the proceeds of slavery in the Americas contributed immensely to the rise of the capitalist bourgeoisie in Europe, as well as to the emergence of a new Euromodern civilisation underpinned by the capitalist world economy. The drive for cheap labour in this economy meant that even the abolition of the slave trade had to be succeeded by another exploitative economic arrangement that was equally slave-like in the conditions it imposed on working people. This reality explains the rise of the indentured labour system of recruiting and exploiting labour – this time bringing the labour of Indians and Chinese to the exploitative economy that arose on the basis of African slave labour. Mbembe is therefore correct in arguing that 'the transnationalization of the Black condition was therefore a constitutive moment for modernity, with the Atlantic serving as its incubator. The Black condition incorporated a range of contrasting states and statuses: those sold through the transatlantic slave trade, convict labourers, subsistence slaves (whose lives were spent as domestics), feudal slaves, house slaves, those who were emancipated, and those who were born slaves' (Mbembe 2017, 15).

When we take into account the resistance that coalesced around the identity of blackness, we can therefore confidently refer to the dynamics of blackism on a world scale in the second sense of 're-membering'. Re-membering encapsulates the consistent attempts of black people at counter-self-creation, self-definition, recovery, restoration of their denied humanity, but also systematic self-re-writing of themselves back into human history. These struggles and initiatives embraced the cultural-cum-intellectual-cum-political-cum-identitarian formations that included Garveyism, Ethiopianism and many other such movements (Ndlovu-Gatsheni 2018a, 2018b). Thus, those who were designated as black people were essentially thrown into the deep end of a problematic liminal state of being that was perpetually transitional in nature – caught between denied humanity and the seductive promise of eventually attaining ontological density so as to return to the human family. It was perhaps this state of limbo that provoked W.E.B. Du Bois ([1903] 2008) to write about 'the souls of black folk' and Lewis R. Gordon to push for 'existentia Africana' thought (2008).

THE INVENTION OF BLACKNESS ON A WORLD SCALE

In a chapter in the *Routledge Handbook of Postcolonial Politics* (Ndlovu-Gatsheni 2018a), one of the present authors makes effective use of Enrique Dussel's important book entitled *Politics of Liberation: A Critical World History* to underscore six interrelated discursive and instrumental technologies of dis-memberment: Hellenocentrism, Westernisation, Eurocentrism, secularism, periodisation and colonialism (Dussel 2011, xv–xviii). These epic colonial and imperial processes framed what David Marriott (2012) correctly articulates as colonial 'inventions of existence' for whiteness. Decoloniality underscores the struggles for (re-)existence of blackness.

It was within this colonial context that Europe defined itself as the centre of the earth, the birthplace of reason, the spring of universal life, the abode of universal truth, the paragon of civilisation and the inventor of the rights of people (Mbembe 2017, 11). Further to this, the European 'Man' self-defined itself as the 'discoverer' of other human species. In the process, this European Man elevated himself to the category of the 'Creator'/God – the superior human being. It is, therefore, not surprising that historians like John M. Headley have been so enchanted by Eurocentric thought, to the extent of believing the nefarious claims of Hellenocentrism, Westernisation, secularism, Eurocentrism and colonialism. Headley's book entitled *The Europeanization of the World: On the Origins of Human Rights and Democracy* (2008) valorises Europe as the progenitor of values of humanism, democracy and human rights. The consequence of this conviction is clearly exemplified in Headley's unproblematic acceptance of the imperial and colonial 'paradigm of discovery' as the basis for common humanity. Listen to him:

> This sudden exposure to a fully inhabited (or so it seemed) yet extra-Christian world, this abruptly expanded ecumene with its variety of peoples, in time created an increasingly secular, religiously neutral lens that gradually revealed humankind's common biological and moral unity. In the terrible shock that Europeans inflicted upon hitherto unknown peoples, the contacts between the peoples posited the fact of humanity as an ideal to be realised in some distant future. Beyond the brutal impact and the immense problem of Adam's newfound children, the intellectual instruments afforded by the decisive re-emergence of Stoicism and natural law, the traditional means of promoting such community, faltered in achieving the universal commitment implicit in the ideal of a single humanity. (Headley 2008, 27–28)

But to argue along the lines of Headley is to reject the undeniable fact that there were other human civilisations and human struggles outside Europe which contributed to the emergence of positive human values such as human rights and democracy. What Headley and other Eurocentric scholars ignore is that the unfolding of Euro-North American-centric modernity not only inaugurated 'rupture' (colonisation of time into pre-modern and modern temporalities) and 'difference' (see Bhambra 2007, 1) but also entailed a consistent stealing of history and denial of the humanity of others. Eurocentric secularism became predicated on what Gordon (1999) articulates as 'bad faith'. Bad faith entails endless proclamations of tenets of humanity at the rhetorical level while practically killing humanity itself everywhere (see also Fanon 1963). Bad faith is claiming humanity for a particular 'race' and denying all other human species of humanity.

Gordon, in *Bad Faith and Antiblack Racism* (1999, 1), poses the question: 'What is the being or ontological limitation of human reality in an antiblack world?' His response is: 'Antiblack racism may embody the extreme poles of the possibility of a universal humankind; it wrenches human beings into the most extreme visual metaphors of difference: from the most light to the most dark, from the fullness of colour (something) to its complete absence (nothing), from "white," that is, to "black".'

In pursuit of bad faith, European secularism invented a science of death that was mobilised to justify coloniality of being. Using bad faith and pseudo-racial science, European secularism consistently pushed God out of the human imagination. Belief in God was only used instrumentally, in Africa and other sites of colonialism, to blind the colonised to the hypocrisy and negative features of the Western civilisational colonial project. Dussel (2011, xvi) emphasises that a new 'periodization', in which human history was cut into a linear chronology of 'Ancient, Middle and Modern Ages', emerged as Europe propelled itself into the future and all others into the past. No wonder, in this periodisation informed by bad faith and pseudo-racial science, that all other civilisations were dismembered and pushed into the category 'Ancient'. The 'modern' was monopolised by Europe.

Thus, the foundational dismemberment of black people took the form of denial of their very humanity. This commenced with Christopher Columbus's questioning of the natives of Latin America about whether they had 'souls' – remember the historic Valladolid Debates (1550–51) in which Bartolome de La Casas and Gines De Sepulveda engaged in intense debates over the ontological question of the humanity of the natives (Castro 2007). This, according to Castro, marked the genesis of the 'colonial death project' that eventually engulfed Asia, Africa and the rest of the world that experienced modern colonisation. The 'death project' was and is a reference to 'the exercise of violence in coloniality, which targets the actual processes of life and the conditions for existence: in short, polarity' (Suárez-Krabbe 2016, 3). 'Necropolitics' (Mbembe 2003, 11) and the 'ethics of war' (Maldonado-Torres 2008, 4) are leitmotifs of the colonial death project; they distinguished those who were to 'live' from those who had to 'die'. Ramón Grosfoguel gives empirical framing to this project when he articulates the 'four genocides/epistemicides of the long 16th century' that were foundational to the politics of dismemberment and the modern colonial death project. These were the conquest of Al-Andalus, the enslavement of Africans in the Americas, the killing of millions of women accused of being witches by burning them alive in Europe, and the extermination of natives of Latin America (Grosfoguel 2013, 74). The conquest of Al-Andalus in 1492 targeted Muslims and Jews, and was propelled by the logic of 'purity of blood' as a form of dismemberment. At that time colour was not yet used as a criterion of exclusion; purity of blood and religion were the key technologies of dismemberment. Here lies the origin of the fundamentalist concept of 'one identity, one political authority, and one religion' (Suárez-Krabbe 2016, 54).

The policies of physical extermination (genocide/ethnocide) targeting the indigenous peoples of the Americas, the Caribbean, Asia and Africa constituted the second technology of coloniality. The black people of Africa did not only experience genocides but also enslavement, through what became known as the 'transatlantic slave trade'. Enslavement naturalised 'the colonial criteria of inferiority, linking racism and capitalism' (Suárez-Krabbe 2016, 56). All of this history is important for an understanding of the genealogies of the invention of blackness on a world scale. For example, the terms 'Negro' and 'black', as racial inferiorising categories, emerged in the context of this inimical colonial/imperial/capitalist history. The time of the enslavement of black people and their transportation across the Atlantic Ocean into the Americas contributed immensely to the birth of 'blackness' as a state of being and an identity (Du Bois 1965, 20).

What has to be emphasised is that even though European discourses of the human were shifting across time and space, what remained constant was the invented inferiority of those deemed to be black. The Caribbean decolonial theorist Sylvia Wynter (2003, 297) correctly captures the historical fact that the enslavement of black people created 'a model for the invention of a by-nature difference between "natural masters" and "natural slaves"'. With specific reference to Africa, Ngũgĩ wa Thiong'o (2009b) argues that the 'dismemberment' of Africa unfolded in two stages. The first stage is traceable to the enslavement of black people and their shipment as 'cargo' across the Atlantic into the Americas and the Caribbean. This is how Wa Thiong'o describes what he considers to be the first phase of this dismemberment: 'During the first of these, the African personhood was divided into two halves: the continent and its diaspora. African slaves, the central commodity in the mercantile phase of capitalism, formed the basis of the sugar, cotton, and tobacco plantations in the Caribbean and American mainland' (Wa Thiong'o 2009b, 5).

The second stage of dismemberment of Africa identified by Wa Thiong'o took place at the Berlin Conference of 1884–85. This second level of 'dismemberment' took the literal form of the fragmentation and reconstitution of 'Africa into British, French, Portuguese, German, Belgian, and Spanish Africa' (Wa Thiong'o 2009b, 5). Wa Thiong'o further argues that those black people who were physically removed from the continent experienced 'an additional dismemberment' in the form of separation 'not only from his[/her] continent and his[/her] labour but also from his[/her] very sovereign being' (2009b, 6). Those who remained on the continent but experienced the 'scramble' for and 'partition' of Africa, were subjected to further dismemberment in the form of dispossession of land: 'The land is taken away from its owner, and the owner is turned into a worker on the same land, thus losing control of his[/her] natural and human resources' (Wa Thiong'o 2009b, 6).

What must be underscored is that the modern school, the Christian church and the 'Westernised' university play an active role in the colonial and even post-colonial process of dismemberment (Ndlovu-Gatsheni 2018a, 2018b). This is so because 'cultural subjugation was a necessary condition for economic and political mastery' (Wa Thiong'o 1997, 9). Colonial education is identified by Wa Thiong'o as the most important force for dismemberment and alienation, because it invades and takes control of the mental universe in order to produce a distorted consciousness among the colonised (Wa Thiong'o 2012, 28).

Ndlovu-Gatsheni (2018a, 2018b) distils six 'dimensions of dismemberment'. The first is the 'foundational dismemberment' involving the questioning of the very humanity of black people, as well as the invention of blackness itself (Ndlovu-Gatsheni 2015; Ndlovu-Gatsheni and Zondi 2016, 5). The second is enslavement, which resulted not only in the reduction of black African people to a commodity but also in the fragmentation of African personhood into continental and diasporic divisions. The third is the scramble for and partition of Africa that took place in Berlin, resulting in the fragmentation of the continent not only into various colonies but also into various invented and contending ethnicities, enclosed within colonially crafted boundaries. The fourth dimension is the theft/usurpation/erasure/silencing of African history so as to deny its very existence, in order to establish the Hegelian notion of a people without history and a continent of darkness and emptiness (Tibebu 2011, xiv). The fifth is the production and reproduction of dismemberment by the 'post-colonial' state, under the leadership of a colonially produced black bourgeoisie who are trapped in a paradigm of neocolonialism/coloniality. The final dimension is the continued reproduction of patriarchy so as to dismember women from power, knowledge and being itself.

Since Euro-North American-centric modernity unfolded as a combination of enslavement, genocides, conquest, colonisation, epistemicides, conversion and linguicides, the major challenge facing 'ex-colonized' people is how to 'recuperate' (Ndlovu-Gatsheni 2018a, 78). This difficult and complex process of recuperation is at the heart of the process of re-membering.

BLACKNESS: FROM DISMEMBERMENT TO RE-MEMBERING

Re-membering is fundamentally a process of recovery and restoration of history. It entails the painstaking processes of re-humanising and humaning. Archie Mafeje (2011, 31–32) captures the centrality of this process when he posits that 'we would not proclaim Africanity, if it had not been denied or degraded; and we would not insist on Afrocentrism, if it had not been for Eurocentric negations'. One can safely state that such re-membering initiatives, ideologies and movements as Garveyism, Ethiopianism, Négritude, African Personality, African Socialism, African Humanism, African Renaissance and many others emerged within a context of realities of dismemberment, and existed as props developed by the dismembered across time to help in the re-membering process. With specific reference to the Négritude movement as a re-membering initiative, Léopold Sédar Senghor explicitly stated that theirs was a form of 'return' to black humanism after centuries of being taken through the French assimilationist colonial project (Senghor quoted in Bâ 1973, 12).

The Négritude movement was part of the broader search for identity within a context of dismemberment. Thus, we are now in a better position to state categorically that Wole Soyinka's critique of Négritude quoted at the start of this chapter, namely that a tiger does not articulate its 'tigritude', was misplaced, as it ignored the context of dislocation and alienation in which the movement had arisen. Négritude was one of the earliest re-membering initiatives. Cheikh Thiam (2014) correctly understands Négritude as an early expression of an 'Afri-centred' conception of the human, one that was consistently critical of a Western universalisation of the human that excluded those with black pigmentation. Négritude was propelled by Césaire's 'tormenting questions' referred to at the start of this chapter: 'Who am I? Who are we? What are we in this world?' (Césaire quoted in Thiam 2014, 2).

But at a global scale, and in black people's struggles for re-membering, the epic Haitian Revolution of 1791–1804 has to occupy a place of pride. In the first instance, this earliest black revolution defied the Eurocentric, colonial and imperial idea, evident in so much Western philosophy, of denial of the humanity of black people (Ndlovu-Gatsheni 2018b). It turned upside down the racist myths of a people who were naturally slaves, and who were said to be unable to develop any notions of fighting for freedom simply because they were not considered to be rational human beings (Ndlovu-Gatsheni 2018a). When enslaved blacks revolted on a large scale in the form of the Haitian Revolution, it became one of those events that were 'unthinkable' for those who had convinced themselves that black, enslaved people were naturally slaves and had no capacity to rebel. The second significance of the Haitian Revolution is that it was not only part of the unfolding modern history of slavery, racism and colonisation, but that this revolt of the enslaved challenged 'the iron bonds of the philosophical milieu in which it was born' (Trouillot 1995, 74).

Any acceptance of the fact that enslaved black people were up in arms against the system of slavery amounted in Western thought to acknowledgement of the humanity of black people. Europeans in general, and speculative plantation owners in particular, were not prepared to concede that they were faced with a people claiming their denied humanity. The Haitian Revolution indeed posed a difficult philosophical and intellectual problem for Western thought: how to think about and conceptualise black revolution in a world in which black people were not considered to be rational and human in the first place? This is why 'international recognition of Haitian independence was even more difficult to gain than military victory over the forces of Napoleon' (Trouillot 1995, 95). The most important but silenced significance of the Haitian Revolution is that it led to the collapse of the entire system of slavery, and constituted a major chapter in the history of re-membering of black people. It was truly an anti-systemic revolution, one that occupies a place of pride in the anti-systemic revolution marked by the definitive entry of the enslaved and colonised into modern history, as human beings opposed to all forms of dismemberment.

The Haitian Revolution forms an important base from which to articulate what Wa Thiong'o (2009a, 35–36) underscores as 're-membering visions'. It laid the foundation for such other formations as Ethiopianism and Garveyism. Wa Thiong'o (2009a, 35) notes that at the centre of Ethiopianism and Garveyism lay 'the quest for wholeness, a quest that has underlain African struggles since the Atlantic slave trade'.

Since the time of the Haitian Revolution and later that of Marcus Garvey's International Negro Improvement Association, those human beings who have been designated as black have continued to fight for their freedom and for the recovery of their denied humanity. Pan-Africanism emerged as one broad re-membering initiative that developed from the time of William Sylvester, who planned and hosted the first Pan-African Congress in 1900, to W.E.B. Du Bois's series of Pan-African Congresses, to Kwame Nkrumah's struggle to unify Africa into a Pan-African Nation. In the USA, black people launched the civil rights movement as part of these initiatives. Re-membering initiatives have taken intellectual and political forms. At their centre has germinated 'the African idea', as opposed to the idea of Africa: 'the African idea as the quest for freedom on a Pan-African scale extended from the diaspora to the continent and back again' (Wa Thiong'o 2009a, 75). The African idea captures the efforts of Africans to define themselves, as opposed to the idea of Africa invoked by Valentin Y. Mudimbe (1994) that speaks to external definition of Africa and Africans.

Linking the question of blackism on a world scale to specific re-membering activities on the African continent, the period from the 1950s to the late 1960s was dominated by struggles for political decolonisation and the emergence of 'post-colonial' states. The major challenge to re-membering initiatives continues to be the active global imperial designs (Mignolo 2017; Ndlovu-Gatsheni 2013a, 2013b). As noted by Grosfoguel (2007, 219), political decolonisation amounted to what he terms 'the most powerful myths of the twentieth century' because the withdrawal of direct colonial administrations and juridical apartheid did not 'amount to the decolonization of the world'.

The admission of the so-called newly independent states into the United Nations simply symbolised their accommodation in an existing and un-decolonised Euro-North American-centric world system and un-deimperialised global order. This was not what re-membering entailed. These so-called newly independent states occupied the lowest echelons in an asymmetrical world system. The new world economic order that was demanded by those who had fought against colonialism did not materialise. As noted by Nkrumah (1965), neocolonialism emerged as a form of coloniality, in which the so-called independent states became entrapped in global coloniality.

At the internal level, the African leaders who had spearheaded the anti-colonial struggle displayed deep-seated 'pitfalls of national consciousness', to borrow a term from Fanon (1963, 98), and the consequences were what Basil Davidson (1992) terms the 'black man's burden' of simply reproducing what had been invented by colonialism and imposing it on Africa. The nation-building project as a re-membering initiative was problematic, and it failed. It failed partly because the leadership that took over the state at the end of direct colonial rule were products of the same colonialism they claimed to be fighting against, and partly because of forms of mimicry involving imposition of external templates as policy on Africa. For example, these leaders imposed the Westphalian template of a tight correspondence between the nation and the state, whereby each modern sovereign state was understood to be a nation state comprised of a people who shared a common language, culture and identity, on Africa (Laakso and Olukoshi 1996, 11–13) - a continent characterised by multiculturalism, multilingualism, multiple identities and multiple religions - revealing how entrapped they were in the thinking of global coloniality. And it was not only the project of nation-building that failed. The Pan-African project itself failed, as territorial sovereignty informed by narrow nationalism was privileged over pan-African unity. The inherited economies of the newly independent states had collapsed by the beginning of the 1970s, because neocolonialism actively reinstated relations marked by coloniality in which the agents were local bourgeois classes in charge of the state. Taking advantage of this desperate situation, agents of coloniality such as the World Bank and the International Monetary Fund presented themselves as the cure for African problems, and they literally took over the policy space in each country as they prescribed Structural Adjustment Programmes to be adhered to by the national governments (Cheru 2009).

To confront this economic colonialism, which took the concrete form of dependency and debt-slavery, organisations representing African people, including the United Nations Economic Commission for Africa (UNECA), the Organisation of African Unity (OAU), later renamed the African Union (AU), and the United Nations General Assembly (UN) produced a number of nationalist, Pan-Africanist inspired economic frameworks, ranging from the *Revised Framework for the Implementation of the New International Economic Order in Africa* (UNECA 1976), the *Lagos Plan of Action For the Economic Development of Africa, 1980–2000* (OAU 1980), *Africa's Priority Programme for Economic Recovery, 1986–1990* (OAU 1986), the *Alternative Framework to Structural Adjustment Programmes for Socio-Economic Recovery and Transformation* (UNECA 1989), the *African Charter for Popular*

Participation in Development and Transformation (UNECA 1990), and the *United Nations New Agenda for the Development of Africa* (UN 1991) to the *New Partnership for Economic Development* (NEPAD, AU 2002). These economic initiatives 'were opposed, undermined, and jettisoned by the Bretton Woods institutions and Africans were impeded from exercising the basic and fundamental right to make decisions about their future' (Adedeji 2002, 4). Adebayo Adedeji (2002), who worked as the Executive Secretary General of the United Nations Economic Commission for Africa, described the colonial matrices of power at play in imposing exogenous ideas and policies on Africa in the 1980s and 1990s as a 'development merchant system'.

Thus, in this chapter we posit that Africa entered the 2000s limping and still dismembered (see Ndlovu-Gatsheni 2018b). The African Renaissance, which was spearheaded by President Thabo Mbeki of South Africa, was meant to provide a discursive framework for the post-2000 re-membering Africa initiatives, but suffered when Mbeki was removed from the presidency in South Africa by his own party, the African National Congress. Among the other re-membering initiatives was the conversion of the Organisation of African Unity, formed in 1963, into the African Union, on 9 July 2002, as part of the galvanisation of the African Renaissance. NEPAD and the African Peer Review Mechanism, as well as the opening of the Pan-African Parliament in South Africa on 18 March 2004, constituted the other concrete initiatives formulated under the aegis of the African Renaissance (Ndlovu-Gatsheni 2013a).

However, after Mbeki left the political scene, the African Renaissance lost one of its most committed advocates. At the continental level, it would seem that the optimism which accompanied these initiatives was based on an incorrect diagnosis and a misunderstanding of how the Euro-North American-centric modern world worked. The developed and industrialised Euro-North American states were never prepared to be genuine partners of Africa. They are beneficiaries of the asymmetrical structure of the modern world system and its global order. We posit that coloniality, as an active global power structure sustaining the dominance of the Global North over the Global South, was somehow forgotten by African leaders.

CONCLUSION

This chapter has presented the history, discursive terrain, ideological productions and resistance initiatives that were meant to enable the re-membering of Africa, while at the same time highlighting how global imperial designs actively worked to undercut these struggles. Today the African Union speaks of a prosperous, united, self-defining and peaceful Africa in 2063 (AU 2015). One wonders whether by 2063 the global imperial designs, including their racist and patriarchal technologies, will have been broken and defeated. Reading David Theo Goldberg's *Are We all Postracial Yet? Debating Race* reminded us that 'Blackness has always been basic to racist definition, and remains so with postraciality' (Goldberg 2015, 123). Goldberg elaborates on the problem of the constitution of blackism on a world scale:

> Roughly, and in broad strokes, the earliest formulation and formation of racial subjects in the making of modern Europe included the Black, the Moor, and the Jew as non-Catholic and heathen interior aliens to be eliminated through conversion, expulsion, or extermination. New World Indians were established as exterior inferiors, savages of the state of nature. The Enlightenment largely produced Negroids, Mongoloids, Asiatics, and Caucasoids. The nineteenth century saw the identification of Negroes in more pernicious terms, and the state classification of Indians or Natives, with whites or Europeans as the driving category of domination. The twentieth century witnessed a proliferation of racial naming, and the hardening of demeaning, and deadly characterizations. As modes of racism came increasingly into question and societies grew more heterogeneous still, blackness stiffened into a variety of name-calling in different societies, each bearing comparable disparagement. (2015, 124–25)

It is within the context described by Goldberg that the question of blackism on a world scale becomes prominent and highly relevant today. At one level, the concept of blackism on a world scale challenges the claims of a post-racial world; at another level it reveals the failure of decolonisation and deimperialisation, as well as of the core claims of modern humanism and the human rights discourse that falsely assert a common humanity while obscuring the resilient forces of dismemberment. The key challenge, as noted by Goldberg (2015, 172), is how to 'un-think racial configuration' so as to enable a new humanism to emerge. Blackism on a world scale is less of an inherent identity than an invented condition created by racism. It will not come to an end until those conditions that are the grounds of its invention have disappeared.

REFERENCES

Adedeji, Adebayo. 2002. 'From Lagos Plan of Action to the New Partnership for African Development and from the Final Act of Lagos to the Constitutive Act: Whither Africa?' Keynote address to the African Forum for Envisioning Africa, Nairobi, 26–29 April. Accessed 15 September 2019. http://archive.niza.nl/uploads/adedeji20020429.pdf?&username=guest@niza.nl&password=9999&groups=NIZA&workgroup=.

Appiah, Kwame A. 1992. *In My Father's House: Africa in the Philosophy of Culture*. Cambridge: Cambridge University Press.

AU (African Union). 2002. *New Partnership for Economic Development*. Addis Ababa: African Union.

AU. 2015. *Agenda 2063: The Africa We Want*. Addis Ababa: African Union.

Bâ, Sylvia W. 1973. *The Concept of Négritude in the Poetry of Léopold Sédar Senghor*. Princeton, NJ: Princeton University Press.

Bhambra, Gurminder K. 2007. *Rethinking Modernity: Postcolonialism and the Sociological Imagination*. London: Palgrave Macmillan.

Castro, Daniel. 2007. *Another Face of Empire: Bartolome de La Casas, Indigenous Rights and Ecclesiastical Imperialism*. Durham, NC: Duke University Press.

Cheru, Fantu. 2009. 'Development in Africa: The Imperial Project versus the National Project and the Need for Policy Space'. *Review of African Political Economy* 120: 275–78.

Davidson, Basil. 1992. *The Black Man's Burden*. London: James Currey.

Du Bois, W.E.B. [William Edward Burghardt]. 1965. *The World and Africa: An Inquiry into the Part Which Africa Has Played in World History*. New York, NY: International Publishers.

Du Bois, W.E.B. [William Edward Burghardt]. 2001. *The Negro*. Mineola, NY: Dover Publications.

Du Bois, W.E.B. [William Edward Burghardt]. [1903] 2012. *The Souls of Black Folk*. Mineola NY: Dover Publications.

Dussel, Enrique. 2011. *Politics of Liberation: A Critical World History*. Translated by Thia Cooper. London: SCM Press.

Fanon, Frantz. 1963. *The Wretched of the Earth*. Translated by Constance Farrington. New York, NY: Grove Press.

Goldberg, David T. 2015. *Are We All Postracial Yet? Debating Race*. Cambridge: Polity Press.

Gordon, Lewis R. 1999. *Bad Faith and Antiblack Racism*. New York, NY: Humanity Books.

Gordon, Lewis R. 2000. *Existentia Africana: Understanding Africana Existential Thought*. New York, NY: Routledge.

Gordon, Lewis R. 2008. *An Introduction to Africana Philosophy*. Cambridge: Cambridge University Press.

Grosfoguel, Ramón. 2007. 'The Epistemic Decolonial Turn: Beyond Political-Economy Paradigms'. *Cultural Studies* 21(2–3): 211–23.

Grosfoguel, Ramón. 2013. 'The Structure of Knowledge in Westernized Universities: Epistemic Racism/Sexism and the Four Genocides/Epistemicides of the Long 16th Century'. *Human Architecture: Journal of the Sociology of Self Knowledge* 11(1): 73–90.

Headley, John M. 2008. *The Europeanization of the World: On the Origins of Human Rights and Democracy*. Princeton, NJ: Princeton University Press.

Ischinger, Barbara. 1974. 'Négritude: Some Dissident Voices'. *African Issues* 4(4): 23–25.

James, C.L.R. [Cyril Lionel Robert]. 1982. *The Black Jacobins: Toussaint L'Ouverture and the San Domingo Revolution*. New York, NY: Vintage Press.

Laakso, Liisa and Olukoshi, Adebayo O. 1996. 'The Crisis of the Post-Colonial Nation-State Project in Africa'. In *Challenges to the Nation-State in Africa*, edited by Adebayo O. Olukoshi and Liisa Laakso, 7–39. Uppsala: Nordic Africa Institute.

Lowe, Lisa. 2006. 'The Intimacies of Four Continents'. In *Haunted by Empire: Geographies of Intimacy in North American History*, edited by Ann Laura Stoler, 191–211. Durham, NC: Duke University Press.

Khunou, Grace, Phaswana, Edith, Koza-Shangase, Katijah and Canham, Hugo, eds. 2019. *Black Academic Voices: The South African Experience*. Cape Town: HSRC Press.

Mafeje, Archie. 2011. 'Africanity: A Combative Ontology'. In *The Postcolonial Turn: Re-Imagining Anthropology and Africa*, edited by Rene Devisch and Francis B. Nyamnjoh, 31–44. Bamenda and Leiden: Langaa and African Studies Centre.

Maldonado-Torres, Nelson. 2007. 'On the Coloniality of Being: Contributions to the Development of a Concept'. *Cultural Studies* 21(2–3): 240–70.

Maldonado-Torres, Nelson. 2008. *Against War: Views from the Underside of Modernity*. Durham, NC: Duke University Press.

Marriott, David. 2012. 'Inventions of Existence: Sylvia Wynter, Frantz Fanon, Sociogeny and the "the Damned"'. *CR: The New Centennial Review* 11(3): 45–90.

Mbembe, Achille. 2001. 'African Modes of Self-Writing'. *Identity, Culture and Politics* 2(1): 1–39.

Mbembe, Achille. 2003. 'Necropolitics'. *Public Culture* 15(1): 11–40.

Mbembe, Achille. 2017. *Critique of Black Reason*. Translated by Laurent Dubois. Durham, NC: Duke University Press.

Mignolo, Walter D. 2017. *Local Histories/Global Designs: Coloniality, Subaltern Knowledges, and Border Thinking*. Princeton, NJ: Princeton University Press.

Mudimbe, Valentin Y. 1994. *The Idea of Africa*. Bloomington, IN: Indiana University Press.

Ndlovu-Gatsheni, Sabelo J. 2013a. *Empire, Global Coloniality and African Subjectivity*. Oxford: Berghahn Books.

Ndlovu-Gatsheni, Sabelo J. 2013b. *Coloniality of Power in Postcolonial Africa: Myths of Decolonization*. Dakar: CODESRIA Books.

Ndlovu-Gatsheni, Sabelo J. 2015. 'Decoloniality in Africa: A Continuing Search for a New World Order'. *Australasian Review of African Studies* 36(2): 22–50.

Ndlovu-Gatsheni, Sabelo J. 2018a. 'Racism and "Blackism" on a World Scale'. In *Routledge Handbook of Postcolonial Politics*, edited by Olivia U. Rutazibwa and Robbie Shillian, 72–85. London: Routledge.

Ndlovu-Gatsheni, Sabelo J. 2018b. *Epistemic Freedom in Africa: Deprovincialization and Decolonization*. London: Routledge.

Ndlovu-Gatsheni, Sabelo J. and Zondi, S. 2016. 'Introduction: The Coloniality of Knowledge: Between Troubled Histories and Uncertain Futures'. In *Decolonizing the University: Knowledge Systems and Disciplines in Africa*, edited by Sabelo J. Ndlovu-Gatsheni and Siphamandla Zondi, 3–24. Durham, NC: Carolina Academic Press.

Nkrumah, Kwame. 1965. *Neo-Colonialism: The Last Stage of Imperialism*. London: PANAF.

OAU (Organisation of African Unity). 1980. *Lagos Plan of Action for the Economic Development of Africa, 1980–2000*. Addis Ababa: Organisation of African Unity.

OAU. 1986. *Africa's Priority Programme for Economic Recovery, 1986–1990*. Addis Ababa: Organisation of African Unity.

Quijano, Anibal. 2000. 'Coloniality of Power, Eurocentrism, and Latin America'. *Nepantla: Views from the South* 1(3): 533–80.

Soyinka, Wole. 2016. 'Repositioning Négritude: The Dialogue Resumes'. Lecture hosted by the Department of Arts and Culture, Africa Month Colloquia, Soweto, 25 May.

Suárez-Krabbe, Julia. 2016. *Race, Rights and Rebels: Alternatives to Human Rights and Development from the Global South*. London: Rowman and Littlefield International.

Thiam, Cheikh. 2014. *Return to the Kingdom of Childhood: Re-Envisioning the Legacy and Philosophical Relevance of Négritude*. Columbus, OH: Ohio State University Press.

Tibebu, Teshale. 2011. *Hegel and the Third World: The Making of Eurocentrism in World History*. New York, NY: Syracuse University Press.

Trouillot, Michel-Rolph. 1995. *Silencing the Past: Power and the Production of History*. Boston, MA: Beacon Press.

UN (United Nations General Assembly). 1991. *United Nations New Agenda for the Development of Africa*. New York, NY: United Nations General Assembly.

UNECA (United Nations Economic Commission for Africa). 1976. *Revised Framework for the Implementation of the New International Economic Order in Africa*. Addis Ababa: United Nations Economic Commission for Africa.

UNECA. 1989. *Alternative Framework to Structural Adjustment Programmes for Socio-Economic Recovery and Transformation*. Addis Ababa: United Nations Economic Commission for Africa.

UNECA. 1990. *African Charter for Popular Participation in Development and Transformation*. Addis Ababa: United Nations Economic Commission for Africa.

Wa Thiong'o, Ngũgĩ. 1997. *Writers in Politics: A Re-Engagement with Issues of Literature and Society*. Oxford: James Currey.

Wa Thiong'o, Ngũgĩ. 2009a. *Something Torn and New: An African Renaissance*. New York, NY: Basic Civitas Books.

Wa Thiong'o, Ngũgĩ. 2009b. *Re-Membering Africa*. Nairobi: East African Educational Publishers.

Wa Thiong'o, Ngũgĩ. 2012. *Globalectics: Theory and the Politics of Knowing*. New York, NY: Columbia University Press.

Wynter, Sylvia. 2003. 'Unsettling the Coloniality of Being/Power/Truth/Freedom Towards the Human, After Man, Its Overrepresentation – An Argument'. *New Centennial Review* 3(3): 257–337.

3 TO WHAT EXTENT ARE WE ALL HUMANS? OF CULTURE, POLITICS, LAW AND LGBT RIGHTS IN NIGERIA

OLAYINKA AKANLE, GBENGA S. ADEJARE AND JOJOLOLA FASUYI

Lesbian, gay, bisexual and transgender (LGBT) issues are very controversial in Africa as they are seen as exceptions to the rule that people are either male or female and sexual relations and marriages are expected to take place only between men and women. While global attitudes to LGBT rights are shifting, African countries generally remain lethargic in regard to LGBT rights, and Nigeria is among the most lethargic of them.[1] What we want to achieve in this chapter is to interrogate whether or not the human identity, and the rights that come with it, are attainable for the LGBT community within cultural, political and economic spaces in Nigeria. Nigeria is currently listed as one of the countries whose harsh social, political, cultural and economic spaces stifle the rights and privileges of non-heterosexual people (Noble 2015; NOI Polls 2015); however issues relating to sexuality and gender remain critical and sensitive globally (Akanle 2011; Akanle and Adejare 2016a; Akanle and Olutayo 2012).

Identity formation relating to the definition of 'who I am' largely concerns the social realities that define *our being human.* George Herbert Mead (1901) did extensive work on the concept of the *social self.* Mead appealed to the principles of social psychology to explain that we are only who we are because we accept the definition that society gives of us – the concept of 'I' is the unsocialised self while the concept of 'me' emanates from a series of socialisation processes (see Ritzer and Stepnisky 2014).

Helen Lyndon (1958) reifies the intangibility of identity or personality struggles amidst various nuclei of institutional and cultural ambiguities that cloud being human; this is of special concern to the same-sex people's liberation struggle in Nigeria, in Africa more broadly, and by extension in the whole world. The mantra 'jail the gays' has become popular in recent times in Nigeria, especially in the period since the former president, Goodluck Ebele Jonathan, signed a bill into law that criminalised amorous relationships between persons of the same sex on 14 January 2014. This bill did not just attract a lot of international attention; it aroused political debate and heightened intellectual agitations aimed at constellating various sociopolitical, cultural and psychoclinical differences of opinion with regard to homosexuality, as well as differences in religious and legal standpoints on the issues of homosexuality, bisexuality and even heterosexuality, with a general convergence of opinions towards disapproval of homosexuality. While the liberal school of thought continues to argue for equality and expressive humanity, conservative minds frown on perceived innovations that negate certain traditional values held by the people. Legal statutes are often deployed to affirm or reaffirm the position of any people or nation; in the case of Nigeria, the enacted law makes it crystal clear that homosexuality goes beyond the perceived and constructed sociocultural anathemas of society, and beyond being a prohibited legal act. The direct implication of this situation is that homosexual and/or transgender people are considered less than fully human and can no longer live freely or enjoy the same benefits that their fellow citizens enjoy relative to their sexual orientations, same-sex activities or gender identities.

Against this background, LGBT people have migrated to places like South Africa, Europe and other developed countries that allow them to be human (Batisai 2015). In fact, many LGBT people have emigrated on account of victimisation due to their sexual orientation or gender identity, and they have successfully secured asylum and integration into more permissive contexts abroad. In this they exemplify the view held by the critical school of thought that the history of human existence has been one of constant struggle (Idyorough 2002). This struggle cuts across geographical boundaries, peoples, cultures, races, classes, genders, economies, entities, identities and, of course, virtually all spheres of life. The apparent consequences of this struggle include emotional crises, political imbalances, economic woes, and sociopsychological eventualities that continue to bedevil human symbiotic co-existence on a daily basis. It is, however, important to recognise that inequality and the struggle for self-assertion assume more intractable dimensions with increases in the level of complexity that defines the human habitat, and the corresponding responses of humans to their social realities which are not the same across societies and groups. Thus, it is pertinent to constantly engage with and re-investigate historical social trajectories that define the past, present and future of a people, in order to foster mutual understanding of 'who/what we are', 'why we are what we are' and 'who/what we ought or want to be'. The main remit of this chapter is to examine the ramifications of culture, legal frameworks, politics and existentialities relating to LGBT people in Nigeria – Africa's most populous country, and one of the most institutionally repressive countries in terms of LGBT rights in Africa.

Hence, this chapter engages with the taken-for-granted question of the humanity of human beings. We do this through an appreciation and examination of the theoretical, philosophical and decolonial issues raised by Maria Lugones and others (Lugones 2003, 2007, 2010), particularly in regard to discourses concerning the relationship between homophobia and coloniality, and the question of the colonial, modern, structural and social institutional production of the human. Our aim here is to present interesting and factually contextualised case study accounts of issues relating to being human within the framework of LGBT rights in Africa, through the example of Nigeria. This is an area that has remained, hitherto, poorly covered in the literature.

THEORETICAL AND PHILOSOPHICAL BASES OF THE HUMANITY OF HUMAN BEINGS: THE LGBT CORRIDOR

Our explanations of contested humanity in this reading are aimed at two things: the first is to reveal the theoretical framework within which we have interrogated the humanity of LGBT people in Nigeria, and the second is to offer a critical lens through which the survival or suppression of the 'being' of LGBT people can be better understood and analysed within the Nigerian context. It is to this end that we have attempted a meta-narration of precolonial, colonial and post-colonial experiences of sexuality.

The work of Shulamith Firestone, *The Dialectic of Sex: The Case for Feminist Revolution,* first published in 1970, takes a significant radical and historical approach to theorising sexuality. Gleaning from the works of Karl Marx and Friedrich Engels, Firestone establishes a link between dominated sexuality and the evolution of capitalism in human society (Firestone 2003).

Capitalism, according to this view, transcends mere economic domination: the oldest form of domination, for Firestone, is sexual domination. For her, sexism in society gives expansive latitude to the subjugation of the weaker sexes (women especially), thereby promoting oppression of these categories of people. By implication, therefore, it requires conscious effort directed at the elimination of sexual diversity to achieve gender balance in human society.

Within the traditional Marxist explanation of sexuality from which Firestone borrows, capitalism is entrenched further in the institution of the family. The family is depicted as structured in such a way that exploitation of the weak is possible during the course of familial relationships; the power relations that exist between husband and wife, parent and children, or even between children themselves, for instance, are evident. One way in which Firestone believes the marginalisation of the female sex can be overcome is through revolution; adopting celibacy as a counter-existential narrative to normative feminine gender oppression is an example of this kind of revolution. Seeing this theoretical position within the traditional and institutional contexts of sexuality in Nigeria, it might be impossible to disconnect the age-old institutionalised gender gaps from the reality of the kind of (deprived) humanity accorded LGBT individuals. Traditional values in Nigeria see to the preservation of cultural barriers and dichotomous perceptions of who is human and who is not, in regard to genders, ages and system of interactions (Akanle and Adejare 2015). The work of Lugones on coloniality and modernity, and that of Gurminder Bhambra (2014) on post-coloniality, are important reference points for theorising the humanity of LGBT people in the past, present and future of Nigeria.

Among other things, Lugones (2010) posits that uncivility or barbarism is a hallmark of those categories of gender relationship that run in opposition to the accepted (or rather imposed) sexuality of colonial modernity. More to the point is the belief that colonialism came with a bifurcation of the sacredness and profanity of sexuality of various kinds: if it was not considered civil by the colonisers, it was uncivil, savage, profane and repulsive; if it was approved by the colonial powers, then it was modern, civil, morally good and sacred. As can be established within the contexts of the dominant religions in Nigeria, within which civility, modernity and sacredness of sexuality are often encapsulated, there seems to be an already drawn line of hierarchical dichotomy between who is human and who is not. A person is human when their sexual orientation conforms to the collective rules of sexuality. Although the work of Lugones focuses on deconstructing colonial strings attached to feminism, it is very important in its analysis of how the colonial experience shaped, and continues to shape, social relationships and the legitimacy of such relationships. This is also true regarding the contestation of the rights, humanity and lived experiences of LGBT people in Nigeria: some schools of thought have attributed the prohibition of homosexuality in the country to the impacts of the colonial experience and inherited legal frameworks.

The theoretical position of Bhambra is the last that we shall consider in this chapter. With roots in an attempt to deconstruct modernity and reinstate the evolution of a post-colonial movement, Bhambra (2014) brings to the fore the argument that the demarcation of human behaviour on the bases of modernity and Western civilisation is fast becoming redundant in the face of post-colonial and decolonial negotiations. What this implies, at least theoretically, is that the post-colonial phase of human existence blurs the gaps in identity discrimination and cultural incompatibility, and promotes convergence of human identities. The post-colonial narrative presented by Bhambra covers a wide range of contexts and themes, among which LGBT falls. Extending the work of Lugones, Bhambra envisages a more sophisticated negotiation of human identity that is entirely decolonised. This development to some extent also furthers the strides being made against the rejection of 'some humans' – like LGBT people. However, it must be noted that in reality, the lived experiences of LGBT people in countries like Nigeria where homophobia exists show that the impact of colonialism continues to be present, side by side with multiple social and historical diversities.

THE TRAJECTORY OF LGBT ISSUES IN NIGERIA

A critical examination of the panoply of perceptual issues associated with the human identity of LGBT people reveals the dynamism of the phenomenon over time. This dynamism is useful for an analysis of the current situation, and of the cross-cutting trajectories and diversity of psychological, cultural, biological and, recently, political explanations of sexualities that differ from heterosexual behaviour. The history of queer sexuality in Nigeria is to a very large extent amorphous. Emmanuel Obidimma and Angela Obidimma (2013) reveal that even though there is no particular date marking the first case of same-sex relations in Nigeria, the phenomenon might have a long clandestine history. While it is often argued that LGBT sexualities and identities are pathological, an anathema and a gross anomaly within the ambit of culture and social symbiosis of Nigerians, there are counter-positions which hold that the question of sexual orientation and gender identity cannot be narrowed down to racial or cultural debates alone. Although it has been documented that the wave of contemporary homophobic movements did not have its roots in Nigeria or elsewhere in Africa, there seem to be a greater number of anti-LGBT measures taken in Africa than in more developed settings like Europe and the USA, perhaps informed by the claim that LGBT practices are un-African (Ibrahim 2015).

In contrast to the definition given by the Institute of Medicine (2011), which depicts 'LGBT' as a phrase that describes an aggregate of groups that are unique in terms of their social, gender and economic means of survival, the collective history of Nigerians as a people subverts the distinction of LGBT as a people of unique history in the country. The category LGBT has been conceived from different angles, including social construction theory and feminist approaches, indicating variation in the practice and appreciation of sexual orientation and how such orientation translates into identity formation. Global recognition of the rights of LGBT people is on the increase by the day (Marks 2006). Different treaties have been signed across climes and continents to accommodate the rights and privileges of LGBT people as part of the fundamental human rights agenda. The cultural and political texture of Nigeria is inadvertently impermissible in the context of this global wave of tolerance for the supposedly 'new' sexuality. That Nigeria is an example of a country with a stern rejection of LGBT rights in Africa and the world is thus no exaggeration. This was clearly expressed in the 'jail the gays' laws promulgated in the country, referred to above.

THE SOCIAL DIMENSION OF LGBT RIGHTS IN NIGERIA

The place of traditional, social and cultural constructions of humanity must be properly contextualised in order to unravel the dynamics of how individuals with same-sex sexual orientation are perceived and treated. Africa at large still prides itself on having strong cultural ligaments. Nigeria is not exempt from this claim (Akanle 2012). There is no gainsaying that while some attribute the immutability of the cultural nexus in Nigeria to backwardness, the seeming reality required for the survival of peoples in developing countries, including Nigeria, is based on the need to galvanise their positive cultural traits for collective development and social stability.

Similarly, Lachenmann (2008) avers that tradition and culture (knowledge) are permanently subject to reinterpretation and they must be located within structural and situational contexts. In other words, there are variations, subject to an individual's world view, in what a culture or tradition means to any people at any particular point in time. Different types of LGBT identity are perceived as anathema, fatalistic, eccentric, debasing and punitive within the ambit of cultural networks in Nigeria, and hence result in the subjugation of the interests or rights of LGBT people (Akanle and Adejare 2016b). Another, cultural dimension of of large-scale discountenancing of LGBT is the pro-natality of Nigerian society. Oka Obono (2003) explains that Nigerians, and by extension Africans, favour procreation, a means by which they believe a society can be reproduced while sustaining traditional ideals. Hence, marriages without offspring tend to suffer from attempts to frustrate them by kinspeople and the society at large. Heterosexuality, as against homosexuality, is thus taken as an ideal form of sexual behaviour for preserving this value. This value system inadvertently debases the chances of LGBT rights being asserted, while promoting homophobic reactions from the generality of the people.

In the same vein, it is much easier to view religion as an integral part of a society's culture than to argue otherwise. In the Nigerian context, the intersection of religion and sexuality cannot be ignored, because religion is a crucial force shaping the realities of existence in the country. And the plural nature of religious orientations in Nigeria makes for more complex interrogation of the interplay of these two aspects of social being (Akanle and Adejare 2016a). The religious dimension of sexuality tends to continue to have an overarching negative influence on how LGBT identity is perceived in the country. All religions in Nigeria – including both the major and the not so popular religions – are inclined to be disapproving of LGBT identities, at least in public. The implication of religious attitudes towards LGBT identity is particularly important given the fact that most Nigerians interpret social issues through a religious lens. Across all institutions, religious sentiments play a central role in determining the directions, processes and outcomes of policies and actions. All religions in Nigeria define LGBT sexuality as a sin, and condemn the act and the people in the strictest terms (Global Legal Research Centre 2014).

Within widespread religious belief systems in Nigeria, LGBT rights do not exist, should not be heard of, and LGBT people and their advocates should be summarily rejected. These are popular sentiments across the country, and they are effective in suppressing the rights of LGBT people in Nigeria.

THE POLITICAL DIMENSION OF LGBT RIGHTS IN NIGERIA

The politics of sexuality in Nigeria is largely unidirectional, non-discursive and simply about playing to the gallery of the electorate, most of whom disapprove of LGBT identities. The political dimension of LGBT rights in the country is concerned with the exclusion or inclusion of these rights. Efforts at protecting LGBT rights in Nigeria have proved difficult due to a lack of political will by past and present governments of the country, which continue to churn out repressive legislation targeted against the LGBT community. The introduction of the anti-gay law referred to earlier in this chapter served as the straw that broke the camel's back. The law heightened homophobia in Nigeria, and made the survival of LGBT people and their rights more intractable and precarious, thereby forcing many to emigrate to more permissive countries (Batisai 2015).

The political space in Nigeria works in opposition to the process described by Ronald Holzhacker (2014), who explicates how the promotion of LGBT rights, which are projected as human rights, will further strengthen the movement for the enhancement of democracy and freedom for all and sundry in the world at large. According to him, there is an emerging perspective arguing on behalf of the equality of LGBT rights with other human rights, which is allowing for legal and political gains to be made. Thus, denying LGBT people their rights is perceived to be tantamount to denying them humanity – a position not encouraged within the ambit of the Universal Declaration of Human Rights (Marks 2006). Similarly, the United Nations' stance against discrimination on the basis of a person's racial or sexual orientation can be pointed to as a positive, in terms of the identity of the LGBT human. Conversely, these 'humans' can only be referred to as such outside the legal and sociocultural spaces of Nigeria. The sharp refusal of Nigeria to embrace LGBT rights as worthy human rights portends, and of course has accounted for, observable strains between Nigeria and other countries of the world where such rights are being upheld. This perhaps explains the diplomatic tensions in the relationship between Nigeria and the USA in recent times (Olanrewaju et al. 2015). The position of Nigerian political leaders is similar to that of the former president of Ghana, John Evans Atta Mills, who declared his country's sovereign stand on the same-sex issue as follows:

> No one can deny Prime Minister Cameron his right to make policies, take initiatives, or make statements that reflect his societal norms and ideals but he does not have the right to direct other sovereign nations as to what they should do especially where their societal norms and ideals are different from those which exist in Prime Minister [Cameron's] society ... I as president of this nation will never initiate or support any attempt to legalise homosexuality in Ghana ... Ghana will continue to operate within its constitution regardless of any threats from any country ... (Solace Brothers Foundation 2016, 9)

A very important point in regard to politics and LGBT rights in Africa is that many political actors and governments of African countries merely maintain positions with which they can score political points. They implement policies and laws that resonate with public anti-LGBT sentiments. Politicians thus apply the anti-LGBT instruments to score political points, uphold traditional cultural values and norms, and maintain deep-seated religious dictates. They do this also because they know full well that their constituents will frown upon their approval of pro-LGBT legislation, and they may be voted out of power and ostracised if they do otherwise. This perhaps explains why the anti-LGBT law in Nigeria was approved at a time when major electoral processes were under way, regardless of pressures from the West, especially from the USA.

THE LAW AND LEGAL FRAMEWORK OF LGBT RIGHTS IN NIGERIA

In reality, the legitimacy of an act or behaviour can best be concretised within the context of the laws (the Constitution, edicts, codes of conduct and other legal statutes) of any nation. Thus, many of the issues related to LBGT identities, as in any other country in the world, are embedded in legal contexts. In some cases, international treaties influence the local content of legislations. Conversely, national sovereignty often pre-empts the overriding effects of these treaties. This is no different in regard to how Nigeria and Nigerians have treated people who exhibited passive or active amorous same-sex behaviour in recent times. Even though the rage against men who have sex with men, women who have sex with women and the transgender community in Nigeria became pronounced in the enactment of the Same-Sex Marriage (Prohibition) Act of 2014, it is pertinent to note that a plethora of attempts had been made in the past to proscribe such acts. This is despite the fact that the stand of the United Nations (UN), as a typical international body, is clear in regard to LGBT rights: 'sexual orientation and gender identity are included among prohibited grounds of discrimination under international human rights law' (United Nations, n.d). LGBT rights are thus presented by the UN as inalienable human rights, expressed in the Universal Declaration of Human Rights of 1948 that all governments at different levels and in different regions of the world must promote and protect.

The flurry of homophobic and transphobic judicial activities in Nigeria has recently placed the country at number five in the top five countries in the world where LGBT rights are impossible to implement, given existing belief systems and social realities (Noble 2015). The plethora of pacts on LGBT rights signed around the world has not translated into liberation of same-sex and transgender people from discriminatory treatment in Nigeria, especially when the contemporary perception of LGBT identity in the country is taken into consideration. LGBT Nigerians practising same-sex relations, as in several other African countries, do so covertly and are liable to punishment under the law. The most stringent legal constraint against such practices is found in the 12 Northern states of Nigeria that have adopted Sharia law: Bauchi, Borno, Gombe, Jigawa, Kaduna, Kano, Katsina, Kebbi, Niger, Sokoto, Yobe and Zamfara. Certain homosexual activities carry the death penalty in these states, while the criminal and penal codes in the country as a whole uphold a 14-year prison term for those found guilty of an attempt at 'carnal knowledge' or 'carnal intercourse' with any person 'against the order of nature' (Human Rights Watch 2014). As Human Rights Watch documented in a 2008 report, these laws are colonial laws that were retained after the end of British colonial rule. Thus, one sees the reverberation of Lugones's view of the coloniality of gender and sexuality, as earlier discussed.

In the 12 Nigerian states where there is strict adherence to Sharia law, men convicted of homosexuality are liable to receive a death sentence, while female 'queer' sexual acts are punishable by flogging or six months' imprisonment. It was a former minister of justice, Bayo Ojo, who initially presented the Same-Sex Marriage (Prohibition) Bill to the national assembly in January 2006, but it did not pass beyond its first reading. A year later, the bill was approved by the Federal Executive Council and sent again to the national assembly for processing. The suggested bill proposed five years' incarceration for individuals who conduct, observe or support same-sex marriage. It also banned public displays of homosexual relations and adoption of children by homosexuals, and proposed a five-year prison term for participation in civic advocacy or groups promoting the rights of LGBT individuals. The intention of the bill was to completely ban homosexuality in the country. It was opposed and criticised, especially by international bodies and human rights organisations, for perceived violations of the rights to freedom of association and assembly as established by international laws and the African Charter on Human and Peoples' Rights (OAU 1981).

In January 2008 another bill to prohibit same-sex marriage was presented to the national assembly. The Same-Sex Marriage (Prohibition) Bill 2008 defined 'Same Gender Marriage' as 'the coming together of persons of the same sex with the purpose of living together as husband and wife or for other purposes of same sexual relationship' (Human Rights Watch 2014). It proposed a three-year jail term for defaulters. It also did not acknowledge homosexual marriages certified internationally. Like the 2006 Same-Sex Marriage (Prohibition) Bill, it went beyond the outlawing of same-sex marriage, and included regulations prohibiting consensual sex between adults, which carries a two-year prison term. The main difference between the 2006 and 2008 bills was the measure in the latter bill which imposed more stringent punishment on individuals who participate in aiding and abetting or witnessing the sanctification of the union between homosexuals, with the intention of further alienating LGBT individuals and denying them access to support and services.

Eventually, in 2014, President Goodluck Jonathan signed into law the Same-Sex Marriage (Prohibition) Bill (commonly referred to by Nigerians as the 'jail the gays law'), which further institutionalises discrimination against the LGBT community as well as threatening the fundamental human rights of all Nigerians. The law bans same-sex unions and the public display of affection by people involved in same-sex relationships, and imposes 14 years' imprisonment for same-sex marriage and a 10-year jail term for individuals who 'aid and abet' or witness same-sex weddings, as well as individuals who operate or participate in homosexual clubs, associations and groups, directly or indirectly, across Nigeria. The law, which forbids any 'public show of same-sex amorous relationship', is designed to inhibit the fundamental human rights and freedom of expression of LGBT individuals and their allies in Nigeria, and promotes persecution and violence against this minority group (Global Legal Research Centre 2014).

The recent focus on LGBT rights under international law has major implications for the legality of Nigeria's anti-LGBT laws because Nigeria is a member of the UN and a state signatory to these laws. The Charter of the UN and its founding treaty clearly establish its functions and objectives, and the binding mandates that its Member States must follow. One of their obligations is to 'reaffirm faith in fundamental human rights, in the dignity and worth of the human person, [and] in the equal rights of men and women' (Human Rights Campaign Foundation 2014). To that end, Member States are required to grant fundamental human rights and equality to all individuals.

The UN established the Human Rights Council in 2006 to identify human rights violations and suggest ways to tackle them effectively. The Council was designed to promote and safeguard human rights globally. In June 2011 it released a report in which it communicated its grave concern at acts of violence and discrimination, in all regions of the world, committed against individuals because of their sexual orientation and gender identity (Human Rights Council 2011). The report notes that the application of international human rights law is directed by the values of universality and non-discrimination as set forth in the Universal Declaration of Human Rights. It then emphasises the statement in the Vienna Declaration and Programme of Action adopted by the World Conference on Human Rights in 1993 (OHCHR n.d.) that, though cultural disparities must be valued, all nations have an obligation to defend the fundamental rights and freedoms of all humans, and argues that therefore cultural values concerning same-sex relationships do not undermine its members' duties to guarantee that individuals are not victims of discrimination based on their sexual orientation or gender identity.

EXISTENTIALITIES OF LGBT RIGHTS IN NIGERIA

With the exception of South Africa, with its more positive legal framework for LGBT rights, African countries generally demonstrate very little sociopolitical and legal tolerance for LGBT acts and people, with homophobia being a common occurrence (UN n.d.). LGBT people are more likely to encounter prejudice, marginalisation, harassment and the threat of violence than heterosexuals (Human Rights Watch 2014). Greatly ingrained homophobic outlooks, often together with restrictions on legal protection on grounds of sexual orientation or gender identity, mean that LGBT individuals in Nigeria are viewed as less human than heterosexuals. The restrictions are experienced at all levels of society and in all spheres – they face discrimination at work, in schools and hospitals, and within the family circle. They are singled out for physical attack, emotional violence, sexual assault and torture (Reid 2013). A poll conducted by NOI Polls (2015) revealed that 87 per cent of Nigerians supported the Same-Sex Marriage (Prohibition) Act.

The major factors that strengthen homophobia across Nigerian society are the moral, religious, traditional and political values of the majority population (UN n.d.). Thus, existing in a homophobic setting forces most LGBT people to conceal their sexual orientation, through fear of the unpleasant reactions and consequences of coming out that they could encounter. There is no unified definition of homophobia; it includes varying standpoints and attitudes. It is most often described as hostility to or fear of gay people, but also includes stigmatisation arising from societal beliefs about homosexuality (Finerty 2012). Negative values or attitudes towards non-heterosexual traits, identity, relationships and communities can lead to homophobic behaviour (Finerty 2012). Homophobia is displayed in different ways, for example through homophobic jokes, emotional violence, physical attacks, discrimination at work and negative media depiction. In February 2006, the national defence school in Nigeria expelled 15 trainees suspected of homosexual acts after anal examinations (Human Dignity Trust 2015). Again, in August 2007, police in Bauchi State arrested 18 men suspected of being homosexuals and charged them with belonging to an illegal society, committing indecent acts and engaging in criminal conspiracy (Human Dignity Trust 2015). In the same year, two civilians and two military men were arrested in Kano for allegedly engaging in same-sex sexual activities, and were only released after the intervention of the Coalition for the Defence of Sexual Rights (Human Dignity Trust 2015).

Within homophobic reactions to different sexualities lie certain tendencies, among others the inability to suppress organised sentimentality and resentment of those considered sexually abnormal, which becomes a dominant trait. On this basis, hatred and rejection of LGBT individuals can be considered inherent in the Africanity of sexual orientation that is, of course, conservative. It is in this respect, also, that the silencing of LGBT individuals in Nigeria as an isolated minority, who explore their sexual orientation or gender identity without any support, should be interpreted (Akanle and Adejare 2016b).

Again, it must be understood that Nigerian social values, as is also observable in other African countries, are predominantly conservative and generally socially exclude the LGBT community. Traditional and institutional support for heterosexuality continually reinforces the illegitimacy of unpopular forms of sexuality as practised by LGBT people. Similarly, there has been an observable lack of official records of any group of Nigerians who have come together to represent LGBT affairs, let alone conduct public advocacies on their behalf. However, there are some structured organisations that do advocate for the rights of the Nigerian LGBT community and seek their social inclusion. These are mostly non-governmental organisations that have publicly affirmed the protection and representation of LGBT rights as one of their areas of focus. They include Alliance Rights Nigeria, the Centre for Youth Policy Research and Advocacy (CYPRAD), the Support Project in Nigeria (SPIN), The Initiative for Equal Rights (TIER), Queer Alliance, Global Rights Nigeria, and the International Centre for Reproductive Health and Sexual Rights (INCRESE).

While the outlawing of LGBT-related activities represents institutionalised or formal constraint inhibiting the diversification of sexuality or gender variability, it must be noted that more often than not, discrimination against LGBT individuals starts within the families into which the individuals are born. As earlier posited, primordial African attitudes towards sexual orientation tend to favour heterosexuality. Since Africans are inclined to family life, the fear of (possible) rejection and severe negative reactions suppresses the instinctive need to express different sexual orientations, as in the case of LGBT identities (Akanle and Adejare 2016b). This narrative has been further strengthened in a study that shows that 89 per cent of individuals who disclosed their 'new' sexual or gender identities to their family members were disowned, while others were forced to undergo therapy or deliverance to 'cure' their 'confusion' (Global Legal Research Centre, 2014).

Corruption is a problem for the police in Nigeria, and the 'jail the gays' Act provides corrupt officers with additional leverage for their profiling and extortion activities, and the blackmailing of individuals with threats of arrest and imprisonment, if they do not pay the requested bribe. The 'jail the gays' Act has definitely increased the vulnerability of LGBT Nigerians to blackmail and abuse. The law instils a fear of imprisonment that discourages LGBT people from reporting violations of their fundamental rights to relevant authorities and, certainly, provides authorities and other individuals with a justification for discrimination (Akanle and Adejare 2016b). This link is very clear in the targeted police abuse against LGBT individuals, because officers can legally arrest people for consensual sex with members of the same sex; therefore the law legitimises homophobia, creating a sense of impunity for those who commit acts of violence.

The outlawing of LGBT acts was not only orchestrated by the interplay of culture, history, politics, law and, to some extent, religious values. These factors are also responsible for upholding the stalled status of negotiations for recognition and protection of LGBT rights in the country. In spite of the plethora of international conventions that constantly forge positive representations of LGBT identity, and work to eliminate all forms of discrimination against them, homophobia and rejection of people living with 'other kinds' of gender and sexuality persist in Nigeria. What is noteworthy in this development is that the current experience of LGBT people in Nigeria has not only been shaped by social factors but is also sustained by them.

CONCLUSION

From the foregoing, it can be concluded that the human identity of LGBT people is compromised by the existing social, political and legal milieus in Nigeria. At the level of social relationships, the history of the people who make up the country does not favour innovative individualism of the kind typified by LGBT identity; collective values regulate the contexts of relationships, and it is these dominant contexts within which acceptance or rejection of an individual's identity can be negotiated. The historical experience of the country is also sewn with the thread of colonial influences. Colonialism especially influenced the development of legal frameworks and religious views on human sexuality. The existing anti-LGBT law lends further credence to public rejection of the humanity of LGBT people, especially through the outlawing of homosexuality. Given the existing situation, it is very unlikely that the human identity of the LGBT population will be accepted by other Nigerians in the near future.

To the extent that both human sexuality and identity are constructed socially – through collective negotiation of ideal relationships, family life, shared historic and cultural experience, aggregated sentiment, and collective definition of humanity – it can be deduced that since Nigerian social, political and legal spaces are averse to same-sex or innovative gender relationships, LGBT people are considered less than fully human in the country.[2] To what extent, then, are they human? To the extent that they can exist and cope with the existing subjugation of their human identity within the dominant cultural, political, legal and religious contexts in the country. Issues around LGBT identity explored in this chapter are relevant to discourses, policies and programmes on citizenship and belonging. They address questions such as: 'who belongs in or to Nigeria?' and 'to what extent do they enjoy their rights in this context, compared to other Nigerians?'

NOTES

1 Uganda, Zimbabwe and Nigeria, for instance, share identical experiences relative to LGBT rights on the continent, as they have equally prohibitive legal frameworks.

2 See Batisai (2016) for parallels that can also be drawn with arguments that emerged from South Africa and other social systems on citizenship, nationality and sexuality.

REFERENCES

Akanle, Olayinka. 2011. 'The Sociology of Gender Equality and Development in Democratizing Nigeria'. *Nigerian Journal of Sociology and Anthropology* 9: 22–36.

Akanle, Olayinka. 2012. 'The Ligament of Culture and Development in Nigeria'. *International Journal of Applied Sociology* 2(3): 16–21.

Akanle, Olayinka and Adejare, Gbenga S. 2015. 'Traditional Institutions and Leadership among the Yoruba People of Western Nigeria'. In *Nigerian Peoples and Culture*, edited by Ikenna M. Alumona and Cynado C. Ezeogidi, 112–24. Enugu: Rhyce Kerex Publishers.

Akanle, Olayinka and Adejare, Gbenga S. 2016a. 'Towards Understanding Gender and Sexuality: Transgender Relational Shift in Contemporary Nigeria'. In *Essentials of Sociology: A Brief Introduction*, edited by Elias Olukorede Wahab, Olanrewaju Emmanuel Ajiboye and Olabisi Sherifat Yusuff, 73–87. Lagos: Department of Sociology, University of Lagos.

Akanle, Olayinka and Adejare, Gbenga S. 2016b. 'Socioeconomic Realities of Burgeoning Pentecostalism in Nigeria: A Study of Pentecostal Gatherings in South-Western Nigeria'. Paper presented at the Sixth Toyin Falola International Conference (TOFAC), Ibadan, July.

Akanle, Olayinka and Olutayo, Akinpelu Olanrewaju. 2012. 'Women's Rights as the Missing Link in Poverty Eradication in Nigeria'. *East African Journal of Human Rights* 18(1): 227–241.

Batisai, Kezia. 2015. 'Being Gendered in Africa's Flag-Democracies: Narratives of Sexual Minorities Living in the Diaspora'. *Gender Questions* 3(1): 25–44.

Batisai, Kezia. 2016. 'Interrogating Questions of National Belonging, Difference and Xenophobia in South Africa'. *Agenda* 30(2): 119–30.

Bhambra, Gurminder K. 2014. 'Postcolonial and Decolonial Dialogues'. *Postcolonial Studies* 17(2): 115–21.

Finerty, Courtney E. 2012. 'Being Gay in Kenya'. *Cornell International Law Journal* 45: 431–56.

Firestone, Shulamith. 2003. *The Dialectic of Sex: The Case for Feminist Revolution.* New York, NY: Farrar, Straus and Giroux.

Global Legal Research Centre. 2014. *Laws on Homosexuality in African Nations.* Accessed 15 May 2020. https://www.loc.gov/law/help/criminal-laws-on-homosexuality/african-nations-laws.php.

Holzhacker, Ronald. 2014. '"Gay Rights are Human Rights": The Framing of New Interpretations of International Human Rights Norms'. In *The Uses and Misuses of Human Rights*, edited by George Andreopoulos and Zehra F. Kabasakal Arat, 29–64. New York, NY: Palgrave Macmillan.

Human Dignity Trust. 2015. 'Criminality of Homosexuality'. Accessed 15 May 2020. https://www.humandignitytrust.org/lgbt-the-law/map-of-criminalisation/?type_filter=crim_lgbt.

Human Rights Campaign Foundation. 2014. 'Report: The State of Human Rights for LGBT People in Africa'. Accessed 10 September 2016. http://allafrica.com/download/resource/main/main/idatcs/00090835:64677debbbebd7098bc2a5d4dddc2cce.pdf.

Human Rights Council. 2011. 'Discriminatory Laws and Practices and Acts of Violence Against Individuals Based on Their Sexual Orientation and Gender Identity'. Accessed 14 September 2016. http://www.ohchr.org/Documents/Issues/Discrimination/A.HRC.19.41_English.pdf.

Human Rights Watch. 2008. 'UN: General Assembly Statement Affirms Rights for All'. Accessed 15 September 2016. https://www.hrw.org/news/2008/12/18/un-general-assembly-statement-affirms-rights-all.

Human Rights Watch. 2014. 'Nigeria: Anti-LGBT Law Threatens Basic Rights'. Accessed 10 September 2016. https://www.hrw.org/news/2014/01/14/nigeria-anti-lgbt-law-threatens-basic-rights.

Ibrahim, Abadir M. 2015. 'LGBT Rights in Africa and the Discursive Role of International Human Rights Law'. *African Human Rights Law Journal*. Accessed 4 September 2016. http://dx.doi.org/10.17159/1996-2096/2015/v15n2a2.

Idyorough, Alamveabee E. 2002. *Sociological Analysis of Social Change in Contemporary Africa*. Jos: Deka Publications.

Institute of Medicine. 2011. *The Health of Lesbian, Gay, Bisexual, and Transgender People: Building a Foundation for Better Understanding*. The National Academies Collection: Reports funded by National Institutes of Health. Washington DC: National Academies Press.

Lachenmann, Gudrun. 2008. 'Localising the State: Gender Policies at Interfaces of Different Knowledge and Social Spaces in West Africa'. Paper presented at the conference of the German African Studies Association in Freiburg and Basel, 14–17 May. Accessed 21 May 2020. https://www.isaportal.org/resources/resource/localising-the-state/.

Lugones, María. 2003. 'Street Walker Theorizing'. In *Pilgrimages/Peregrinajes: Theorizing Coalition Against Multiple Oppression*, edited by María Lugones, 207–37. Lanham, MD: Rowman & Littlefield.

Lugones, María. 2007. 'Heterosexualism and the Colonial/Modern Gender System'. *Hypatia* 22(1): 186–209.

Lugones, María. 2010. 'Toward a Decolonial Feminism'. *Hypatia* 25(4): 743–59.

Lyndon, Helen M. 1958. *On Shame and the Search for Identity*. New York, NY: Hartcourt, Brace and Company.

Marks, Suzanne M. 2006. 'Global Recognition of Human Rights for Lesbian, Gay, Bisexual, and Transgender People'. *Health and Human Rights* 9(1): 33–42.

Mead, George Herbert. 1901. *The Social Self*. Accessed 24 December 2014. www.marxists.org/reference/subject/philosophy/works/us/mead3.htm.A

Noble, Breana. 2015. 'Top 5 Countries with Strictest Anti-Gay Laws'. *Newsmax*, 15 June. Accessed 15 May 2020. https://www.newsmax.com/fastfeatures/anti-gay-laws-strictest-countries/2015/06/15/id/650638/.

NOI Polls. 2015. 'A Year-And-Half after Legislation, Nigerians Still Support Anti-Same Sex Marriage Law'. Accessed 15 May 2020. https://noi-polls.com/a-year-and-half-after-legislation-nigerians-still-support-anti-same-sex-marriage-law/.

OAU (Organisation of African Unity). 1981. *African Charter on Human and Peoples' Rights (Banjul Charter)*. Accessed 21 June 2020. https://www.achpr.org/legalinstruments/detail?id=49.

Obidimma, Emmanuel and Obidimma, Angela. 2013. 'The Travails of Same-Sex Relation under Nigerian Law'. *Journal of Law Policy and Globalization* 17: 43–47.

Obono, Oka. 2003. 'Cultural Diversity and Population Policy in Nigeria'. *Population and Development Review* 29(1): 103–11. Accessed 3 September 2014. http://www.jstor.org/stable/3092736.

OHCHR (Office of the High Commissioner on Human Rights, United Nations). n.d. 'Vienna Declaration and Programme of Action'. Accessed 28 September 2016. http://www.ohchr.org/EN/ProfessionalInterest/Pages/Vienna.aspx.

Olanrewaju, Faith, Chidozie, Felix and Olanrewaju, Adekunle. 2015. 'International Politics of Gay and Nigeria-US Diplomatic Relations'. *European Scientific Journal* 11(4): 505–20.

Reid, Graeme. 2013. 'The Trouble with Tradition: When "Values" Trample Over Rights'. Accessed 28 September 2016. https://www.hrw.org/world-report/2013/country-chapters/africa.

Ritzer, George and Stepnisky, Jeff. 2014. *Sociological Theory*, 9th edition. Singapore: McGraw-Hill Education.

Solace Brothers Foundation. 2016. 'Human Rights Violation against Lesbian, Gay, Bisexual, and Transgender (LGBT) People in Ghana: A Shadow Report'. Paper submitted for consideration at the 115th Session of the Human Rights Committee in Geneva, 15 October.

UN (United Nations). n.d. 'Fact Sheet: International Human Rights Law and Sexual Orientation and Gender Identity'. Accessed 15 May 2020. https://www.ohchr.org/EN/Issues/Discrimination/Pages/LGBTFactSheets.aspx.

4

HUMANNESS AND ABLEISM: CONSTRUCTION AND DECONSTRUCTION OF DISABILITY

SIBONOKUHLE NDLOVU

Without denial of difference and diversity, all people are human and equal. However, dominant powers in society categorise people using the concept 'normalcy' as the standard, leading to the emergence of 'human' and 'subhuman' as categories for labelling people. One such group of people that have continued to emerge from this categorisation, in which the 'normal body' and the 'normal mind' are used as a measure of ability and the 'abled', are persons with impairments. 'Disabled' is thus an identity label, a social construct used to define and describe those who do not meet the criteria of body and mind that are used to construct a 'normal' human being. There has been a realisation, however, that being 'disabled' is a by-product of this process of categorisation and labelling, and critical voices are emerging to claim humanness for people in all their diversity, including those with impairments.

Drawing from secondary data on disability, impairment issues and critical disability theory, as well as decolonial theory, this chapter makes use of the conceptual toolkit offered by these theories for understanding the deconstruction of disability. It demonstrates how disability has been socially constructed from the past to the present, and how this identity is being deconstructed to reclaim the humanness of persons with impairments. The concept of coloniality, drawn from decolonial theory, is used to illuminate an understanding of how disability is socially constructed, resulting in those with impairments losing their humanness. Sabelo Ndlovu-Gatsheni (2001) argues that it is the categorisation process implemented by the dominant powers which culminates in other social groups losing their humanness. From a decolonial perspective, humanness considers and accepts all human beings as fully human, in all their diversity. Decoloniality is also used in this chapter as the theory with the most traction for explaining the deconstruction of disability in terms of emancipation through consciousness, awareness of oppression, and agency, all with the over-arching aim of reclaiming humanness.

The concepts of ableism and body corporeality are drawn from critical disability theory, and enable a deeper analysis of how disability is constructed. Ableism involves preference of ability over disability (Hehir 2002), and an 'able body' is preferred over an impaired one (Goodley 2014). Thus, society places value on those identified as 'able' and dehumanises those with impaired bodies. The concept of body corporeality specifically explains the dichotomy abled/disabled as constructed categories, and shows how the concept of an impaired body is now being deconstructed to enable a more positive understanding of impairment. Deconstruction of disability and reclamation of humanness are therefore understood in the light of work towards dismantling oppression, so as to restore the dignity to persons with impairments which has been lost through their dehumanisation.

Barriers confronted in the deconstruction process are also discussed in this chapter, because reclaiming humanness is not without its challenges and it should be understood as a struggle. I will argue that while persons with impairments have been dehumanised, and struggle under the banner imposed on them by the dominant society, an understanding of body corporeality, emancipation through consciousness and awareness of oppression and agency could be useful ways to reclaim their humanness. However, doing so would not be without challenges, as there are issues involved that need to be addressed such as structure, context, inertia and intersectionality, among many others.

MAKING THE INVISIBLE VISIBLE

Making the invisible visible means using theory to unveil and reveal the deeper meaning of what might not be seen at face value, which in this chapter is the construction of disability, and its deconstruction to reclaim the humanness of persons with impairment. The hidden is brought to light, through the illumination offered by the specific theoretical concepts highlighted in the introduction.

Critical disability theory has been developed by post-conventionalists, post-structuralists and post-colonial scholars who draw most of their ideas from Michel Foucault, Judith Butler and Jacques Derrida. These scholars acknowledge the achievements of the conventional scholars as pioneers in their disability work, for example Oliver (1990), who proposed the traditional social model in which disability is located in the social environment and not in an individual. However, they also constructively problematise and critique specific disability- and impairment-related issues, with the aim of bringing to light different ways of understanding them, in order to improve the life conditions of all persons, including persons with impairments, whom they all agree are dehumanised, undervalued and discriminated against. The theory critiques the established discourse on disability and impairment in conventional disability studies, with the aim of constructing new meanings for these terms and a new understanding in which the humanness of persons with impairments can be reclaimed (Meekosha and Shuttleworth 2009).

Critical disability scholars such as Dan Goodley (2013, 2014) contest the essentialising of disability, ableism and disablism, arguing for a different understanding of them in the light of, among other things, intra/intersectionality, acknowledgement of difference, and allowing the voices of persons with impairments to be heard. These theorists critique the social model of disability, and propose resistance theories in its place. Shelley Tremain (2002, 2005) draws on the Foucauldian concept of modern power repressively regulating political lives; she sees disability and impairment as constituting each other and not as separate entities. She critiques the paradoxical reasoning of those who see the two as separate, and seem not to consider other categories of people who are also excluded and stigmatised (on grounds of their skin colour or queer bodies, for example) as 'disabled', only those with impairments (Tremain 2005). For her, disability is a social construct, as is impairment, because being categorised as impaired involves meeting specific requirements that are defined socially and politically. As such, she argues that there is a causal relationship between disability and impairment. I do not agree with Tremain's assertion, because disability exists in a social context while impairment is experienced in the individual realm and can limit one's functionality. It does not automatically follow that when one has an impairment one is disabled.

The post-colonialists Shaun Grech (2015) and Karen Soldatic (2015) seek to shift the understanding of disability and impairment from ethnocentric

Global North perspectives, to include the voices from the South. Within critical disability theory there are efforts to introduce change and influence thinking in ways that depart from the long-established and dominant discourse of disability and impairment, so as to include all persons, including those with impairments, in a space where everyone has a dignified life as a human being. Intersectionality is used as a key lens to guard against generalisations about the oppression of persons with impairments; it should always be at the back of one's mind if disability is not to be overgeneralised. Disability should be thought of as intersecting with multiple identities such as sexuality, race, gender, ethnicity and class, and should be placed at the centre of them (Sherry 2009), so as to heighten awareness of the social dynamics and power relations that shape lived realities.

Decolonial theory extensively explains coloniality in ways that provide useful insights for understanding how the *other* is socially constructed in the context of coloniality of being, and how the humanness of this other can be reclaimed. The theory is described as different from other theories of coloniality, and based on a different logic (Mignolo 2007), in that it not only exposes the ills of coloniality but also offers a method of fighting it, namely decoloniality. It provides a different understanding of the long-established hegemonic structures and practices of oppression, in terms of their underlying causes, that can lead to enlightenment, awareness, consciousness and agency on the part of the other. It not only unveils coloniality in its various guises but proposes ways of overcoming the oppression and related prejudices that coloniality imposed (Rose 2004). Decolonial theory hinges primarily on unmasking and exposing the ills of coloniality and Western modernity, and offers decoloniality as a way of self-liberation. The theory starts from the failures of post-modernism, which sought to address the problems of modernity without unmasking it as a power structure. I argue that it is only when the invisible underlying cause of dehumanisation is exposed that humanness can be reclaimed.

The key proponents of decolonial theory include Anibal Quijano (2000), Nelson Maldonaldo-Torres (2007), Ramón Grosfoguel (2011) and Walter D. Mignolo (2007). Other scholars from the Global South such as Ndlovu-Gatsheni have used decolonial theory to contribute to debates on transformation, poverty and oppression in specific African contexts, including xenophobia in South Africa (Ndlovu-Gatsheni 2013). The theory can be useful in stimulating positive change in and emancipation of those categorised as the other. The concepts of coloniality of being and ableism are therefore used to explain the construction of disability, which underlies dehumanisation of persons with impairment.

TRACING DISABILITY CONSTRUCTION

Disability was, and has continued to be, constructed differently at different times. During the pre-colonial era, African societies' construction of disabilities was informed by religious and cultural beliefs. Religion influenced positive or negative conceptions of disability in traditional communities. Robert Murphy (1990) explains that where Christian beliefs in God or African traditional beliefs in gods dominated, disability was understood by parents either as a punishment or a curse, seen as the result of having been bewitched for wrongdoing, or considered as something that befell innocent victims of fate. When reactions to their presence were informed by traditional beliefs, persons with impairments and their families were feared, ostracised, discriminated against, treated with cruelty and even killed because of fear that they could bring the curse onto the whole community. When the reactions were informed by Christianity, these individuals were accepted as a gift from the supernatural, and as a result they were over-protected, patronised and exempted from doing ordinary daily chores. Mike Oliver and Colin Barnes (2012) argue that only small-scale studies of these reactions were conducted in a few rural communities, and it cannot be concluded that all African societies' view of disability was informed by religion. But the overarching factor is that persons with impairments in traditional communities were dehumanised in one way or another.

In the West, some forms of impairments were conceived in a positive way during feudal times (Stone 1999). People were able to participate in the primitive collective activities in their communities as members of society, and as such not all persons with impairments were seen as disabled (Oliver 1990). The view changed during the period of the Industrial Revolution, when attitudes towards disability were informed by historical materialism (Finkelstein 1980). During this period, all people were expected to contribute to economic production. Members of a society had to work in the factories, and those who could not participate because of their physical impairments were viewed as disabled. They were seen as unproductive economically, and were excluded from the labour force because of their impairments. Such exclusion was a form of dehumanisation. When the social context is transformed and becomes inclusive of all forms of diversity, even those with impairments will be able to contribute to economic development.

Disability continued to be constructed negatively during the colonial and post-colonial periods. It was viewed as a limitation of the individual, being based on an individual model of understanding disability. In that view, disability was understood to be a tragedy, a misfortune that befalls individuals and renders them malfunctional within a 'normal' society; hence persons with impairments are viewed as victims who are to be pitied. Conceived in this way, there was and still is an attitude of patronisation towards people with impairments, one characterised by professional interventions such as rehabilitation, medical correction and institutionalisation, with charity, care and special education being used as ways to 'normalise' such people (Barnes and Mercer 2010).

The limitations of the individual view of disability weigh heavily on the humanity of persons with impairments. Depending on the severity of their impairments, individuals can be isolated and removed from the mainstream and from their families, and placed in institutions intended only for them. Separation of this kind can be understood as implying that those who are different from the norm in some way should be taken out of society, and be grouped together according to their impairments. When their limitations have been identified, they are removed from society and placed in specialised institutions, where professionals make decisions on their behalf and dictate how they should be normalised – resulting in discrimination and patronisation. Grech (2015) argues that these professionals also experiment on their bodies. This suggests that they are deprived of their own voices in regard to the lived experience of their impairments, how they are disabled by the social contexts, and what they want and need as individuals. This is the reason why intervention is directed at individuals, rather than at transforming their social contexts. Such interventions thus perpetuate dehumanisation.

With specific reference to the South African context, Collen Howell (2006) argues that the previous system of apartheid-era education was divided into mainstream and special education. Learners with impairments were educated in special schools. This system of education could be viewed as segregationist, discriminatory and dehumanising on grounds of impairments. However, the positive elements in this kind of education must not be glossed over. On the one hand the system could be viewed as segregationist; but on the other hand it recognised the humanness of learners with impairments. In segregated special schools, these learners accessed learning through specialised equipment designed specifically to cater for their different impairments. The teachers were trained to teach different learners with specific impairments. The built environment in these institutions was accessible, because it was specifically designed from the outset for learners with different types of impairment. Though the overarching consequence of such a system is dehumanisation embedded in segregationist education, the provisions made for learners with impairments that can potentially lead to humanness should not be understated, because being separated enabled learning to take place in special and unique ways suited to learners with impairments. It should therefore be acknowledged that though the individual model dehumanises persons with impairments, it also has a positive influence on the provision of facilities and support for them. Their unique needs are met, more specifically in terms of education.

As the struggle for independence and liberation of the disabled continues, there has been a shift from the individual to the social model. The limitations of the individual model have been widely contested in conventional (mainstream) disability studies by scholars such as Oliver (1990), Barnes and Mercer (2010) and Oliver and Barnes (2012). The social model locates disability in the environment; that is, it argues that it is the social and the physical environments that disable. Oliver (1990) argues that while it is understood that impairments in themselves might 'disable' persons with these impairments, this should not be over-emphasised as that could result in the responsible government stakeholders in society – that is, those responsible for creating an inclusive social environment for all the people of the country, including those with disabilities – not taking on the task of constructing an inclusive environment that caters for all. The social model also led to positive changes being made for persons with physical impairments in the 1970s (UPIAS, 1976) in terms of society meeting their needs, because it transformed the thinking on how to overcome the restrictions that were imposed on people with physical impairments. The shift to the social model could thus be viewed as a way in which society could empower persons with impairments, so that they are treated in a dignified way, gain their independence and claim their humanness.

The social model is, however, also critiqued in both the conventional and the critical disability scholarship. The main criticism of it is that it separates disability and impairment, defining them as different entities (Tremain 2005). In the social model of disability there is denial that an individual could be disabled because they have an impairment. The critics of this model argue that separating disability and impairments overlooks the effects of impairments, and limits those with impairments from sharing their lived experiences of how the impairments restrict them (Shakespeare and Watson 2001). They further argue that the social model emphasises the simple material benefits of access to infrastructure, amenities and education, rather than also considering the psychological being of persons with impairments (Shildrick 2012). Justifying the present criticisms, Grech (2015) argues that the realities of disability, the experiences of persons with impairment, and their voices, concepts and knowledge, more specifically in the Global South, are over-simplified and over-generalised as homogeneous and decontextualised. There has been further argument by critical disability scholars such as Goodley (2013, 2014) for a different way of looking into disability in a broader context. It needs to be reiterated that disability and impairment are separate things. I am in agreement with Tom Shakespeare and Nick Watson (2001) that the two are not mutually exclusive and should be treated separately.

CONSTRUCTION OF DISABILITY: THE NOTION OF DEHUMANISATION

It is important to understand how disability has been and continues to be constructed in day-to-day life. From the decolonial perspective, the categorisation and labelling of humanity in terms of normative standards by dominant powers constructs certain humans as the other. Disability is also socially constructed in the process, and persons with impairments emerge as disabled because of the different ways in which their identities are constructed.

In a society based on hierachisation, the group labelled as 'normal' is placed higher in the hierarchy and any other group diverting from the 'normal' is placed lower down. Those placed in lower positions are inferiorised, because they are viewed as of low status. Ndlovu-Gatsheni (2001) explains the process of categorisation and naming in which persons with impairments are dehumanised. He reiterates that the standard measure of 'normal body and mind' is used as the yardstick. All those with a body and mind that meet the specific criteria for 'normalcy' are labelled as the 'abled', while those who fall outside the margins of this category and do not meet the specific criteria for normalcy are named the 'disabled'. Multiplicity, diversity and difference are denied in the process (Ndlovu-Gatsheni 2001). The idea of normalcy in itself is subject to contestation because it is also a social construct, constructed by the powerful and imposed on the powerless. The process and the criteria used in the categorisation and naming of individuals and groups are a form of dehumanisation, because normalcy is a concept that cannot be universalised: it is a subjective and contextual phenomenon.

In critical disability scholarship, the construction of disability and consequent dehumanising of those with impairments is understood in the light of ableism. In ableism, 'normal' ways of doing things are preferred to ways that depart from what is understood as the norm. For example, a child who walks is preferred to one who rolls. A person who reads print is viewed as better than one who reads Braille. Hearing is prioritised over signing (Hehir 2002). In the modern world, Goodley (2014) explains this way of thinking as one informed by the capitalist system and the ethos of entrepreneurship, whereby all people are expected to contribute to economic production in society and to be independent individuals. It is the able-bodied who, it is assumed by society, can meet the demands of production, hence the need for normalcy to take this form (Goodley 2014). It does not end there; society then views itself as responsible for making those who have impaired bodies 'normal', 'normalising' them to fit in and function in sociocultural contexts in which all the structures and practices have been designed for the 'normal'. The process of normalisation is, however, heavily critiqued, because it implies an assumption on the part of the 'able' that the 'disabled' want to be 'normal' like them. It could be argued that normalisation is tantamount to dehumanisation, because according to Rod Milchako (2002), persons with impairments have not said they want to be anything that they are not. However, what they have said, and continue to say, is that they want accessible social contexts in which they are also able to participate, succeed, achieve and lead independent lives, different as they are (Oliver 1990). Persons with impairments do not want to be changed, but want both the social and physical contexts to be transformed so that they are also included in mainstream society. They argue in this way because they understand themselves to be like all other beings, only disabled by restrictions imposed on them. Milchako (2002) argues that society should be barrier-free, so that all people can genuinely belong to it, even the easy and hard-core cases of persons with impairments. It is therefore the society and the environment that should be transformed, rather than persons with impairments.

BARRIERS CONFRONTED BY PERSONS WITH IMPAIRMENTS

By constructing the 'normal' and the 'able', society is designed for the functioning of such categories. Its social and physical structures and practices have been designed for the 'normal' person. Persons with impairments are then 'disabled', and find themselves excluded. They confront a number of barriers and disabling conditions in different social contexts, although the infrastructural barriers and low expectations placed on them are viewed as the most disabling. These barriers dehumanise and limit persons with impairments in both physical and psychological ways, and society sees them as indeed disabled. Lack of accessibility and being understood in negative terms are core in making persons with impairments less human, leading them to live a life of dependence. Limited mobility has numerous consequences that lead to entrenched limitations. Society's low expectations of an individual lead to withdrawal and waste of potential and capabilities. In this chapter these barriers are discussed in the context of South Africa, which has the most comprehensive policies of inclusion of any country in Africa. If persons with impairments are confronted with so many barriers that dehumanise them in the South African context, the situation could be worse for such people in less advanced countries that do not even have comprehensive policies of inclusion.

The physical infrastructure in South Africa does not cater for diversity, and the issue of inaccessibility affects mainly those with physical impairments. Public transport is one major barrier: buses, cars and trains are still inaccessible, specifically to those who use wheelchairs and those with visual limitations (Parliamentary Monitoring Group 2013). The transport system was designed for a 'normal' being and not for people in all their diversity. Khuzwayo (2011) argues that the problem of inaccessible transport is more pronounced in rural areas. However, even in urban areas there are still very few accessible modes of transport. Given such transport barriers, persons with impairments who are working might find it difficult to get to their workplace, or could always arrive late. This could result in them losing their jobs and becoming dependent, and then being viewed as unproductive. It is a form of dehumanisation of persons with impairments, when their mobility is limited while they need to be mobile like all other human beings.

The built environment is also a barrier to persons with impairments, because of its inaccessibility. Most buildings still do not have rails, ramps and lifts. Some have lifts, but there is no voice mechanism to alert those with total visual loss of their destination. Leslie Swartz and Marguerite Schneider (2006) explain that for persons with impairments in South Africa, accessibility is still a pipe dream because of the costs involved in renovating and retrofitting old buildings, which were originally built without consideration for the accessibility needs of persons with impairments. Even though there has been a start in the retrofitting and renovation of the built environment to also cater for persons with impairments, the National Building Regulations impose restrictions in terms of the extent to which the specific alterations can be made (SANS 2011). When physical spaces are inaccessible, persons with impairments, more specifically those using wheelchairs and those who have visual challenges, encounter mobility problems in general, including manoeuvring in their workplaces. Of interest in regard to such dehumanisation is what happens when architectural design and heritage are valued over humanness. Clive Chipkin (1993) reveals that in one institution of higher education in South Africa there are buildings which cannot be renovated or retrofitted because they are being preserved for their architectural design and heritage value. Students with mobility and visual limitations can be confronted with barriers to access when they are expected to use such buildings for learning; they might have to spend time negotiating access and lose out on learning, and this can affect them negatively. It could be argued that it is typical of dehumanisation for the design of a building to be valued over the mobility, access and learning needs of persons with impairments.

Negative perceptions of the intellectual capabilities and abilities of persons with disabilities are another dehumanising tendency that is prevalent in society. There are assumptions that those people are incapable of intellectual work, and might not meet the academic demands of higher learning programmes. In this regard Sheila Riddel (1998), in agreement with Howell (2006), argues that academic staff at university level have negative perceptions of the capabilities and potential for learning of students with impairments. Those with impairments are pre-judged as being intellectually incapable even before they have the opportunity to prove themselves capable or not. When having an impairment is reduced to incapability, capable students with impairments could be denied equal opportunities for access to higher education. The few who make it into higher education courses of study, and can make positive contributions socially and economically, are further confronted with infrastructural obstacles to accessing employment, as discussed above. This is common in the South African context (Swartz and Schneider 2006). Without employment, they are stripped of their independent lives and framed as disabled, when it is society that disables them.

EVERYONE IS HUMAN: DECONSTRUCTION OF DISABILITY

Critical voices have emerged and debates are fierce in regard to the social construction of the identity of disability. Critical disability scholars problematise the narrow understanding of impairment as equal to disability, and the way in which persons with impairments are, as a collective group, categorised and labelled as the disabled. They argue that this view is reductionist, because it simplifies and reduces disability to a product of impairment, neglecting its broader, complex and deeper meanings that go beyond being impaired. Diane Pothier and Richard Devlin's (2006) reflections suggest that disability should be understood in terms of, among other things, social values, and also in terms of power and how it is used at the institutional and broader political levels. The concept of disability should not be reduced to meaning only impairments, but should also be located in social contexts so as to be better understood.

The binary able/disabled is viewed as oppressive in critical disability scholarship. There has been a proposition to deconstruct this binary (Shildrick 2012), in order to place all people of diverse types on the same plane. This is because binaries are viewed as creating hierarchical differences, and privileging one category over the other. The argument is that such binaries yield differential power relations, as those placed in the lower category as disabled are assigned lower status than those said to be abled. Pothier and Devlin (2006) argue that binaries are othering – hence the social constructs in which there are 'them' and 'us', with 'them' being labelled as 'disabled' and 'us' being the 'able'. It could be argued that these binaries dehumanise those in the lower rank. Goodley (2011) argues that this is done for political reasons so that one group dominates the other. Thus, when binaries have been deconstructed, all people are placed on a continuum. In this way they become equal, and as such there are no distinct boundaries where ability ends and disability begins. When that is put into practice, persons with impairments can be empowered and they can genuinely belong with others to mainstream society.

BRINGING BACK THE BODY: THE CORPOREALITY OF DISABILITY

There is widespread agreement among scholars that an impaired body is the reason for the dehumanisation of persons with impairments. But placing emphasis on the impaired body has not gone far enough in unmasking the reasons for this dehumanisation, and moving away from understanding the body as simply biological (Meekosha 1998). Goodley (2013) critiques the essentialist understanding that an impaired body is deficient. He argues that instead the emphasis should be on the corporeality of disability, as 'bodies are lived in but in the social setting that they inhabit' (Goodley 2013, 635). The body is brought back into its social context; as social entities all bodies, including those with impairments, need to be recast in terms of value in this context. All bodies should be understood as important for their uniqueness. The understanding is that all bodies matter and should be considered valuable. Goodley argues further that an impaired body should not only be understood in the context of oppression, because persons with impairments are intersectional subjects – they embody other positions which are valued in the ableist cultures (Goodley 2013).

Assistive devices and technology can be useful to support impaired bodies. Helen Meekosha and Russel Shuttleworth (2009) propose technologies and mechanical devices to be used to enhance bodies with impairments. Through the use of such technologies positive self-images are developed to overcome feelings of inadequacy. This might seem to contradict earlier intimations that persons with impairment do not want to be transformed but instead want the social contexts to be transformed to suit their unique needs; but analytical attention is invited to address the necessity of providing support in the form of assistive devices and technology, as they could be useful for their aesthetic value and for restoring confidence and self-value to bodies with impairments. However, as Shakespeare (2010) explains, no amount of environmental transformation can totally overcome all impairments, and it is important that the realities of impairments are brought to the fore so that when rethinking disability, genuine and feasible ways of bringing back humanness are considered.

EMANCIPATION THROUGH DECOLONIALITY

From the decolonial perspective, the voices of the oppressed could also be stifled by different epistemic locations. Boaventura de Sousa Santos (2007, 45) explains that the zones of these locations are the spaces into which humanity is categorised and placed through Western 'abyssal thinking'. This is the social reality in which the world is divided into two realms by an invisible line and by the creation of the West and the South. On one side of the line is the *zone of being* where the metropolitan is located, and on the other side of the line is the *zone of non-being* which constitutes the other (Santos 2007). Persons with impairments, by virtue of their different bodies, are othered and located in the zone of non-being. However, although these persons are located in the zone of non-being, some epistemically think and speak from the dominant side (Ndlovu 2014). In other words, some persons with impairments epistemically locate themselves in the zone of being, because of their way of thinking. Those who do so find their conditions of dehumanisation exacerbated, because on top of society dehumanising them, they also dehumanise themselves. Viewing internalised dehumanisation as the worst form of mental colonisation, Stuart Hall (1990, 225) argues that 'it is one thing to position subjects as the other in a dominant discourse, it is quite another to subject them to that knowledge'. Hall's argument is that when the oppressed have internalised oppression they might not even be aware that they are oppressed. Liberation therefore starts from being conscious, and aware of oppression. It might be difficult for persons with impairments who are not aware that they are oppressed to use their agency to bring about change. However, as Grosfoguel (2011) argues, the two zones are not fixed, and not permanent categories. The epistemic location of such persons could also transform as they are conscientised.

Consciousness of oppression could be viewed as the starting point for emancipation for persons with impairments. Proceeding from the argument that disability is constructed through coloniality of being and placement in the zone of non-being, Grech's (2015) argument of an 'alternative way of being' could be emancipatory. Those with impairments should resist and dismantle a normative conceptualisation of being prescribed and imposed on them by the dominant society. Self-value, self-love and embracing the reality that they are different and diverse can be the starting point for those with impairments. A positive self-concept and identity can enable persons with impairments to offer an alternative to coloniality, one which can be appreciated as plurality by other people such as those without impairments. Persons with impairments can reclaim their humanness through awareness of their oppression as a key point of departure. But while consciousness and awareness of oppression are pivotal in reclaiming humanness, casting the net wider to consider context and structure illuminates ways of thinking about the production of power and the attendant oppression of persons with impairment. The social structure and context might not be conducive to persons with impairments liberating themselves, thus rendering consciousness and awareness of oppression inadequate for reclaiming humanness.

Persons with impairments could also emancipate themselves through resisting practices and structures that are oppressive, as it has been emphasised that limitations are imposed by social contexts. Grech (2015) observes that historically the colonisers and colonised had a dialectical relationship, which included resistance. Gayatri Spivak (1988) understands resistance and speaking against oppression as aspects of agency. In most societies, both in the South and the West, the able-bodied have been speaking and continue to speak for persons with impairments. This trend has resulted in the construction of those with impairments as powerless and voiceless. The experience of being impaired has been and continues to be understood from the able-bodied perspective (Hosking 2008); hence it is reported that the voices of persons with impairments are suppressed and silenced by the mainstream. When persons with impairments say things that the mainstream society wants to hear they are listened to, but when they speak of what society does not want to hear, that is considered as an inappropriate response to their impairments (Titchkosky 2003).

The critical voices contest this, and are fighting to change it by calling for the privileging of the voices of lived experience from persons with impairments (Hosking 2008). Essentially, there should be a shift from understanding the experience of impairment on terms set by those without impairments, to understanding it from the perspective of those with lived experience of it.

To allow these stifled voices to emerge, there has been a proposal to adopt bottom-up approaches (Pothier and Devlin 2006). In ongoing struggles to overcome the limitations associated with impairments, the focus should be on proposals made by people who have lived experiences of impairment. Through their agency to resist, fight and speak against oppression, persons with impairments can push back against the circumstances imposed by oppressive structures. This can be done through a collective voice, which can attract more attention than individual voices. Ndlovu-Gatsheni (2013) argues that coloniality must be unmasked, resisted and destroyed. Those with disabilities should not normalise coloniality, but instead should collaborate with other oppressed groups such as women and blacks in the struggle to regain humanness. Through such efforts an 'alternative way of being' can be conceived in their minds and in those of the dominant society. It is, however, important to highlight that the struggles for reclaiming humanness need to take into consideration questions of whether or not actions are being taken on the basis of proposals from persons with impairment. This is important, because it is not always the case that when someone speaks they are listened to and what they say is implemented.

INTERSECTIONALITY

It is important to understand that disability does not always equal oppression. Critical disability scholars engage with the intersectionality of disabled identity to nuance the debates on disability (Goodley 2013, 2014). Their proposition is that an impairment should be understood in the context of multiple identities, because it intersects with other identities such as race, gender and class which might bring some privileges. Sherry (2009) argues that impairments should be thought of as intersecting with multiple identities, and as a result should be placed at the centre of them. It should be viewed as a fluid and ever-changing entity shared by people with and without impairments, and not a specific absolute category that is stable. Furthermore, an impairment should be viewed as occupying a position of possibility, because it is an aspect of a multi-layered position in which it converges with gender, race, class, ethnicity or sexuality (Goodley 2013), which are considered normative within the ableist context. The result of this convergence is subversion, connection and a reappraisal of identities (Goodley 2013). Thus persons with impairments should not always be viewed as oppressed and dehumanised.

What bears emphasising is that impairments centre other positions of power. Goodley (2011) argues that impairments should be understood in terms of a springboard, a space from which to think through a host of political and theoretical issues that apply to all identities. Engaging with intersectionality as a key aspect has enabled critical disability scholarship to bring to light the view that impairments should not always be understood in terms of disadvantage and double oppression (Crenshaw 1989), with impairments always seen as the intersection of one axis of oppression with another. The 'disabled' body is not only understood in the context of oppression, because persons with impairments are intersectional subjects, and they therefore embody other positions which can be powerful and valued in an ableist culture (Goodley 2013, 2014). For example, an impaired body from a middle-class family might have better opportunities for access to education and employment that constitute a set of privileges than an able-bodied person from a lower socio-economic class. Also, an impaired body of a white female student from a high socio-economic class could be privileged over a black able-bodied student from a lower class.

It bears noting that when impairment intersects with other axes of oppression, it yields double oppression (Crenshaw 1989). For example, blackness is not an impairment, a medical condition or a lack of operational efficiency. However, Ndlovu-Gatsheni (2016), making reference to Ngũgĩ wa Thiongo's discussion of 'dismemberment', argues that black people's humanness is questioned, resulting in their exclusion from the human family. In the same way, those with impairments are dismembered from society. Though blackness cannot be equated with an impairment, it functions as a disabling condition, and by virtue of both persons with impairments and black people being viewed as inhuman, black persons with impairments could be more oppressed than white people with impairments, because of the intersection of their impairment with blackness. A woman with impairments could also be understood as doubly oppressed because of the stereotypes related to gender. In a nutshell, intersectionality is important in reclaiming humanity because it helps us to understand impairments and disability more broadly in the context of multiple identities and the workings of power dynamics that shape privileges and oppression, as impairments intersect with other identities (Goodley 2013; Soldatic and Meekosha 2012).

Drawing attention to intersectionality enables an understanding of persons with impairments that goes beyond seeing them as a group on their own 'with special needs'. Furthermore, while speaking with one voice against oppression could be one way of reclaiming humanness for persons with impairments, the effects of being privileged or underprivileged within the category of disabled persons themselves could defeat the purpose. As disability intersects with other identities, class dynamics play themselves out in ways that shape forms of oppression and privilege. As a result, a deeper understanding of intersectionality leads to a more nuanced analysis of persons with impairment, one that renders generalisations about speaking with a collective voice in reclaiming humanness inadequate.

CONCLUSION

This chapter has discussed how disability is constructed and how persons with impairments have been dehumanised in the process. By virtue of their dehumanisation, impaired people find themselves confronted with specific barriers that limit their access to, and participation and achievements in, society – more specifically in the spheres of education and employment. It is against this background that critical voices seek to reclaim humanness for and restore dignity to all people, especially persons with impairments. The issue at stake, however, is whether or not the voices of those who seek to reclaim humanness, and of the persons with impairments themselves, are being listened to, are being heard and acted upon. Without addressing this point of contention, reclaiming humanness might not be without its challenges.

Intersection with other identities of power in a disablist society could also stifle the voices of persons with impairments, as not all of them are oppressed. Those in a privileged position do not have the same experiences of disablement and oppression as the underprivileged. In addition, the epistemic location in which oppressed persons with impairments think and talk like the oppressor could also work against bringing humanness back to them. It is these counter-productive issues that should be addressed as a priority to push the struggles for humanness to its desired conclusion. Bringing to the fore the value of the body through corporeality and decoloniality, in terms of consciousness of agency expressed by persons with impairments themselves, and listening to the voices of those with lived experience of impairment, are some of the ways in which the humanness of persons with impairments can be reclaimed and they can be given the dignity due to them just as it is given to those without impairments.

REFERENCES

Barnes, Colin and Mercer, Geoff. 2010. *Exploring Disability: A Sociological Introduction*. Cambridge: Polity Press.

Chipkin, Clive M. 1993. *Johannesburg Style, Architecture and Society: 1880–1960s*. Cape Town: David Philip.

Crenshaw, Kimberley. 1989. 'Demarginalizing the Intersection of Race and Sex: A Black Feminist Critique of Antidiscrimination Doctrine, Feminist Theory and Antiracist Politics'. University of Chicago Legal Forum 1989: Article 8. Accessed 12 May 2020. https://chicagounbound.uchicago.edu/uclf/vol1989/iss1/8.

Finkelstein, Vic. 1980. *Attitudes and Disabled People*. New York, NY: World Rehabilitation Fund Inc.

Goodley, Dan. 2011. *Disability Studies: An Interdisciplinary Introduction*. London: SAGE Publications.

Goodley, Dan. 2013. 'Dis/entangling Critical Disability Studies'. *Disability and Society* 28(5): 631–44.

Goodley, Dan. 2014. *Dis/ability Studies: Theorising Disablism and Ableism.*London: Routledge.

Grech, Shaun. 2015. 'Decolonising Eurocentric Disability Studies: Why Colonialism Matters in Disability and Global South Debate.' *Social Identities* 21(1): 6–12.

Grosfoguel, Ramón. 2011. 'Decolonising Post-Colonial Studies and Paradigms of Political Economy: Transmodernity, Decolonial Thinking and Coloniality'. *Journal of Peripheral Cultural Production of the Luso-Hispanic World* 1(1): 1–5.

Hall, Stuart. 1990. 'Cultural Identity and Diaspora'. *Identity: Community Culture Difference* 2: 222–37.

Hehir, Thomas. 2002. 'Eliminating Ableism in Education'. *Harvard Educational Review* 72(1): 1–33.

Hosking, David. 2008. 'Critical Disability Theory'. *Disability Studies* 2(4): 7.

Howell, Collen. 2006. 'Disabled Students and Higher Education in South Africa'. In *Disability and Social Change: A South African Agenda*, edited by Brian Watermeyer, Leslie Swartz, Theresa Lorenzo, Marguerite Schneider and Mark Priestley, 164–78. Cape Town: HSRC Press.

Khuzwayo, Zuki. 2011. 'Providing Accessible Transport for People with Disabilities in the Ethekwini Municipal Area: Unpacking the Options'. Paper presented at the Southern African Transport Conference, Pretoria, 11–14 July.

Maldonaldo-Torres, Nelson. 2007. 'On the Coloniality of Being: Contributions to the Development of a Concept'. *Cultural Studies* 21(2–3): 240–70.

Meekosha, Helen. 1998. 'Body Battles: Bodies, Gender and Disability'. In *The Disability Reader: The Social Science Perspective*, edited by Tom Shakespeare, 163–80. London: Cassell.

Meekosha, Helen and Shuttleworth, Russel. 2009. 'What's so Critical about Critical Disability Studies?' *Australian Journal of Human Rights* 15(1): 47–76.

Mignolo, Walter D. 2007. 'Introduction: Coloniality of Power and De-Colonial Thinking'. *Cultural Studies* 21(2–3): 240–70.

Milchako, Rod. 2002. *The Difference that Disability Makes*. Philadelphia, PA: Temple University Press.

Murphy, Robert. 1990. *The Body Silent.*New York: W.W. Norton.

Ndlovu, Morgan. 2014. 'Cultural Villages in Post-Apartheid South Africa: A Decolonial Perspective'. PhD diss., Monash University.

Ndlovu-Gatsheni, Sabelo J. 2001. 'Imperial Hypocrisy, Settler Colonial Double Standards and Denial of Human Rights to Africans in Colonial Zimbabwe'. In *The Historical Dimensions of Democracy and Human Rights in Zimbabwe. Volume One: Precolonial and Colonial Legacies*, edited by Ngwabi Bhebe and Terence Ranger, 53–83. Harare: University of Zimbabwe Publications.

Ndlovu-Gatsheni, Sabelo J. 2013. *Empire, Global Coloniality and Subjectivity*. Oxford: Berghahn Books.

Ndlovu-Gatsheni, Sabelo. 2016. 'The Imperative of Decolonising the Modern Westernised University'. In *Decolonising the University Knowledge Systems and Disciplines in Africa*, edited by Sabelo J. Ndlovu and Siphamandla Zondi, 27–45. Durham, NC: Carolina Academic Press.

Oliver, Mike. 1990. *The Politics of Disablement: Critical Texts in Social Work and the Welfare State*. Basingstoke: Macmillan.

Oliver, Mike and Barnes, Colin. 2012. *The New Politics of Disablement.* Basingstoke: Palgrave Macmillan.

Parliamentary Monitoring Group. 2013. 'Disabled People South Africa: Briefing on Education, Employment and Accessibility Challenges'. Accessed 17 May 2017. http://www.pmg.org.za/committe-meeting/15509/.

Pothier, Diane and Devlin, Richard. 2006. *Critical Disability Theory: Essays in Philosophy, Politics and Law*. Vancouver: UBC Press.

Quijano, Anibal. 2000. 'Coloniality of Power, Eurocentrism, and Latin America'. *Nepantla: Views from the South* 1(3): 533–80.

Riddel, Sheila. 1998. 'Chipping Away at the Mountain: Disabled Students' Experience of Higher Education'. *International Studies in Sociology of Education* 8: 203–22.

Rose, Deborah Bird. 2004. *Reports from a Wild Country: Ethics for Decolonisation*. Sydney: University of South Wales Press.

SANS (South African National Standard SANS 10400-S). 2011. *The Application of the National Building Regulations Part S: Facilities for Persons with Disabilities*. SABS Standards Division: Pretoria.

Santos, Boaventura de Sousa. 2007. 'Beyond Abyssal Thinking: From Global Lines to Ecologies of Knowledges'. *Review* 30(1): 45–89.

Shakespeare, Tom. 2010. 'The Social Model of Disability'. In *The Disability Studies Reader*, edited by Lennard Davis, 266–73. London: Routledge.

Shakespeare, Tom and Watson, Nick. 2001. 'The Social Model of Disability: An Outdated Ideology?' *Research in Social Science and Disability* 2: 9–28.

Sherry, Mark. 2009. *Disability and Diversity: A Sociological Perspective*. New York, NY: Nova Science Publishers.

Shildrick, Margrit. 2012. 'Critical Disability Studies: Rethinking the Conventions for the Age of Postmodernity'. In *Routledge Handbook of Disability Studies*, edited by Nick Watson, Alan Roulstone and Carol Thomas, 30–41. London: Routledge.

Soldatic, Karen. 2015. 'Postcolonial Reproductions: Disability, Indigeneity and the Formation of the White Masculine Settler of Australia'. *Social Identities* 21(1): 53–68.

Soldatic, Karen and Meekosha, Helen. 2012. 'Disability and Neoliberal State Formation'. In *Routledge Handbook of Disability Studies*, edited by Nick Watson, Alan Roulstone and Carol Thomas, 195–210. London: Routledge.

Spivak, Gayatri. 1988. 'Can the Subaltern Speak?' In *Marxism and the Interpretation of Culture*, edited by Cary Nelson and Lawrence Grossberg, 21–78. London: Macmillan.

Stone, Emma, ed. 1999. *Disability and Development*. Leeds: Leeds Disability Press.

Swartz, Leslie and Schneider, Marguerite. 2006. 'Tough Choices: Disability and Social Security in South Africa'. In *Disability and Social Change: A South African Agenda*, edited by Brian Watermeyer, Leslie Swartz, Theresa Lorenzo, Marguerite Schneider and Mark Priestley, 234–43. Cape Town: HSRC Press.

Titchkosky, Tanya. 2003. *Disability, Self and Society*. Toronto: University of Toronto Press.

Tremain, Shelley. 2002. 'On the Subject of Impairment'. In *Disability/Postmodernity: Embodying Political Theory*, edited by Mairian Corker and Tom Shakespeare, 32–47. London: Continuum Press.

Tremain, Shelley. 2005. *Foucault and the Government of Disability*. Ann Arbor, MI: University of Michigan Press.

UPIAS (Union of Physically Impaired Against Segregation). 1976. *Fundamental Principles of Disability*. London: Union of Physically Impaired Against Segregation.

5 DOING THE OLD HUMAN

CARY BURNETT

Creative endeavours can provide a powerful means of reflecting, and reflecting on, human experience and can therefore extend our understanding of the human other. My feature-length screenplay *When Granny Went on the Internet* is a creative product which takes as its centre an '-ism' that sits low on the radar of public comment or concern: ageism. The story revolves around Granny who, at 75 years of age and after the unexpected death of her husband, suddenly finds herself alone and unable to operate any twenty-first-century technology. I use the creative product of the screenplay to explore the link between technology, patriarchy and sexism, and the traditional alignment between technology and men, as well as the alignment between technology and youth. Granny, as an old woman, is an outsider to digital technology and her sons, believing they are acting in her best interests and are 'protecting her from herself', attempt to gatekeep her access to such technology.

The relationship between gender and technology is not static, but evolves over time. Eugenia Siapera (2012, 181–82) describes both technology and gender as 'moving targets, involved in a fluid relationship in which they co-constitute each other', along with other influencing elements. I sense that new media such as the Internet provide an opportunity for the traditional alignment between technology, gender and age to be disrupted. Through my screenplay I explore the notion that new media may provide a portal through which definitions of self can be reconstructed: Granny's story disrupts the traditional alignment between technology, patriarchy, sexism and ageism described by Siapera, and re-imagines it.

INT. GRANNY'S BEDROOM – DAY

The harsh sound of an alarm clock heralds the start of the big day. Granny's eyes snap open. She switches on the light and puts on her hearing aid. She tries to jump out of bed but ends up rocking back and forth on the edge before she can finally stand. She is chatting ten to the dozen.

GRANNY

Ho-kay! Let's get the show on the road. Today is the day! Can you believe it! I want you to tell me which outfit is better for the ship.

She opens the cupboard and starts taking out one vividly bright outfit after another, tossing them behind her onto the bed.

GRANNY (CONT'D)

What do you think? This one OR . . . this one?

Grandad lies silently. Granny pauses and turns, holding another colourful outfit in her hands. She faces the bed and Grandad.

GRANNY (CONT'D)

Sweetheart?

Granny's expression changes as she realises that something is not quite right. She goes over and shakes Grandad. No response. She shakes him harder. He lies motionless. Granny drops to her knees next to the bed. She places her hand on Grandad's chest, but there is no breathing. She grabs for the phone next to the bed and dials furiously. It rings for a long time before someone answers.

*

This is an early scene from *When Granny Went on the Internet*, a feature-length screenplay I wrote about a 75-year-old grandmother who suddenly finds herself alone after the death of her husband. Through this screenplay, I explore what it means to be old, female, alone and out of step with the technological world around you. The protagonist, Granny, has to find her feet again without the partner who 'did it all' for her. In the aftermath of her husband's passing she learns how to use a computer and then the Internet, which leads to a changed perception of herself and to renegotiated relationships with her two sons.

I chose the title of my screenplay before I had encountered the work of pioneering feminist writer Barbara McDonald. The title *When Granny Went on the Internet* speaks on various levels: first, hailing old women and families as an important target audience through the use of the word 'Granny' (although they are not the only audience); second, positioning the screenplay as a comedy and therefore as non-threatening; and third, as an *agent provocateur* asserting that old women have the right to engage with new media.

The dialogue in the screenplay includes use of the word 'old'. The decision to refer to the protagonist as old, rather than with a euphemism such as 'senior citizen', or the more innocuous-sounding term 'older woman', was influenced by McDonald's writings about identity and difference in old women (McDonald and Rich 1984). McDonald has been described as the first person to really draw attention to the fact that old women are ignored, excluded and rendered invisible in society (see Adams 2008). She identified society's view that 'old is ugly, old is powerless, old is the end and therefore … old is what no one could possibly want to be' (McDonald and Rich 1984, 91). Her powerful and clear writing encouraged me to use the word 'old' deliberately, and to choose that the protagonist of my screenplay challenge the stereotype of the old woman as benign, non-productive and inconsequential. I hope that the screenplay will provide a form of advocacy for the right of old women to experiment with new media and to enjoy its affordances, such as easy access to information and connection with people who live far away.

Another view is that it is life stages, rather than age, that better predict engagement with and use of new media (Helsper 2010). I have deliberately tried to highlight the protagonist's life stage of widowhood. The norms and conventions associated with Granny's life stage of advanced age and widowhood are clearly displayed by one of her sons, Aaron, when he tries to persuade her to move to a retirement centre. He believes she is old, unskilled, should not be trying anything new, and needs looking after. Josh, her other son, on the other hand, believes that Granny's new life stage of widowhood is as good a time as any for her to try out new things. As such, Josh focuses more on Granny's life stage than on her age.

Through McDonald I came to understand that the identity of grandmother is a safe one for women to occupy, given that the role stereotypically emphasises the nurturing of the young and is seen as supportive, useful and non-threatening. The choice of name for the protagonist – 'Granny' – conjures up the stereotype of the benign, inconsequential individual whose uses do not extend much beyond child-minding. However, Granny does have a real name: Sylvia Human. I chose the name Sylvia for her as it provides a connection to the phrase 'Silver Surfers' being used in the online press to describe old people using the Internet.[1] Her surname – 'Human' – suggests that she is an 'everywoman' and her experiences and feelings reflect those of many other old people. As such, she is a mirror of the human condition.

However, McDonald also says that 'age in our society also gives us a second opportunity … to move out of that safe harbour of acceptability' (McDonald and Rich 1984, 2). The two sons, Aaron and Josh, represent these two positions – the safe harbour and the move away from it. I trade on the stereotype of the granny, and pull the audience in through the use of comedy, but ultimately I invert expectations since my protagonist does indeed move out of that 'safe harbour of acceptability' as she engages with new media and starts to create a new self.

Aaron and Josh represent two polarised views of old women that can be found in the broader society: on the one hand, the view that an old woman is at the end of her life and should not be disturbing the status quo – this is Aaron's position – and, on the other, that an old woman still has much living to do – this is Josh's eventual position (although it takes him a little while to reach it).

It is interesting to me that the basis of ageism might be the family. Lise Weil (2007) maintains that McDonald's recognition of family as the source of ageism is one of her most significant contributions to feminist thought. Granny's elder son, Aaron, is the one who displays ageism most clearly, having fixed and preconceived ideas about what is and is not appropriate for a woman of Granny's age. Aaron personifies the conservative, restrictive voice of traditional roles and expectations. As such, he serves to hamper her activities, and Granny is always concerned about what he will say. McDonald points out that 'the need in an ageist society to rely on children for acceptance … results in a profoundly unbalanced power relationship, in which the old woman must often bend to her children's definition of herself' (McDonald and Rich 1984, 60).

Aaron believes that as Granny is approaching the end of her life, she should not be starting anything new or engaging with anything of consequence. Expressing a desire to revive an old skill, in this case driving, is interpreted by Aaron as proof of his mother's lack of judgement. Despite her grief and insecurities Granny is an independent woman at heart. She strives to maintain her independence and declares that she wants to start driving again, a notion that is met with resistance from her two sons, as in the following extract.

EXT. GARAGE – DAY

Granny enters the garage clutching car keys and a remote control. She surveys the old car uncertainly. She tries the car door. It is locked. She points the remote at the car and presses a button. The garage door starts to close behind her.

GRANNY

Woopsie.

She quickly presses the remote again and the garage door rises. She presses the remote and tries to open the car door again, but this time she triggers the car alarm, which begins to wail and screech. Josh and Aaron appear in the background. Josh rushes in looking worried while Aaron stays in the driveway, covering his ears.

JOSH

Shouting.

Ma, what's happening?

Granny looks somewhat bewildered as he takes the keys and remote from her and stops the alarm. She composes herself, and after a moment she puts out her hand for the keys. Josh hands them over hesitantly.

JOSH (CONT'D)

Do you need to go somewhere, Ma? I'll take you.

GRANNY

I'm just wondering what to do. I'm going to need to start driving again.

Josh processes this information and tries to choose his words carefully.

JOSH

Ma, do you really think that's the best thing?

GRANNY

Why not? I've had my licence for 40 years.

JOSH

Ya, but you haven't driven for 25 of those.

GRANNY

And so?

JOSH

Aaron won't like it.

GRANNY

Oh, Aaron. He worries too much. One or two little accidents and he thinks I can't cope.

*

For Granny, the car and being able to drive represent autonomy of movement and choice. Much has been written about women and technology, and Julie Wosk's work, *Women and the Machine: Representations from the Spinning Wheel to the Electronic Age* (2001), elucidates the link between technology, patriarchy and sexism. Following Wosk, I try to show in the scene above and throughout the screenplay how technology is aligned with gender and, following Siapera (2012), that technology is gendered as masculine. When issues of gender intersect with issues of age, as in Granny's story, the exclusionary aspects of technology are amplified, resulting in the scene above where Granny's sons try to stop her from driving.

Later in the screenplay I suggest that, although technology has historically been perceived as gendered and masculine, new media such as the Internet provide the opportunity for such an alignment to be re-imagined. In order to convince her sons that she should continue living alone, and to prove that she can cope on her own, Granny learns how to go on the Internet.

The storyline suggests that acquiring digital technological expertise can lead to an expanded definition of self, and can empower the individual to break free of expectations related to their role in the family and in society. Thus, it offers a challenge to stereotypes about age and gender, and suggests that new media may provide a portal through which definitions of self can be re-imagined.

The person that Granny becomes can be understood as an example of a 'resistance identity'. The idea of resistance identities was formulated by Manuel Castells (1997), who describes them as 'stigmatised identities that seek recognition – identities that do not enjoy a high material and symbolic status' (Castells cited in Siapera 2012, 173–74). This is precisely what Granny's experiences elucidate. An old woman online is not taken seriously. An old woman as a teacher of new technologies is oxymoronic, and yet this is indeed what Granny becomes in the end.

The script functions as a form of consciousness-raising and advocacy for old people to be included in new media, and for the younger generation to be the conduit that allows this to happen. However, a film must still work as a film, and so I have created a multilayered script that is, on the one hand, a comedy aimed at a family audience, and on the other, a serious social commentary which uses flips in tone to create provocative content for those who care to look beyond the surface humour. My reasons for choosing the subject matter for my screenplay stem mainly from considerations about my late mother who, at 88, with a hearing impairment and with Parkinson's disease, found herself increasingly isolated from life around her – the plight of many an old person. At the same time, her independent spirit led her to search for ways to become mobile and autonomous, including expressing a desire to learn to drive, which led to alarm among her adult children, and a desire to learn how to use the Internet.

My interest in notions of digital insiders and outsiders is reflected in the character of Granny, and was partly inspired by my mother's situation. The Internet, along with Skype, email and social networking sites, holds positive potential for old people to expand their virtual horizons at a time when their real world is shrinking. I therefore constructed the events of the plot by researching and considering the multiple opportunities provided by new media, especially the Internet. The comic storyline rests on a bed of both realities and possibilities related to new media and their affordances, particularly in regard to how these apply to old women.

I was inspired by the National Aeronautics and Space Administration (NASA) Clickworkers' project, in which members of the public were invited to volunteer a few minutes or more to map and identify areas on the surface of Mars, meaning that people without scientific knowledge could do this (Benkler 2006). Another intriguing NASA project is 'Target Asteroids', through which amateur astronomers are invited to discover and study near-earth objects (Benkler 2006). It struck me that such Internet-based initiatives provide the ideal opportunity for old, retired or immobile persons to contribute to important projects and, in so doing, gain a sense of self-worth. This presupposes, however, that the old person has access to a connected device, is reasonably new media-literate, has a support system to help them navigate online problems, and possesses a degree of self-confidence, all of which would enable them to take advantage of such opportunities. Without access, skills, assistance and confidence, the old person is an outsider to new media and the prospects they afford. Although I did not specifically include the Clickworkers' project and Target Asteroids in the storyline of the screenplay, these initiatives and the issues they raise sparked my ideas.

At the outset of the story Granny is neither digital native nor digital immigrant, and is not located anywhere in the digital dimension. Initially she is not particularly interested in the Internet and is not bothered by her lack of techno know-how. If it were not for her younger son Josh's insistence, she would happily continue with a life lived 'unconnected'. I have extended Marc Prensky's (2001) digital native hypothesis and invented the category of the 'digital stateless' to refer to those who are indifferent to or unaware of new media, and do not belong to either the category of digital native or that of digital immigrant. Granny embodies the digital stateless person. Aaron, her elder son, tries to ensure that she remain stateless in this sense. Josh, by contrast, believes that Granny has the potential to become an 'immigrant', as demonstrated in the following scenes which follow on from Granny's money being stolen at an ATM.

*

INT. KITCHEN – DAY

Josh and Granny sit at the kitchen table having a cup of tea, the rain visible through the window behind them.

GRANNY

I feel bad about the money. Don't tell Aaron.

JOSH

Ma, you have to be careful at ATMs. You can't trust anyone to help you. Don't give your card to anyone.

GRANNY

I didn't.

JOSH

Don't tell anyone your pin number.

GRANNY

I didn't!

GRANNY (CONT'D)

He just looked so helpful. And I wasn't really sure how to use the stupid machine. That woman showed me so quickly. Boom, boom, boom, just like that. It's easier to go into the bank. Your father always used to go into the bank.

Granny starts to cry. Josh moves to comfort her. He puts his arm around her tenderly.

JOSH

It's okay, Ma. I'll show you. We'll go over it step by step.

Josh sits in silence for a moment, thinking.

JOSH (CONT'D)

Actually, Ma, there is a way of avoiding the ATM altogether. Online banking. With the computer.

GRANNY

That'll be even worse. You know I can't use that thing.

JOSH

But I can show you. It's much safer and it's easy. You can do your banking and everything. You can even order stuff online. Do shopping.

GRANNY

Shopping?

JOSH

Ja, and crosswords.

INT. GRANNY'S STUDY – DAY

The camera follows a cable up to a laptop which rests on a desk in front of Granny and Josh.

JOSH

Okay. Now I've connected the mouse. I think it'll be easier than using the trackpad.

GRANNY

Maybe this is a mistake.

JOSH

Just trust me. You'll like it once you know how. It's easy, I promise.

Granny looks sceptical.

JOSH (CONT'D)

Okay. You switch it on at the side here.

The familiar sound of a computer booting up is heard.

JOSH (CONT'D)

I'll use 3G because you haven't got the Internet yet.

He puts a dongle into the side of the laptop. He points to an Internet icon on the desktop.

JOSH (CONT'D)

That is for the Internet. You just double left-click on it and …

GRANNY

(*Interrupting*)

I don't want to try this thing right now, Josh. It's too much. And I'm tired. And I don't understand it.

JOSH

That's the beauty of it, Ma. You don't have to understand it. You just do it. You just click.

They face off for a long moment.

JOSH

Just click.

JOSH (CONT'D)

Just click, man. Please.

Granny clicks her fingers and laughs at her own joke.

JOSH (CONT'D)

Come on, Ma, please man. Just click.

GRANNY

Oh, for heaven's sake! Okay, here.

She takes the mouse and clicks.

JOSH

No, on the left button.

Granny tries again.

JOSH (CONT'D)

No, actually double click.

Granny gives him a withering look. She clicks twice, slowly.

JOSH (CONT'D)

No, fast like this (*he takes the mouse*). Click, click, fast.

Granny folds her arms, looking stubborn.

GRANNY

At my age I don't do anything fast.

JOSH

Ma, I know you can do this.

GRANNY

Make me.

JOSH

Now you're just being silly.

Granny sits with folded arms and raised eyebrows.

JOSH (CONT'D)

Okay. Well, you know what, I'll just demonstrate and you watch. Then if you feel like it later you can try on your own. Okay, so you double click, fast, on this 'I' which stands for Internet. Then you type the word 'crossword' here and then you double click here, and there you go!

A crossword puzzle fills the screen. Granny perks up a bit and leans forward, trying to disguise her interest. Josh looks pleased with himself.

*

After noticing the possibility of online shopping, Granny ultimately embarks on a journey of acquiring expertise and surprises everyone, including herself, with her ability to learn how to use the Internet. She gains confidence and discovers an aptitude she never knew she possessed, and starts to refer to herself as 'a natural'. All of this is possible through her grandson Max's help. He personifies Paul DiMaggio and Eszter Hargittai's (2001) concept of a social support network or system, and without his encouragement it is unlikely that Granny would have continued with her online journey and been able to traverse the 'digital divide'. Without support and help, old people are unlikely to enjoy the maximum affordances of new media.

Granny personifies the South African who is venturing online for the first time. She is an unthreatening figure with whom South African audiences can identify. The idea of outsiders and insiders to the Internet and new media has been conceptualised as a digital divide and much has been written about it (see Dan Schiller 2007). The divide is most often seen as a case of 'information haves and have-nots' (Siapera 2012, 69). In unequal societies such as South Africa, it is easy to mistakenly conceive of the digital divide as a fault line between those who are rich and those who are poor. However, it is somewhat simplistic to envision the digital divide as merely a question of financial affordability. Furthermore, one cannot assume that once a person owns a connected device they are on the right side of the digital divide, or that if they are young they possess techno know-how. In the screenplay I present factors other than the overly deterministic conditions of age and class that have clouded early considerations about new media access and affordances, and show that stereotypes about where, how and by whom new media are used are not necessarily accurate.

Granny's plight as a widow, her conflicts with family members, and her predicament as an outsider to digital technology are the primary features of her life that are likely to resonate with the audience. In addition, her initial reluctance to learn how to use the Internet, perhaps because she fears making a fool of herself, could be an experience with which many digital outsiders identify, irrespective of age, race or class. It is not uncommon to approach new technology with a degree of resistance and a lack of confidence, and it is not uncommon to make mistakes when using new technology. Yet, as the storyline charts Granny's adventures online, it demonstrates that not even the formidable intersection of age, gender, race, middle-class financial status and lack of confidence can prevent her growing technological proficiency, and that it is possible to cross the so-called digital divide, or traverse the digital hierarchy, and become an insider to new media.

Current events, issues and theories concerning new media and the Internet provided me with multiple story opportunities, and they form the foundation of the action and the events of the plot of my screenplay. The screenplay rests on a bed of both realities and possibilities related to new media and the affordances of the Internet, particularly in how these apply to old women. News media often report on acts of hacking, and it was one such case that became a foundational idea for the screenplay. Some years ago I read a newspaper article about a teenager who hacked into NASA and accidently moved a satellite.[2] The humour as well as the potential for disaster inherent in this act struck me as very powerful, and I used it as the trigger incident in my screenplay, the event that sets the plot in motion. There are many similar stories of hacking, including several cases of hacking the NASA website.[3] There are also reports of numerous NASA mobile computing devices being lost or stolen, including one containing details of the algorithms used to control the International Space Station (BBC 2012). Based on this, the events of the plot are entirely plausible, and having 'even' a digital newcomer such as Granny capable of carrying out such a hack, albeit by accident, serves to highlight the fragile nature of NASA's security. Furthermore, hacking, as opposed to cybercrime, might actually have positive spin-offs such as improving the security of the system being hacked. Thus, in the screenplay, the audience may actually be sympathetic towards Granny when she becomes involved, albeit unintentionally, in hacking.

For some hackers, their online exploits can be construed as a job interview, if you will; an example is George Hotz, a teenage US hacker going by the hacker name GeoHot, who hacked the Apple iPhone and the Sony Playstation 3. Although he was sued by Sony, he subsequently worked for Facebook and Google.[4] This is not unlike what happens to Granny in the screenplay, when the attention she gains through her accidental hacking leads to her landing a job teaching old people how to use the Internet.

There can be no doubt that Granny is asserting herself as mistress of her own life and, as such, is carving out a new identity for herself and a new relationship with her adult children. In Granny's case the Internet provides her with the opportunity to act differently to how she performs in real life. Judith Butler's (1993) writings introduce the concept of performativity, and the idea that we acquire our gender identities through repeating expected practices. Such gender performances are not limited to the real world and may take place via new media devices and activities, such as going online and entering the cyberworld. Granny's experiments with the Internet result in her developing abilities hitherto unrelated to her concept of herself. She begins to see herself in a new way. For example, she starts buying things online. In her life up until this point she was only able to go shopping if someone, usually Granddad, gave her a lift to the shops; and once there, he would moderate her choices. Her shopping excursions were thus mediated by his needs and presence. Shopping online, however, frees her from all of this. She ends up shopping whenever she wants, spending as much as she wants, and choosing anything she wants.

However, her emerging new identity is threatened in the following scene, which is the midpoint of the screenplay, when Aaron is helping her to install all the new computer equipment she has bought and suddenly realises that she has accidentally moved a satellite.

*

INT. GRANNY'S LOUNGE – DAY

Aaron busies himself installing the new computer. While he sorts through cables and connections Granny takes a break.

GRANNY

My feet are killing me. I've got to sit for a bit.

AARON

This guy saw you coming, Ma. You don't need half this crap. Why don't you just keep using the laptop Josh lent you?

GRANNY

Because it isn't Josh's laptop. He has to give it back soon. And I want my own.

AARON

What are you actually going to do with a computer anyway, Ma, I mean, at your age and everything?

GRANNY

I'll have you know that I'm quite good at the computer. I've been using it for shopping and I need it now.

AARON

What shopping? Haven't you just been to the centre?

GRANNY

Not groceries. Other things. I'll show you. It was delivered yesterday.

Granny goes off and quickly returns with a small package, a shoe box and a certificate. Aaron looks on, bracing himself.

GRANNY (CONT'D)

Okay. Now, you're not going to believe it but THIS (*she holds a mouldy piece of toasted cheese aloft*) actually does look like the Virgin Mary.

Gob-smacked, Aaron stares at the piece of mouldy toast that Granny holds out towards him.

AARON

Oh my God. How much did you pay for this?

GRANNY

It doesn't matter. Because THESE were a bargain.

She pulls out a pair of platform shoes with plastic goldfish swimming in glitter in the soles. Chuckling to herself, she starts to put them on. Aaron splutters incoherently. He notices the certificate, which Granny has placed on the floor while she changes her shoes. He picks it up and begins to read.

AARON

You now have the 'title' Lady Gloucestershire?

GRANNY

It wasn't expensive.

AARON

You bought a title? This can't be real. For God's sake Mom please, you can't do this!

A tense silence descends instantly. Aaron does his utmost to remain calm. Granny feels assertive.

GRANNY

Why not? It makes me feel better.

AARON

For one thing, you've got to watch your money.

GRANNY

It wasn't expensive. And I can handle my money just fine.

AARON

It's all just too much for me, Mom. I can't keep up with you. Driving and accidents and computers and buying crap online.

Granny remains silent as they face off.

AARON (CONT'D)

Why can't you just relax and take it easy?

GRANNY

You want me to just sit at home and do nothing? Just stop everything?

AARON

No. Just the online shopping and the bladdy driving. Just stop. Please. We can still find a nice retirement place for you. There's got to be one out there.

GRANNY

I doubt it.

AARON

There must be. That's where you should go. They help you if you want to do anything, drive, shop (A LONG BEAT), go on the Internet (*he shudders*).

GRANNY

No.

AARON

Mom.

GRANNY

No.

Granny clicks her tongue and ignores Aaron. She picks up the newspaper. The front page article is something about a 'Satellite Sleuth'. She sits for a moment contemplating the picture and headline. Aaron reluctantly returns to installing the computer, aggressively and noisily moving things around. Granny looks up.

GRANNY

This picture in the paper is just like the one I saw when I went inline. You know when I was helping Max with his project? I copied and pasted this exact picture for him. That's a coincidence, hey?

Aaron abandons the cables and connectors and goes over to Granny. He takes the newspaper from her.

AARON

Let's have a look. (*He reads from the newspaper.*) 'NASA system engineers believe they are up against a hacking genius. NASA confirmed today that the orbital path of the DAS 5 weather satellite was altered from a source. Authorities are baffled as to how their system, which features state-of-the-art security protocols, could have been breached. The hacker …' (A BEAT)

Granny and Aaron drift in a long moment of silence as Aaron puts two and two together.

AARON (CONT'D)

Hacker?

INT. HOSPITAL – NIGHT (FLASHBACK) CONTINUOUS

A speeded-up flashback of the hospital scene shows Granny and Max working on the laptop, the NASA logo visible among the satellites on the screen.

INT. GRANNY'S LOUNGE – DAY (CONTINUOUS)

We screech back to real time while Aaron's face registers the full spectrum of emotions and expressions as the penny drops. He finally bursts out with:

AARON

Oh my God! You're the one who moved this thing!

GRANNY

No, I didn't.

AARON

No, I think you bladdy did!

GRANNY

Surely not. How is it possible?

AARON

If you go on the Internet, no, if YOU go on the Internet, anything's bladdy possible! Besides, people are always hacking into NASA. Their security's bladdy appalling.

Granny looks scared. She eventually answers.

GRANNY

It says here they managed to put it back.

Aaron collapses into a chair and puts his head in his hands.

AARON

Fuck.

GRANNY

I didn't do it.

AARON

I strongly suspect you did.

Aaron gets up and crosses to the boxes. He starts packing the computer away aggressively.

AARON

All this crap is going back. You moved a bladdy satellite. What the hell's next??? You can't have this. You mustn't go online any more. And it's ONline, not bladdy INline. You don't know what you're doing. You're dangerous. It's got to stop now before we get into big trouble.

GRANNY

No. I want the computer. I like it. I'm a natural.

Aaron kicks the boxes out of the way. Granny flinches. He grabs his car keys.

AARON

A natural? A natural? I'm going. I can't take this any more. I have to process all of this. My mother moved a fucking satellite.

He storms out.

GRANNY (*to herself*)

It's not like they couldn't put it back.

Aaron is out of earshot, already at the front door. He screams back at her.

AARON (*offstage*)

And Max has to stay here tonight, I'm working late and there's no one to look after him.

He slams the door with an almighty bang. Granny flinches.

*

The scene above illustrates that the Internet has provided Granny with a portal to a new self, manifested through her shopping online, on her own terms. Back in the real world Aaron tries to regain control over Granny, but it is too late. Her new independence has provided her with a surplus of self-confidence.

As the plot unfolds, the question is posed: once Granny has access to a connected computer and the ability to operate it, what difference will this make in her life? Will her access to the Internet only get her into trouble, as when she inadvertently hacks into NASA and accidentally moves a satellite, or can it provide her with something positive? Throughout the screenplay we see the affordances of new media in Granny's life, some of which are quite unexpected, particularly the construction of a different self as she moves from the stereotypical 'old person' position of resisting new technology towards embracing it. Another affordance of her engagement with the computer is that it ultimately helps bring the family together, as they try to solve the predicament that Granny has got herself into. In this way I link the concept of the digital outsider, or the digital stateless person, to questions of new media affordances, and connect all of this to questions of identity and family relationships.

Granny's journey is one that takes her across the digital spectrum and up the digital hierarchy as she traverses DiMaggio and Hargittai's (2001) five dimensions of digital inequality. Factors other than the overly deterministic conditions of age and class are presented, and stereotypes about where, how and by whom new media are used are interrogated through the fabric of the story and the lives of the characters. Granny's story disrupts the traditional alignment between technology, patriarchy and sexism, and re-imagines it.

The screenplay suggests that the modification of self can continue even into old age and, furthermore, that new media provide a means for this modification to occur, the latter point also made by Donna Haraway (Haraway cited in Siapera 2012). Granny questions and changes not only who she is, but who she is in relation to new media, as she moves from epitomising the digital stateless to being a self-described new media 'natural'.

The Internet allows us to move far beyond our neighbourhood and thus, as Manuel Castells points out, personal identity is 'no longer limited or determined by the immediate socio-political context of values, requirements and expectations' (Castells cited in Siapera 2012, 174–75). This manifests in the screenplay when Granny experiences immense online support for her predicament, made possible when her grandson Max and his teacher set up a Facebook support group for her. This online support translates into validation of her new self: she comes to see that it is permissible to be an old woman who enjoys experimenting with new media, even if she makes a few mistakes along the way. The online support mediates and modifies the pressures from members of her immediate family who want her to conform to gender and age expectations. Thus, her reconstructed self is fostered and impacted upon by her online supporters, who are diverse and geographically dispersed.

A final significant affordance is revealed at the end of the screenplay, when we realise that Granny's access to new media and her proficiency have landed her a fabulous job opportunity – teaching old people how to use the Internet. This in turn suggests that she can continue to live independently, and the major axis of conflict in the screenplay is thus resolved, albeit in an open-ended manner.

When Granny goes online she enters another reality and is free to be who she wants to be, unfettered by Aaron's expectations. The nuances of this other side, or cyber side, of Granny are revealed to Aaron when he realises not only the havoc she has caused on the NASA website, but also that she has been looking at support group websites for the newly widowed. He begins to realise that his mother may be more than he thinks she is, or wishes she were, and that her children, himself included, may no longer be the centre of her universe or able to influence and control her. Granny's changing identity has consequences for Aaron, and for his perception of himself as being in charge of her life. This is manifested in the dialogue between Granny and Josh in the scene where she wakes up from her nightmare about trying to put the satellite back in its correct position, after the concert where her Grandson Josh played the part of a satellite, and tries to correct her misadventures on the NASA website.

*

JOSH

Ma, Aaron says you shouldn't …

GRANNY (*interrupting*)

Fuck Aaron.

Aaron reels and Josh practically takes a step back at his mother's use of the 'f-' word, something he has never heard from her before.

*

A symbol I use in the screenplay is Granny's hair colour. Later in the plot Granny meets Jack, a charming man who lives in the retirement home she visits, and decides to throw a party, before which she elects to colour her hair. The subtext of this episode is that she is attracted to Jack and wants to look 'nice', in other words 'young'. I played this part of the storyline for humour, having the hair colour turn out to be a bright pink, to add a subtext to the main plot critiquing age-modifying attempts by old women. McDonald (McDonald and Rich 1984) is critical of women who try to 'pass' as younger than they are, believing that this is a denial of self, and Ann E. Gerike states that hair dyeing 'represents the attempt of aging people to "pass" as members of a group with greater power, privilege and prestige than that to which they belong' (Gerike cited in Rosenthal 1990, 37). That Granny chooses to dye her hair illustrates that she has internalised some of the ageism that permeates our culture.

However, by the end of story, when Granny is released from prison (her NASA misadventure did not go unpunished), her hair has returned to its natural grey, symbolising that she is at peace with who she is and is becoming her authentic self. Women should be free to choose whether they want to colour their hair or not, but because of the association of coloured hair with sexual attractiveness and reproductive potential and, conversely, of grey hair with being past one's physical prime, it is not difficult to understand why women would choose to conceal their grey hair. That Granny finally lets her hair return to its natural grey is physical proof of her internal growth. She is owning who she is, and is proud to be herself.

Through advertising and social interaction we are constantly surrounded by messages of what is age-appropriate and gender-appropriate, and the fact that the audience might laugh at Granny experimenting with products aimed at the youth market shows how ingrained these notions are. Other notions of this ilk are that 'old people, especially women, should not drive', 'old people should not live alone', and 'old people cannot handle new technology'. Throughout the screenplay I try to contest these popular notions, and at the end of the story Granny drives her own car to the location where she will be teaching other old people how to use the Internet. On arrival there she successfully performs a complicated parking manoeuvre. The fact that she is able to drive independently and teach others how to use the Internet shows how much she has changed, and that she is mistress of her own life. Her 'age-inappropriate' choices remain, in terms of her dress sense – she loves very bright dresses and high heels, and has no problem wearing a swimsuit - and are proof that she is resisting the suffocating, societally imposed prescriptions of image. She is doing it her way, regardless of what 'people' may think.

NOTES

1 See *The Telegraph*. 2017. 'Rise in "silver surfers" as over-65s learn computer skills', 19 May. Accessed 22 June 2020. https://www.telegraph.co.uk/news/2017/05/19/rise-silver-surfers-over-65s-learn-computer-skills/.

2 Wilson, Catherine. 2006. '15-Year-Old Admits Hacking NASA Computers'. *ABC News*, 7 January. Accessed 20 May 2020. https://abcnews.go.com/Technology/story?id=119423&page=1

3 See *The New York Times*. 2000. 'Youth Sentenced in Government Hacking Case', 23 September. Accessed 22 May 2020. https://www.nytimes.com/2000/09/23/us/youth-sentenced-in-government-hacking-case.html.

4 *Eurogamer*. 2014. 'Remember PS3 Hacker Geohot? Now He Works for Google', 17 July. Accessed 22 May 2020. https://www.eurogamer.net/articles/2014-07-17-remember-ps3-hacker-geohot-now-he-works-for-google.

REFERENCES

Adams, Jan. 2008. 'Barbara MacDonald: A Pioneer Theorist of Ageism'. Accessed 22 May 2020. https://www.timegoesby.net/weblog/2008/10/barbara-macdonald-a-pioneer-theorist-of-ageism.html.

BBC (British Broadcasting Corporation). 2012. 'Hackers had "full functional control" of Nasa computers'. 8 March 2012. Accessed 15 May 2020. https://www.bbc.com/news/technology-17231695.

Benkler Y. 2006. *The Wealth of Networks*. New Haven, CT: Yale University Press.

Butler, Judith. 1993. *Bodies That Matter: On the Discursive Limits of Sex*. London: Routledge.

Castells, Manuel. 1997. *The Power of Identity, The Information Age: Economy, Society and Culture*. Volume 2. Cambridge, MA: Blackwell.

DiMaggio, Paul and Hargittai, Eszter. 2001. *From the 'Digital Divide' to 'Digital Inequality': Studying Internet Use as Penetration Increases*. Working Paper Number 15, Centre for Arts and Cultural Policy Studies, Woodrow Wilson School of Public and International Affairs, Princeton University.

Helsper, Ellen. 2010. 'Gendered Internet Use across Generations and Life Stages'. *Communication Research* 37(3): 352–74. Accessed 26 August 2014. https://doi.org/10.1177/0093650209356439.

McDonald, Barbara and Rich, Cynthia. 1984. *Look Me In The Eye: Old Women, Aging and Ageism*. London: Women's Press.

Prensky, Marc. 2001. 'Digital Natives, Digital Immigrants'. *On the Horizon* 9(5): 1–6.

Rosenthal, Evelyn R. 1990. *Women, Aging and Ageism*. New York: Haworth Press.

Schiller, Dan. 2007. *How to Think about Information*. Urbana, IL: University of Illinois Press.

Siapera, Eugenia. 2012. *Understanding New Media*. London: Sage.

Weil, Lise. 2007. 'In the Service of Truth: Remembering Barbara McDonald'. *Trivia Voices of Feminism* 5. Accessed 15 May 2020. https://www.triviavoices.com/remembering-barbara-macdonald.html.

Wosk, Julie. 2001. *Women and the Machine: Representations from the Spinning Wheel to the Electronic Age*. Baltimore, MD: Johns Hopkins University Press.

BEING A MINEWORKER IN POST-APARTHEID SOUTH AFRICA: A DECOLONIAL PERSPECTIVE

ROBERT MASEKO

Being a black mineworker in South Africa is neither a racial nor a class question; it is a multifaceted experience, one that challenges the presently dominant interpretations of what it means to be a black mineworker. These interpretations, characterised as they are by a logic of exclusive, singular extrapolations, do not allow for a holistic approach to understanding the experiences of the mineworkers, that is, an approach that encompasses economic issues, class issues, politics, gender, race and sexuality. A number of critical analyses of what it means to be a black mineworker within a non-Western spatio-historical temporality such as South Africa are based on a Marxist political economy paradigm (Allen 1992, 2003; Crush et al. 1991; Jeeves 1985; Yudelman 1984). These analyses reduce the experience of being a black mineworker to that of entering the proletariat, as though blackness as a racial category were not a problematic dimension of the experiences of black mineworkers. This approach to the meaning of being a black mineworker obscures rather than reveals the multiple concrete experiences of black mineworkers, as opposed to just mineworkers, within the present modern world in general and South Africa and the non-Western world in particular.

A second dominant paradigm underpinning analyses of what it means to be a black mineworker within a spatio-historical temporality such as South Africa is that of critical race theory (Magubane 2007; Pollard 1984), which reduces the experience of black mineworkers to a problem of identity politics. Thus, by privileging the question of identity over that of economic power relations, critical race theories, like many other cultural studies paradigms such as gender-based or disability-oriented critical analyses, obscure rather than reveal the multifaceted nature of the experience of black mineworkers in South Africa.

The mineworker is disposable and dispensable (Magubane 2007), and lives and works in the shadow of death. In pursuing this course of reasoning, I deploy the epistemic method of 'shifting the geography of reason' in order to read the experience of mineworkers in South Africa from the locus of enunciation of the oppressed subject, within the scheme of a colonial power differential based on a hierarchy of humanity. This method allows me to speak with and from the perspective of black mineworkers – in this chapter, specifically black mineworkers in the Platinum Belt of South Africa – as opposed to speaking for and about them. I reach the conclusion that being a platinum mineworker in post-apartheid South Africa is a racially and market-determined identity of colonised subjectivity, one that that relegates the dominated subject (the black mineworker) to the realm of the subhuman. This chapter, therefore, transcends the limits of current dominant reductionist perspectives on what it means to be a black mineworker in South Africa.

THE HISTORY OF MINING IN SOUTH AFRICA

Commercial mining of minerals in South Africa started with colonialism; the first mining operations took place in Namaqualand in 1852, and were followed by the discovery of diamonds in Kimberly in 1870 (MMSD 2002). The rise of capitalism saw the beginning of proletarianisation (or at least semi-proletarianisation) of the local populations due to land dispossession and forced removals; hence, many men were forced to sell their labour to the newly-formed mines as part of the migratory labour system (Worger 1987). In these mines, black male mineworkers were housed in well-secured, single-sex compounds and their movement was restricted to limit interaction with the surrounding communities. The compounds resembled prison-like conditions, with many of these workers dying of work-related diseases such as silicosis (a disease which of course also affected white workers) and starvation (Crush et al. 1991; Demissie 1998; James 1992; Worger 1987). The same system of black oppression in the diamond mines was transferred to the Witwatersrand goldfields in 1886, when black workers were sourced from various independent and colonised territories in southern Africa (Crush et al. 1991; James 1992).

From the time that the Union of South Africa was formed in 1910, and throughout the apartheid era until 1979, labour laws in the country were based on colour distinctions. Black mineworkers were semi-slaves, and were not allowed to participate in any strike action; they had their own labour unions, but these were excluded from participation in bargaining processes. This situation was supported initially by the Industrial Conciliation Act No. 11 of 1924, the Wages Act No. 27 of 1925, the Mines, Works Amendment Act No. 25 of 1926 and the Labour Relations Act No. 28 of 1956. This entire legislative framework (as well as later legislation) was designed to protect the employment security of white workers, while black workers were employed as cheap labour, thereby reducing production costs, and were not allowed to hold even low-level supervisory positions as these were reserved for white workers (McBean 1978). Labour on the mines in South Africa continued to be sourced from neighbouring countries, notably Mozambique, Lesotho, Swaziland and Southern Rhodesia (later Rhodesia) (Department of Labour 2007; Jeeves 1985). The Witwatersrand Labour Organisation recruited most of the foreign workers. The work-induced death rate was high among mineworkers (Harington et al. 2004), with an estimated 470 deaths for every 100 000 mineworkers per year (this figure included white mineworkers).

The life of black mineworkers was a daily struggle for existence. They were paid sub-poverty wages to cover their own expenses only (to the exclusion of their dependents), on the assumption that the wages they earned were subsidised by agricultural and other activities in their home areas. On arrival at the mine, they were often given loans or advance payments and this practice was repeated on an ongoing basis to maintain them in a state of perpetual debt, therefore trapping them in a relationship of never-ending dependency (Allen 1992; Demissie 1998; Van Onselen 1976). For those who did not die on the mines, there were no pension funds for them when they retired, although they were given a small amount of money to take back to their rural homes. But according to Charles van Onselen (1976), the amount was too little, only enough to pay the transport costs to return to their countries of origin or their homelands. The majority of these mineworkers would suffer a life of poverty, and would soon die of the diseases acquired while working in the mines; some ended up committing suicide (Meel 2003). This misery arising from the employment relationship was reinforced by the misery of the compound. The compound housing system was out of reach for the spouses and children of mineworkers, and it perpetuated a lonely existence. In addition, during incidents of illegal labour unrest on the mines, compounds were quickly converted into actual prisons to inhibit and undermine the blossoming of such labour activity. At times, mineworkers' strikes were subjected to brutal suppression by the repressive apparatuses of the South African state (Allen 1992; James 1992; Worger 1987).

This brutal site of economic production by, and social reproduction of, black mineworkers remained in existence until the end of apartheid. Significant changes did arise during the reform era of apartheid in the late 1970s and 1980s, at least with respect to the whittling away of the employment colour bar (because of the sheer demand for skilled labour on the mines) and the right to strike. Despite this, however, a combination of mine security forces and state repression was used to brutally suppress strikes by mineworkers during a period of mine unrest that lasted from 1985 to 1987 (Moodie 2009, 2013). During this time, surrogate forces were also planted among the mineworkers by the mine management to divide their union along ethnic lines and, as a result, workers were killed in uprisings between rival ethnic groups (Moodie 2013).

Up until the end of apartheid, there is no doubt that the semi-proletarianised status of black mineworkers also entailed a condition of racial capitalism such that their rights as citizens and as workers were both denied. This is what Halisi (1999) called racial proletarianisation – a process whereby black mineworkers were denied their citizenship rights in the city, with the result that they were forced to live half their life in the city and half in the rural areas. But, even in post-apartheid South Africa, mining has been resistant to broader processes of decolonisation and democratisation which are, arguably, taking place nationally. This was also articulated by Cyril Ramaphosa, one of the beneficiaries of the government's black economic empowerment policies (Phillips 2004; Ponte et al. 2007), who argued that the mining industry in South Africa today is resistant to change because black people are co-opted into the mining industry but they are not given influential positions that will allow them to initiate change (Desai 2014). In short, black people do not have control of the mining industry, and the industry still operates on an apartheid template. Black mineworkers, as 'subjects' – in the sense used, in another context, by Mahmood Mamdani (1996) – and as workers continue to be subjugated socially, economically and politically through the specific form of proletarianisation that took place historically in South Africa, and which saw them dispossessed of land and forced to be workers on the mines as well as in factories and on farms (James 1992; Worger 1987). This systemic condition, a condition of colonisation in the zone of ontological non-being (Fanon 1967; Gordon 2005, 2007) remains today (Maldonado-Torres 2007). Since 1994, certain reforms have been implemented to rectify past injustices and imbalances, but there have also been changes indicative of more fully integrating the South African economy into global neoliberal restructuring processes. Mineworkers are still not free to withdraw their labour, and when they do, they are usually subjected to coercive force from the state, as witnessed during the Marikana Massacre (Alexander et al. 2012; Bond and Mottiar 2013; Magaziner and Jacobs 2013; Ndebele 2013; Sorensen 2012).

Despite the non-existence of an employment colour bar, black South Africans have not made significant advances into managerial and supervisory positions on the mines. The black workforce continues to be subjected to dangerous working conditions, with low pay and living in conditions of poverty, either in mine compounds or in informal settlements near the mines (Ndebele 2013; Sorensen 2012). For example, in Rustenburg, mineworkers live in compounds and informal settlements around the town while new housing development sites are reserved for white mineworkers and the black middle classes (Macmillan 2012). What makes it more difficult for the mineworkers is that the majority of them are migrant workers from the rural areas of South Africa or from neighbouring countries such as Lesotho and Mozambique; these workers need to maintain two households with their wages (Bond 2013).

In addition, economic instability in the mining sector has led to new challenges; the industry has experienced major retrenchments, leading for example to a decrease in employment levels from 800 000 in 1987 to just over 400 000 in 2001 (Sorensen 2011). Statistics gathered in September 2018 show a slight increase in the number of people employed in the mining industry, from 457 290 in 2016 to 464 667 in 2018 (Minerals Council of South Africa 2018). A number of factors have increased production costs in mining, such as the political uprisings of the 'Arab Spring' and the concomitant sharp rise in oil prices, the devaluation of the South African rand, and labour unrest. Lower-grade ore has also resulted in lower profits, mine closures and retrenchments (Sorensen 2011). Following the gold seam deeper underground through tunnelling, ventilation and locomotives has also resulted in higher costs of production and lower profits, and in even more inhospitable working conditions for mineworkers (Diering 2000).

The events in Marikana in August 2012, when 34 mineworkers were shot dead by police officers, show that the challenges faced by mineworkers in the country are still far from over despite 25 years of democracy. The wildcat strikes by mineworkers in Marikana, and the discontent of mineworkers in the country in general (Ndebele 2013; Sorensen 2012) are manifestations of the experience of being a mineworker in South Africa. The Marikana incident can in large part be viewed as an anti-colonial rebellion and a struggle against continued imperialism (Jacobs 2013).

DECOLONIAL UNDERSTANDING OF A MINEWORKER IN SOUTH AFRICA

Decolonial theory helps us to understand the processes that created a black mineworker, as well as the social, political and structural conditions under which black mineworkers continue to exist. As defined by Nelson Maldonado-Torres (2007), decoloniality consists of a family of thoughts that identify coloniality as the main cause of the problems faced by those people who happened to be affected by the negative aspects of Euro-North American modernity. These problems have included mercantilism, the slave trade, imperialism, colonialism, apartheid, neocolonialism, underdevelopment, structural adjustment programmes and the current neoliberal coloniality of markets. Coloniality is defined as a global power structure cascading from the above-mentioned processes, but surviving the decolonisation project and continuing to underpin asymmetrical power relations between the Global North and the Global South and to sustain a racially hierarchised modern capitalist world order.

This section of the chapter posits that it is difficult to fully understand the predicament of black mineworkers today without delving deeper into historical, discursive and structural processes unleashed by Euro-North American-centric modernity on those epistemic sites, such as Africa, that were subject to the darker underside – the more negative aspects – of this modernity, such as colonial dispossession, displacements, forced proleteri-anisation, peasantisation and impoverishment. It is within this context that the category of a worker named 'mineworker' emerged as a market-defined identity. In this context, I approach South Africa as a neo-apartheid polity where mineworkers continue to exist as a category of the working poor, with no right to withhold their labour.

The specific entry point for this analysis is the concept of 'coloniality of being', as introduced by Maldonado-Torres (2007) and elaborated on by Walter Mignolo (2011). Coloniality of being is a concept that helps in understanding how blackness was produced by Euro-North American-centric modernity as a deficient and lacking subjectivity, one that was uncivilised and had less ontological density than white subjectivity, under whose tutelage it had to remain. Besides forced conversion to Christianity, manual labour was articulated as one of the means for civilising black people by drawing them into the evolving capitalist system as providers of cheap labour. But coloniality of being also speaks to the dispensability of black life, as happened in Marikana in August 2012. From a decolonial perspective, the mining sector is understood as a site of hyper-exploitation of labour just like the plantation in the period of the slave trade, and the factory under industrial capitalism.

Colonialism has left its mark, and in many ways continues to structure, for instance, present-day cultures, labour relations, sexualities and knowledge production. Coloniality stands on three pillars: coloniality of knowledge, coloniality of power and coloniality of being. Decolonial theory is an attempt to challenge the coloniality of knowledge, or the dominance of so-called Northern theories. Coloniality of being raises critical questions about the humanity (or, more specifically, the inhuman condition) of colonial-type subjects (Maldonado-Torres 2007); as Ndlovu-Gatsheni states: 'coloniality of being is a useful tool that helps analyse the [contemporary] realities of dehumanisation and depersonalisation of colonized Africans into *damnés*' (Ndlovu-Gatsheni 2013, 8), or those living in the zone of non-being (Fanon 1967; Santos 2007). Coloniality of power, or the colonial matrix of power, entails global power structures which continue to reproduce and re-inscribe – on an international scale – colonial-type economies, cultures, political landscapes and social reproduction practices (Quijano 2000, 2007).

Decoloniality therefore helps us to unmask the challenges and problems created by current Euro-North American modernity or civilisation. It is beyond doubt that the South African mining industry of today inherited the colonial template for managing its activities; it is a direct product of a brutal colonial and apartheid structure that produced the mineworker as a category of the poor. There is therefore a need to decolonise the industry in order to imagine a future beyond modernity, one that will recover the lost ontological density of black mineworkers in the country. And decolonising it will not only lead the recovery of this lost ontological density, but will also be a starting point in the project of imagining a future society beyond the rhetoric of modernity. The current black political leadership in the country have become gatekeepers of the system created by the colonial and apartheid-era oppressors, and have in effect become worse oppressors of the very people who elected them into office. Thus there is also a need to decolonise the Westernised elites holding influential positions of power in the government and in the mining industry.

Frantz Fanon argued that black people are generally viewed as a problem, and they live in what he called the 'zone of nonbeing' (Gordon 2005, 2007). Those who live in this zone have their humanity and their souls questioned, and their rights to satisfaction of their basic human needs are denied (Maldonado-Torres 2007). The globalisation of the political economy is still embedded in Western philosophy, which believes in the subalternisation of the world other, or the non-European world, and what is needed is a decolonisation of this epistemic view (Grosfoguel 2007). Therefore, to understand the situation of mineworkers it is necessary to incorporate new research techniques. W.E.B. Du Bois argued that to understand the oppressed people, particularly African subjects, within coloniality, the current conventional scientific methods were not helpful. Knowledge based on scientific investigation did not provide answers to the question of race. Understanding the system that was oppressing them was the best way to achieve this (Du Bois [1903] 2008). Hence decolonial theory is deployed here to understand the system behind the oppression of black mineworkers. Deploying a decolonial critique of the mining sector will enable me to assess whether the dignity of the African mineworker has been recovered.

The so-called discovery of diamonds in Kimberley in 1867 unleashed devastating consequences for the black indigenous peoples in the region that became the Union of South Africa in 1910, and the aftermath is being felt even today. The process of proletarianisation, based on accumulation by dispossession, was a violent one, as it involved forced removals, expropriation of land and slavery-like conditions to satisfy the mining industry's labour needs, with labour seen as a civilising process for the subjugated (Allen 1992; Magubane 2007; Worger 1987). Capitalism took a pronounced racial turn when it reached Africa and other non-European lands, and black people bore the brunt of this racialised capitalism (Halisi 1999; Magubane 2007). As Magubane (2007, 180) argues: 'Every settler in the colonies wants to own slaves and thus avoid manual work. The use of slaves in the process of colonization was a calculated strategy to ensure a captive labour force to reap high profits, on territory appropriated without regard to any rights of indigenous owners ... The question of slavery became a crucial issue for the rising bourgeois "civilization".' Cecil John Rhodes created a system of forced segregation on the Kimberley diamond mines, and this system was used over time as a crucial framework for social regulation on the mines and in the cities around South Africa (Allen 1992; Callinicos 1987).

In the South African mining industry, a mineworker can be fired at any time, and can be disciplined thoroughly for withdrawing their labour without the approval of their employer (Alexander et al. 2012). The abundant availability of potential mineworkers, and their possession of a widely available skill, make them 'the dispensable other' as described by Bernard Magubane in his book *Race and the Construction of the Dispensable Other* (2007). The dispensability of a mineworker's life is evidenced by the events that took place at Marikana on 16 August 2012, when 34 mineworkers were slain for withdrawing their labour and demanding higher wages (Alexander et al. 2012; Bond and Mottiar 2013; Magaziner and Jacobs 2013; Ndebele 2013; Sorensen 2012). Being a mineworker in the South African context, as I have shown above, has always meant being reduced to the category of the miserable working poor, with the mineworker both past and present being paid a wage that Magubane (1984) describes as a slave wage. Trapped in extreme poverty, mineworkers continue to live in beastly conditions in hostels and shacks, unable to free themselves from this misery.

THE SOCIO-ECONOMIC CONDITION OF A BLACK MINEWORKER

In interviews, mineworkers on South African platinum mines recounted their varied experiences in the mining industry; despite these variations, the majority of them gave similar accounts of poor working conditions and low wages.[1] Others articulated personal experiences of ill health, while a few lucky ones who had no experience of illness were concerned about their friends who had succumbed to diseases. They also pointed to the continued experiences of racism and discrimination they endured.

Sondela informal settlement

Sondela informal settlement is a mixture of Reconstruction and Development Programme (RDP) houses and shacks that make up the housing infrastructure of the settlement. It houses mineworkers from the mines around Rustenburg, the largest urban area in what is known as the Platinum Belt – an area of platinum mining in North West Province.[2] Overcrowding in Sondela is common, as a result of high demand for accommodation there. The situation in the settlement clearly resembles Frantz Fanon's description of a 'Native city' where people live on top of one another (Fanon 1967, 30). Around 15–20 people share a toilet and a tap for water in the RDP section of the settlement, while the shacks are devoid of any source of running water and electricity.

In fact, the Rustenburg Integrated Development Plan (IDP) for 2012–2017 demonstrates that Sondela is not necessarily unique in the mining area (Rustenburg Local Municipality n.d.). According to this IDP, in 2011 21 per cent of the houses in the city of Rustenburg were informal or backyard shacks, while 16 per cent were in informal squatter camps. There were about 20 000 RDP houses, 30 000 houses in informal settlements and 10 000 houses in newly developed areas that had neither waste management services nor sanitation facilities. As a result, residents revealed that they eased themselves in bucket toilets and nearby bushes. The Rustenburg Local Municipality *IDP Review Final Report for 2018–2019* indicates that there are 24 informal settlements and 24 000 households in and around Rustenburg characterised by high levels of poverty and lack of security and shortage of housing; the total of backyard and informal units in Rustenburg numbers about 68 800 (Rustenburg Local Municipality 2018–2019, 14).

In the poorer section of the informal settlement, it is easy to find vacant shacks to rent because most of the mineworkers, on receiving some income, quickly vacate them for relatively better accommodation in the RDP section. Besides the absence of sanitary facilities, the shacks are rat-infested. The presence of large numbers of stray dogs at the dumpsites poses a danger to the residents. Some residents maintain the rural practice of keeping livestock with them such as goats and sheep, which occasionally feed from the dumpsites as well. Sondela is also a hub for unemployed rural immigrants and retrenched mineworkers, who turn to the dumpsites to search for recyclable materials such as plastics, paper and metal objects that can be sold.

Jabula Hostel

Jabula Hostel is located about 200 metres south of Sondela, and it houses more than 1 000 mineworkers from the Anglo Platinum Khuseleka Mine. Violence is common in this settlement, as witnessed during the platinum mining strikes in early 2014. Such violence and strikes often spread to the nearby Sondela informal settlement, where foreign-owned shops mostly owned by Somali, Ethiopian and Chinese nationals are targeted. Attacks are also directed by members of the Association of Mineworkers and Construction Union (AMCU) at members of the rival union, the National Union of Mineworkers (NUM), and often result in serious injuries and fatalities.[3]

This is unlike the housing situation for mineworkers during the period of official segregation under colonial rule and the apartheid era, when black mineworkers were housed in overcrowded compounds (Allen 1992; Van Onselen 1976; Worger 1987). At the Anglo Platinum Jabula Hostel, communal accommodation has been renovated and divided into tiny single rooms with room for only a small bed. Apparently mineworkers are free to own a television set and a fridge, but no cooking is allowed in the rooms (interview, Leketo, 18 August 2014; interview, Mzala, 18 August 2014). Contrary to the claim made by Andries Bezuidenhout and Sakhela Buhlungu (2011) that, in post-apartheid South Africa, mining compounds (or hostels) are exclusively for lowly-paid contract workers at Anglo Platinum, permanently employed mineworkers are the ones housed in the compounds, while contract workers seek accommodation in the informal settlements in and around Sondela.

The monthly rent for the housing units in Jabula Hostel is R1 000, and another R1 000 is paid for food in the dining hall. Those staying outside the hostel are entitled to a 'living out allowance' of R1 000 for accommodation and R1 000 for living expenses. Contract workers are entitled to similar allowances, although their payment is regulated by their labour broker who determines the terms of their remuneration. In effect, a hostel dweller, in terms of their monthly wage, earns R2 000 less than a non-hostel dweller. Nonetheless, the lower-paid contract workers who live in Sondela must somehow ensure that the living out allowance, assuming they actually receive it in full, is sufficient for all purposes. Whether the allowance is sufficient to meet the needs of such workers is not a concern for management. This makes staying in the hostel more advantageous for the mineworkers, because they are closer to the mine and do not have to spend time cooking as they all eat in the dining hall. Besides, there is more security and safety for them at the hostel than in Sondela.

Surprisingly, access of women, children and other visitors to the hostel is still tightly restricted. If a spouse intends to visit her mineworker husband, she has to make an application to the hostel manager so that alternative accommodation can be sought for the couple for a short period of time (usually four weeks). By virtue of the fact that mineworkers number in their thousands, many stay on this waiting list for long periods before they can secure alternative accommodation for themselves and their visiting wives. The frustration experienced by mineworkers who fail to have access to their spouses is a concern for most of them. The branch chairperson of AMCU at Khuseleka Mine, Siphamandla Makhanya, who had a particular understanding of the role of Jabula Hostel and the state of housing for black mineworkers in the shacks around Sondela, provided a summary of all the problems of accommodation and living conditions experienced by the mineworkers:

> Look at these shacks where they live, there is no electricity, no water and no sewage system but they [mineworkers] are the ones who extract this precious metal. Look at the hostels, if you go back to history these were designed purposefully to accommodate slaves, meaning they will stay ten of them in one room, and secondly they were not supposed to sleep with a woman because that was going to make him weak, unable to work the following morning and this is the case today with those hostels. (Interview, Siphamandla Makhanya, 20 August 2014)

What he claims clearly resonates with the thoughts of the black mineworkers interviewed. To a large extent, Makhanya's viewpoint implies that black mineworkers are treated as labour units used for extracting and accumulating surplus value. Even with rooms of their own in Jabula, they are still not permitted visits from women and are denied their sexual rights; ongoing struggles for these rights are still being waged by the union and the affected mineworkers.

In speaking about how living conditions determine the working conditions of the mineworkers, Makhanya is not trying to give analytical significance to the former. Rather, he is simply claiming that an examination of their living conditions probably speaks volumes about their working conditions (which I discuss below). Specifically, the low wages they receive make it difficult for them to find better accommodation of their own. Unlike in the past, when hostel accommodation was free of charge, charges are now deducted from their wages; and yet some problems still exist and restrictions continue to be upheld. In the next section I discuss the presence of diseases on the mines, and how this has impacted on the mineworkers.

DISEASES, INJURIES AND COMPENSATION

Those interviewed for this research, including union leaders, stressed disease outbreaks and high death rates among mineworkers. This was also highlighted by the then minister of health, Dr Aaron Motsoaledi, on 19 June 2014 in a parliamentary debate (Motsoaledi 2014). Silicosis and tuberculosis (TB) remain the biggest killers of mineworkers since colonial and apartheid times, as articulated by Allen (1992), Jeeves (1985), Van Onselen (1976) and many others. However, what is devastating is that the prevalence of silicosis is concealed by the mines as well as by the medical practitioners who diagnose and treat the mineworkers, in order to spare the employers from having to pay compensation to the families of dead mineworkers. Generally, mining companies are unwilling to pay for such ill health or death of mineworkers, as the law requires.

During an interview with the AMCU chairperson of education at Anglo Platinum Khuseleka Mine, Lazarus Khoza, on the prevalence of diseases among mineworkers, he had this to say: 'Per day we have more than 300 people who are sick … Most of these diseases they get them at work but some diseases are those gotten outside such as HIV and Aids, but these become serious because of the conditions underground' (interview, Lazarus Khoza, 3 September 2014). This statement by Mr Khoza is a gruesome revelation of how serious the question of health is among the mineworkers, and this of course threatens the viability of the mining industry as most of these diseases are acquired while working in the mines. The majority of the workers were reported to have spinal cord TB when they actually suffered from silicosis (interview, Siphamandla Makhanya, 20 August 2014).

Unlike the situation in previous years, when silicosis and TB killed black mineworkers together with white mineworkers (Allen 1992; Maloka 1996; Nicol and Leger 2011), today these diseases have become 'a black man's diseases', mainly because of reduced numbers of white underground mineworkers in the country. Accordingly, most white mineworkers at Anglo Platinum hold supervisory positions. One of the mineworkers, Nkulumo, revealed that blast smoke kills more people than dust, because it is very poisonous (interview, Nkulumo, 17 August 2014). Unfortunately, black workers are coerced into going underground, even when the tunnels are still filled with smoke and dust.

Unfortunately, as reported by mineworkers in the interviews, the contracts of those who fell sick were often terminated without compensation. Ngqeleni lamented: 'When you are sick the mine is losing because you are no longer productive' (interview, Ngqeleni, 14 August 2014) The mine does not want to keep sick people on its payroll, and this is when the relationship between a mineworker and the mine becomes most tense. Another mineworker, Mzala equated the treatment of black mineworkers who fell sick at Anglo Platinum to a cow that stops giving milk to its owner (interview, Mzala, 14 August 2014).

Mine management sends the majority of mineworkers who are diagnosed with silicosis and TB home to die; those who seem fit can develop signs of silicosis years after they have left the mine (for example, after retirement). Usually, when black mineworkers are no longer wanted by the mines, they will go back to their rural homelands where they will die in poverty, as Meel (2003) argues in his research on the suicide rate among former mineworkers. And yet due to fear of losing their jobs, the majority of mineworkers conceal their sicknesses:

> When you are sick they will send you to hospital and you will be given medication there ... some people hide their illness for fear of losing their jobs because once you became sick all the time the mine will say you have a bad record and they will eventually send you to the Medical Board, which will then send you home and this will be the end of you ... Once you are gone the company will forget about you and you will get nothing. (Interview, Mfundo, 18 August 2014)

Hence, to remove all responsibility for the ill health of mineworkers, the mine reconstructs the health problem as emanating from outside the mine and therefore washes its hands clean of all guilt.

But, even if in fact these illnesses emanate from outside the work environment, the mine cannot disclaim all responsibility for them. Indeed, not all diseases arise through underground work, because some are acquired from where mineworkers stay, notably under the inhumane conditions in shack accommodation at Sondela informal settlement described earlier. Sondela is a key site of accommodation for mineworkers because the wages paid by the mine are inadequate to obtain decent accommodation.

Similarly, many of the mineworkers who suffer injuries associated with mining accidents are neglected, receiving limited or no compensation. Instead, blame is heaped on them for negligence and they are at times suspended or fired. According to mineworker Mkhonza, there is a need for the mine to make payment to a worker who is injured. Families of workers who die as a result of accidents are only paid if it can be proved that the accident was not in any way the fault of the worker (interview, Mkhonza, 15 August 2014). For example, if a mineworker is hit and injured by a rock, the mine always looks for minor issues that suggest worker guilt. They pose questions such as: when the rock fell, did the mineworker have his gloves on? Did the mineworker have good quality boots? Was he in overall good health? Any negative answer to these questions would suggest to the mine management that the worker should be held in some way accountable for the accident.

The strategy of shifting the blame to the victim ignores the dangers associated with the mining environment. It also seeks to promote the colonial mentality of denying any authentic humanity to black workers, and denying their capacity to act in a reasonable manner underground. In this regard, the lives of black mineworkers can easily be sacrificed in the pursuit of mining profits.

The education chairperson of AMCU, Lazarus Khoza, thus emphasises a racial dimension to accidents and deaths at Anglo Platinum. In his view, white fatalities are unheard of. When asked about the life of a black mineworker in the mining industry, Khoza expressed the following view: 'I would say it's a very difficult life because a black person is still working under very difficult conditions, and we have many fatalities that lead to death. Ever since in my time here I have never seen a white person who has died because of accidents; only black mineworkers do. Black people are the ones working very hard extracting this platinum, the conditions are very dangerous' (interview, Lazarus Khoza, 3 September 2014).

Thus, accidents, diseases, injury and death are the lived reality of black mineworkers. These, combined with other diseases such as HIV and Aids, mean that the health and safety of black mineworkers are currently severely compromised. This also leads to many social problems outside the mines, such as grinding poverty and the presence of numerous orphans in black communities such as Sondela.

According to another mineworker, David, the system of payment for injured and dead mineworkers has been complicated by the agreements accepted by the previous union (NUM), which mostly connived with mine management. According to him, NUM ensured that the families of dead mineworkers were not paid any money due to these mineworkers, including their pensions, so that the money could be shared between NUM representatives and some corrupt mine managers. He said this was also the case with respect to diseases:

> When you are sick, this is the time when the mine dumps you, here they want people who are healthy, even if you have worked for more than 20 years for the mine without having health problems, but the day you will get sick everything changes. This is the time Anglo wants you out of their premises. What they will do is to send you to the hospital and doctors will recommend you unfit, then you are sent back home and you are given only R4 000 and that's all. (Interview, David, 17 August 2014)

Based on interviews with mineworkers, there appear to be different understandings of the time period that should elapse before a worker starts receiving compensation payments while recovering at home or in hospital during an illness, insofar as compensation is received. The variance in the interviewees' understanding of this issue might have arisen because many of them had never had the experience of being sent home as a result of ill health; but, for those who had, it took from two to five months for the worker to access the money, which was usually paid in instalments.

CONCLUSION

The mining industry in South Africa needs to be understood in the context of coloniality, as it continues to function on an apartheid template with race in large part structuring social relationships and social status on the mines. It is an industry that remains resistant to change, and thus a decolonial critique of it becomes fundamental not only analytically but ultimately for transforming the industry to the benefit of black mineworkers. The AMCU branch chairperson, Siphamandla Makhanya, speaks about 'the living and housing conditions of mineworkers reflect[ing] their working conditions underground' (interview, Siphamandla Makhanya, 20 August 2014). This statement is important in the sense that it highlights the conditions of existence and experiences of black mineworkers both inside and outside the work environment. These conditions, as this chapter highlights with specific reference to the case study of a mine in the Platinum Belt, are marked by poverty, frustration and indignity – as indicated in relation to daily work activities, wages, hostel and informal settlement accommodation, and health and safety. The question of dignity is particularly crucial, because coloniality of being is a condition in which people are stripped of their human dignity and their very humanity is questioned. By extension, mineworkers need decent accommodation and social protection against unhealthy and unsafe work conditions. This is what black mineworkers are saying, and I have sought to give voice to their far-reaching concerns in this chapter. But, within the mining industry itself, their voices are rarely heard unless they engage in overt struggles around their demands. In line with the coloniality of knowledge, black mineworkers are treated by the mines (and by government) as unworthy of being heard, as if their thoughts are not sufficiently rational and reasonable. All this reflects the enduring prevalence of the coloniality of power in the mining industry in post-apartheid South Africa.

NOTES

1 The mineworkers quoted in this section of the chapter were interviewed for a broader research project I undertook from 2013 to 2016. Pseudonyms were used to protect the identities of the interviewees, with the exception of AMCU union representatives who agreed to be identified by their full names.

2 The Platinum Belt is located in what is called the Bushveld Igneous Complex (BIC), which harbours the largest platinum reserves in the world. The BIC is so vast that it covers several heavily populated urban centres such as Rustenburg, Polokwane and Pretoria (Davenport 2013). The North West Province, in which the Platinum Belt is located, produces 65 per cent of South Africa's platinum as well as 35 per cent of its chrome (Davenport 2013; Manson 2013).

3 See for example reports of such attacks published in the *Mail & Guardian* (19 September 2012), *Drum* (22 May 2014) and *News24* (3 May 2014). AMCU has been the dominant union in the Platinum Belt since 2014, taking over from the National Union of Mineworkers (NUM), which was the dominant union there for many years. Soon after the Marikana massacre that saw 34 mineworkers gunned down by police officers in August 2012, NUM lost its majority of the workers on the mine, who defected to the rival AMCU because they felt that NUM was siding with the employers and that mineworkers had been reduced to a life of poverty under its leadership (Bond 2013; Bond and Mottiar 2013; Saul and Bond 2014).

REFERENCES

Alexander, Peter, Lekgowa, Thapelo, Mmope, Botsang, Sinwell, Luke and Xezwi, Bongani. 2012. *Marikana: A View from the Mountain and a Case to Answer*. Johannesburg: Jacana Media.

Allen, Victor L. 1992. *The History of Black Mineworkers in South Africa: The Techniques of Resistance 1871–1948*. Volume 1. Keighley: Moor Press.

Allen, Victor Leonard. 2003. *The History of Black Mineworkers in South Africa*. Volume 2. Keighley: Moor Press.

Bezuidenhout, Andries and Buhlungu, Sakhela. 2011. 'From Compounded to Fragmented Labour: Mineworkers and the Demise of Compounds in South Africa'. *Antipode* 43(2): 237–63.

Bond, Patrick. 2013. 'Debt, Uneven Development and Capitalist Crisis in South Africa: From Moody's Macroeconomic Monitoring to Marikana Microfinance Mashonisas'. *Third World Quarterly* 34(4): 569–92.

Bond, Patrick and Mottiar, Shauna. 2013. 'Movements, Protests and a Massacre in South Africa'. *Journal of Contemporary African Studies* 31(2): 283–302.

Callinicos, Luli. 1987. *A People's History of South Africa. Volume Two: Working Life 1886–1940: Factories, Townships, and Popular Culture on the Rand*. Johannesburg: Ravan Press.

Crush, Jonathan, Jeeves, Alan and Yudelman, David. 1991. *South Africa's Labour Empire: A History of Black Migrancy to the Gold Mines*. Oxford: Westview Press.

Davenport, Jade. 2013. *Digging Deep: A History of Mining in South Africa, 1852–2002*. Johannesburg: Jonathan Ball.

Demissie, Fassil. 1998. 'In the Shadow of the Gold Mines: Migrancy and Mine Housing in South Africa'. *Housing Studies* 13(4): 445–69.

Department of Labour. 2007. *Labour Market Review 2007. Labour Migration and South Africa: Towards a Fairer Deal for Migrants in the South African Economy*. Pretoria: Department of Labour.

Desai, Rehad (dir.). 2014. *Mineworkers Shot Down*. DVD. Johannesburg: Uhuru Productions.

Diering, D.H. 2000. 'Tunnels Under Pressure in an Ultra-Deep Witwatersrand Gold Mine'. *Journal of the Southern African Institute of Mining and Metallurgy* 100(6): 319–24.

Du Bois, W.E.B. [William Edward Burghardt]. [1903] 2008. *The Souls of Black Folk*. Edited by Brent Hayes Edwards. Oxford: Oxford University Press.

Fanon, Frantz. 1967. *Black Skin, White Masks*. Translated by Charles Lam Markmann. New York, NY: Grove Press.

Gordon, Lewis R. 2005. 'Through the Zone of Nonbeing: A Reading of *Black Skin, White Masks* in Celebration of Fanon's Eightieth Birthday'. *The C.L.R. Journal* 11(1): 1–45.

Gordon, Lewis R. 2007. 'Through the Hellish Zone of Nonbeing: Thinking through Fanon, Disaster, and the Damned of the Earth'. *Human Architecture: Journal of the Sociology of Self-Knowledge* 5(3): 5–11.

Grosfoguel, Ramón. 2007. 'The Epistemic Decolonial Turn: Beyond Political-Economy Paradigms'. *Cultural Studies* 21(2–3): 211–23.

Halisi, C.R.D. 1999. *Black Political Thought in the Making of South African Democracy*. Bloomington, IN: Indiana University Press.

Harington, J.S., McGlashan, N.D. and Chelkoska, E.Z. 2004. 'A Century of Migrant Labour in the Gold Mines of South Africa'. *Journal of the Southern African Institute of Mining and Metallurgy* 104(2): 65–71.

Jacobs, Sean. 2013. 'Notes from Marikana, South Africa: The Platinum Mines' Strike, the Massacre, and the Struggle for Equivalence'. *International Labour and Working-Class History* 83: 137–42.

James, Wilmot. 1992. *Our Precious Metal: African Labour in South Africa's Gold Industry, 1970–1990*. London: James Currey.

Jeeves, Alan H. 1985. *Migrant Labour in South Africa's Mining Economy: The Struggle for the Gold Mines' Labour Supply, 1820–1920*. Johannesburg: Wits University Press.

Macmillan, Hugh. 2012. 'Mining, Housing and Welfare in South Africa and Zambia: An Historical Perspective'. *Journal of Contemporary African Studies* 30(4): 539–50.

Magaziner, Daniel and Jacobs, Sean. 2013. 'Notes from Marikana, South Africa: The Platinum Miners' Strike, the Massacre, and the Struggle for Equivalence'. *International Labor and Working-Class History* 83: 137–42.

Magubane, Bernard. 1984. 'The Mounting Class and National Struggles in South Africa'. *Review* 8(2): 197–231.

Magubane, Bernard. 2007. *Race and the Construction of the Dispensable Other*. Pretoria: Unisa Press.

Maldonado-Torres, Nelson. 2007. 'On the Coloniality of Being: Contributions to the Development of a Concept'. *Cultural Studies* 21(2–3): 240–70.

Maloka, Tshidiso. 1996. '"White Death" and "Africa Disease": Silicosis on the Witwatersrand Gold Mines'. *South African Historical Journal* 34(1): 249–54.

Mamdani, Mahmood. 1996. *Citizen and Subject: Contemporary Africa and the Legacy of Late Colonialism*. Princeton, NJ: Princeton University Press.

Manson, Andrew. 2013. 'Mining and "Traditional Communities" in South Africa's "Platinum Belt": Contestations over Land, Leadership and Assets in North-West Province c. 1996–2012'. *Journal of Southern African Studies* 39(2): 409–23.

McBean, J.C. 1978. 'Opposition to the Mines and Works Amendment Act of 1926'. PhD diss., University of Natal, Durban.

Meel, Banwari. 2003. 'Suicide among Former Mineworkers in the Sub Region of Transkei, South Africa: Case Reports'. *Archives of Suicide Research* 7(3): 287–92.

Mignolo, Walter D. 2011. *The Darker Side of Western Modernity: Global Futures, Decolonial Options*. Durham, NC: Duke University Press.

Minerals Council of South Africa. 2018. 'Facts and Figures'. Accessed 21 May 2018. https://www.mineralscouncil.org.za/industry-news/publications/facts-and-figures.

MMSD (Mining, Minerals and Sustainable Development Project). 2002. *Breaking New Ground: Mining, Minerals and Sustainable Development*. London: International Institute for Environment and Development.

Moodie, T. Dunbar. 2009. 'Managing the 1987 Mine Workers' Strike'. *Journal of Southern African Studies* 35(1): 45–64.

Moodie, T. Dunbar. 2013. 'Bra Soks: An Inside Story of the Rise of the National Union of Mineworkers at Vaal Reefs Gold Mine'. *South African Historical Journal* 65(3): 383–402.

Motsoaledi, Aaron. 2014. 'Health Budget Vote Speech by the Minister of Health Dr. Aaron Motsoaledi, MP'. Accessed 23 June 2020. http://www. health-e.org.za/wp-content/uploads/2014/07/Minister-of-Health-Budget-Vote-Speech-2014-15-.pdf.

Ndebele, Njabulo S. 2013. 'Liberation Betrayed by Bloodshed'. *Social Dynamics: A Journal of African Studies* 39(1): 111–14.

Ndlovu-Gatsheni, Sabelo J. 2013. *Coloniality of Power in Postcolonial Africa: Myths of Decolonization*. Dakar: CODESRIA Books.

Nicol, Martin and Leger, Jean. 2011. 'Reflections on South Africa's Gold Mining Crisis: Challenges for Restructuring'. *Transformation* 75(1): 173–84.

Phillips, N.E. 2004. 'The Funding of Black Economic Empowerment in South Africa'. PhD diss., University of Stellenbosch, Stellenbosch.

Pollard, Michael. 1984. *The Hardest Work under Heaven: The Life and Death of the British Coal Miner*. London: Hutchinson.

Ponte, Stefano, Roberts, Simon and Van Sittert, Lance. 2007. '"Black Economic Empowerment", Business and the State in South Africa'. *Development and Change* 38(5): 933–55.

Quijano, Anibal. 2000. 'Coloniality of Power, Eurocentrism and Latin America'. *Nepantla: Views from the South* 1(3): 533–80.

Quijano, Anibal. 2007. 'Coloniality and Modernity/Rationality'. *Cultural Studies* 21(2–3): 168–78.

Rustenburg Local Municipality. n.d. *Integrated Development Plan*. Accessed 23 June 2020. www.rustenburg.gov.za/IDP-2017-2022-May-2017.pdf.

Rustenburg Local Municipality. 2018–2019. *Integrated Development Plan, IDP Review Final Report 2018–2019*. Accessed 22 May 2020. https://www.rustenburg.gov.za/wp-content/uploads/2018/06/IDP-REVIEW-FINAL-REPORT-2018-2019.pdf

Santos, Boaventura de Sousa. 2007. 'Beyond Abyssal Thinking: From Global Lines to Ecologies of Knowledge'. *Review* 30(1): 45–89.

Saul, John S. and Bond, Patrick. 2014. *South Africa – the Present as History: From Mrs Ples to Mandela and Marikana*. Woodbridge: Boydell and Brewer.

Sorensen, Paul, 2011. 'Mining in South Africa: A Mature Industry?' *International Journal of Environmental Studies* 68(5): 625–49.

Sorensen, Paul. 2012. 'The Marikana Tragedy'. *International Journal of Environmental Studies* 69(6): 871–73.

Van Onselen, Charles. 1976. *Chibaro: African Mine Labour in Southern Rhodesia 1900-1933*. London: Pluto Press.

Worger, William H. 1987. South Africa's City of Diamonds: Mine Workers and Monopoly Capitalism in Kimberley, *1867–1895*. New Haven, CT: Yale University Press.

Yudelman, David. 1984. *The Emergence of Modern South Africa: State, Capital, and the Incorporation of Organized Labor on the South African Gold Fields, 1902–1939*. Cape Town: New Africa Books.

Interviews

David, mineworker, Sondela Informal Settlement, Rustenburg, 17 August 2014.

Lazarus Khoza, AMCU education secretary, Meriting Township, Rustenburg, 3 September 2014.

Leketo, mineworker, Jabula Hostel, Anglo Platinum Khuseleka Mine, Rustenburg, 18 August 2014.

Siphamandla Makhanya, AMCU branch chairperson at Khuseleka Mine, Seraleng Township, 20 August 2014.

Mfundo, mineworker, Sondela Informal Settlement, Rustenburg, 18 August 2014.

Mkhonza, mineworker, Sondela Informal Settlement, Rustenburg, 15 August 2014.

Mzala, mineworker, Sondela Informal Settlement, Rustenburg, 14 August 2014.

Mzala, mineworker, Jabula Hostel, Anglo Platinum Khuseleka Mine, Rustenburg, 18 August 2014.

Ngqeleni, mineworker, Sondela Informal Settlement, Rustenburg, 14 August 2014.

Nkulumo, mineworker, Sondela Informal Settlement, Rustenburg, 17 August 2014.

7 MEDITATIONS ON THE DEHUMANISATION OF THE SLAVE

TENDAYI SITHOLE

If the human is a given, then the human exists in the world. In a sense, the human is inseparable from humanity; for there to be humanity there must be life. However, the mutual standing of the human and humanity has allowed an ontologically absurd separation, one that suggests the human can exist without humanity. The conception of the human has to do with certainty about, and mastery of, the ways of life of the human who is a subject in an antiblack world, that is, a white human. The subject that is fully embodied, the full subject as opposed to the figure of lacks and deficits, is one that is in control of its existence. The subject is, therefore, the transcendental and free agent of its own making.

First, it is important to ask: what is the subject in relation to the human question? Why pose the question of the human now? What does it mean to think of the human? Is it that the human and the subject are the same? Or, put simply, what is the human in the matrix of power relations? It is important to claim, in relation to these questions, that the human has a relational capacity to the world. There are institutions, structures and reality as such, the reality of the antiblack world, that support the human. The formation of the subject and its constitution is not the preoccupation here; rather, the human question will be pursued, through a critique of the subject. The silent scandal – the non-human, the slave, in relation to the subject – is what foregrounds this meditation.

What is understood to be the human has nothing to do with the slave. The human and the non-human, as ontological axes structurally imposed by antiblack racism, provide a clear determination of who lives and who must die. The slave exists in the realm of non-existence. Therefore, this existence is not a meaningful one, but one of humanity called into question. What emerges then is the question of the non-human. What does it mean to think from the positionality of the non-human? The subject is incompatible with the existence of the slave. The question that preoccupies the slave has to do with being prefigured as non-human – it is the question of life and death, of knowing that it is possible to be killed at any time, without any form of accounting being required. The burden of life assigns a different weight to the human (the subject) and the non-human (the slave). It is this ontological axis that I will deal with in this chapter, drawing on an episode that Frederick Douglass ([1845] 1995) recounts, in his *Narrative of the Life of Frederick Douglass*, about his aunt (named Aunt Hester) being whipped by the slaveholder Captain Anthony. It is not the cruelty of this episode that is my preoccupation, but the understanding of the mechanics of dehumanisation that leads to the invention of the flesh, where the non-existence of the slave is affixed to absolute ontological destruction.

At stake here is the politics of the slave, the figure who is denied any form of being. The life and death of Aunt Hester, as immortalised by Douglass, are dependent on the will of her master, Captain Anthony, who is human after all, and has the prerogative to lord over her existence because she is the slave, his possession, his property, his thing – that is, nothing human. The way of seeing through the eyes of the subject is not the perspective of the slave, but rather, of the subject imposing the world onto the other – the world that crushes the existence of the slave as the non-human who has no place in the world. The construction of the coherent embodiment of existence has to do with the subject, and the human question revolves around making the world a better place - and this better place means glossing over the question of enslavement.

Clearly, the question of life as primal falls within the realm of a discursive code that does not pertain to the slave. Thus, the subject will render it absurd to extend its ontological privileges to that which is not human. The slave as the figure of the impossible is structurally positioned outside the subject. It is outside the capacity to acquire – what can Aunt Hester acquire that will free her from the brutality of her master? The affirmation of the constituent subject has a place in things human, and it is the inscription of antiblackness that instils the discursive code which fixes the binary of who is human and who is non-human. It is this discursive code that belongs to Aunt Hester's master, as its definer and chronicler.

The subject acquires the package of existence from the discursive code, while conversely it extracts life from the slave. The merciless whipping of Aunt Hester that Douglass describes attests to this, and she has no structure of power, no world, to stand upon as there is nothing that gives validity to her existence. She cannot acquire anything that is deemed important for the human. She does not own her own life. The symbolic practices that have to do with life are for subjects, and they are constituted in the structure of white power. The constitutive subject sees itself as an individual in the world, and also as the subject of self-mastery. The subject is not reducible to the symbolic order, as it is the subject that creates this order. In other words, there is mutual reinforcement between the subject and the symbolic order. If both the subject and the symbolic order are in favour of dehumanisation, then the brutalisation of Aunt Hester will not call for any moral response or any form of sanction. The subject creates the world, structuring it through violence and making sense of reality through control and possession of the other. The possession of Aunt Hester by Captain Anthony reveals how the slave is compelled to see herself as that which is unseen and non-existent as human.

Taking Aunt Hester's flesh as the point of departure, my aim here is to wrestle with the question of the flesh, and to dwell on the modalities of its inscription. It is only the will of the master that determines the degree of dehumanisation of the slave. It is clear that no ethical and moral codes can come to Aunt Hester's defence, or exempt her from the structure of reality. The lashes that are directed at Aunt Hester's flesh can only be started, continued and stopped by Captain Anthony, and not by the posing of ethical questions about the human. By virtue of his whipping of her, he is exempted from responsibility in the ethical realm because these are his ethics, and the antiblack world protects him. Thus, he is whipping the slave – that is, nothing is being whipped. There is no violation of the human. No violation at all. For the slave is the thing that cannot be violated. The suspension of ethics is what Captain Anthony enacts, and thus he confirms that Aunt Hester is nothing but flesh. Indeed, what is whipped is the flesh and not the human being. What, then, does it mean to be abstracted and structured as nothing but flesh?

Aunt Hester is structured by Captain Anthony's will as the master subject. His absolute truth is to be obeyed by Aunt Hester – she should not do what the master does not want. Her whipping is indicative of the fact that Captain Anthony's 'Word' should be obeyed at all times. At no point should there be a contravention. It is this Word – the absolute truth - that Aunt Hester happened to contravene. His encounter with the scene causes Douglass to vividly describe 'the blood-stained gate' (Douglass [1845] 1995, 5), which is not a metaphor but the real picture of slavery. To enter through this gate is what Douglass equates with hell. Even if that blood can be wiped off or cleaned afterwards to leave the gate spotless, blood will always be there. The sadistic drive of the whip serves as the impulse of the visual orgy – the blood must be there – a spectacle, a scopic discipline imposed on those who witness it – everlasting, haunting. Captain Anthony's sadistic drive engraves marks on the flesh through the merciless lashes of the whip; the bleeding that results from it and the intensification of the whipping are pleasurable in that nothing can stop the whipping. It is the drive, the overdrive, the deadly drive.

Hortense Spillers (2003, 21) evokes what she calls 'the hieroglyphics of the flesh' in order to account for Aunt Hester's sadistic brutalisation as a result of her contravention of the master's Word. Anthony Farley (2005, 223) writes: 'The mark must be made on the flesh because that is where we start from.' It is the flesh that determines difference, human hierarchy, and reveals, in the account of Aunt Hester's whipping, how she cannot be treated as a human being. Within this context, Alexander Weheliye (2014, 32) calls upon us to 'understand the workings of the flesh'. This is underpinned by Spillers's revelation of the flesh as the site to be violated at will. There is no recourse to its irreparability, but the continuation of terror exercised upon it through '*prescribed* internecine degradation' (Weheliye 2014, 66 emphasis in the original). For Spillers, the markings of the flesh signify the entity that is written in blood, and a scene of radical expulsion that shows the nakedness of dehumanisation. It is misrecognition and disregard; the whipping by the master as the hieroglyphics of the flesh, the whip being the writing instrument upon the surface that is the flesh, and the ink being the blood that comes from ceaseless lashes marked upon Aunt Hester's flesh. What then emerges is that the body ceases to be such. It becomes non-corporeal, it becomes property. It can be itemised, catalogued, tagged, indexed, classified, ordered, priced, exchanged, replaced, sold, dispatched, liquidated, expunged, and undergo whatever else can be done to a thing. Through capture, birth, inheritance and transaction, the slave is the property of the master. The flesh, according to Spillers (2003), is the entity that stands as evidence against the high crimes committed against it. The flesh is the witness. Alas, there is no juridical structure that can listen to its testimony.

The subject is the human, and a thing is not human. In other words, to do violence to the subject is not equivalent to doing violence to a thing. The subject can be accounted for because it has ontological weight as the figure of the human. In the event of death, the subject dies and there is mourning that follows. There cannot be mourning for a thing, as it has never existed. The ontological difference remains stark, and this shows the different lived experience of those who dehumanise and those who are dehumanised. The birth of the subject is possible in the realm of the human, and this is the subject that possesses humanity – that is, humanity is born. Things are not born; they are invented (in this case it is violent invention as absolute destruction, as that is what dehumanisation is). Things are outside humanity as such.

Achille Mbembe's (2001) conception of the subject is tied to its subjection. Both are in close physical contact and violence becomes, as Mbembe (2001, 174) notes, 'a labyrinth of forces at work'. This violence, Mbembe insists, is saturated in structures and institutions.

The slave is not a usable human, but the object of value – the value accumulated by the master; the slave is nothing in the domain of being human. The exterior of the human is what the slave is – nothing. The master determines the fate of the slave, and this is not in the realm of choice. The slave does not know what satisfies the master, even if the slave thinks they do, as their fate is contingent upon knowing that they will die under the brutality of the master anyway. The life of the slave is that of the master. Having no value on their own, and having value in terms of their overuse and misuse, deprivation and degradation, shame and humiliation, dehumanisation and death, the slave has nothing that counts as human. The slave, Mbembe insists, is deemed by the master to have no reason and transcendence to aspire to. The value of the slave lies in being a tool of the master, a *thing* and *nothing* at the ontological level. Mbembe writes: 'The "thing" – and, by extension, others, the Other – can be made mine. In this sense, I have ownership of it; I possess it. It can be absorbed in, and by, my *I*. I can submit by myself. I can realize myself at its expense. Thus I create myself as a free, autonomous individual in a class of my own: as a subject' (Mbembe 2001, 191 emphasis in the original).

This is the 'objective thought' of the master subject, the human in their own right, the individual who relates to the world, their world – the figure who lords over everything that is there in the world. The master subject is the 'I' whose objective thought not only justifies himself as human but himself as lord – the individual as the transcendental subject. His existence is that of *I for I*; it denies the existence of the other by creating *I and Other* wherein dehumanisation and death are rendered possible. The ontological justification of the 'I' is the master himself, who claims not to need any form of justification because he is justification in himself. The master subject owns a thing that he lords over, the thing is his by virtue of his own justification. This excess of justification is nothing but narcissism. The master subject sees the world from his 'objective thought'. His thought is not only definitive, it is absolute truth. Everything that has to do with reality and existence rests with the master himself. Narcissism creates the possibility of boundlessness; everything dwells in the 'objective thought' of the definer and chronicler of objective truth. It thus remains a dubious fact – that is, the master is the absolute truth and the slave, as a thing, signifies a lie.

If Aunt Hester's flesh is to be located in this violence, what emerges is the collapse of the narrative that seeks to narrate it. It is the spirit of violence that haunts Aunt Hester's flesh. She is violated because the spirit of violence signifies her to be vulnerable to violence – or, the spirit of violence annihilates her as her flesh is incarcerated. This not only occurs at the level of possession, but also through Aunt Hester not being allowed to be on her own. She is violated by the structure that makes Captain Anthony her master, the institution that makes her the flesh that is commanded by Captain Anthony's will. The spirit of violence is directed to its referent – Aunt Hester's flesh. What haunts this flesh is the sadistic drive, its impulses, its excess and its fulfilment of perverted fantasies. Why would there be an acute narrative to give an account of such madness?

Douglass provides the narration, but he still has no narrative, and no grammar to account for the violence that befell Aunt Hester. Even though he gives a vivid explanation, it does not capture the extent or excess of the violence enacted against that which is nothing. For Douglass, Aunt Hester is the subject qua human and not a thing. By giving an elegant description of her as a woman of note, the spirit of violence that unmakes her as such and makes her as a thing becomes interesting. What would the narration have been like if Douglass had given the account of Aunt Hester through the register of Mbembe's ontological question – 'But what does it mean to do violence to what is nothing?' Clearly, what is fundamental here is not simply the violence, but its sadistic proportion, its arbitrariness, its inescapably firm grip, one that mutes the language that seeks to narrate it, blinds the eye that seeks to see it, deafens the faculty of hearing. This violence is the spirit: it is not the human spirit, it is the spirit of human suspension, of dehumanisation. To see Aunt Hester is not to see the human. Thus, her violation is that of a thing – that is, nothing is violated, there is no violence. Spillers (2003) shows how the inscription of the slave is nothing but violence – the topology and topography of terror – the abstraction of the body from its form, which then results in ontological erasure. The flesh signifies 'an empty vessel, a commodity, an unsuffering property' (McKittrick 2006, 70). It is clear that this is not the body of the human. Aunt Hester's body is relegated to what Katherine McKittrick (2006) calls the 'ungeographic', as it belongs nowhere but to the master. It is the body that has no interiority or corporeality – the abstracted and extracted entity – the flesh.

The analytics of the flesh are necessary, if not fundamental, to an understanding of Aunt Hester's flesh. The flesh is the site upon which violence is exercised and where it makes its marks visible. Spillers (2003, 21) amplifies the point thus, by referring to 'slavery's technologies through marking, [that] also … suggest that "beyond" the violating hand that laid on the stigmata of a recognition that was misrecognition, or the regard that was disregard, there was a *semiosis* of procedure that had enabled such a moment in the first place'.

The flesh as the analytic serves as the perspective through which Aunt Hester is looked at. As the slave, she lives the life that is not life - a void, a delirium, and nothingness. She finds herself there, and this is the life that is determined by Captain Anthony – the master in the capacity qua master. Aunt Hester's life and death rest in his hands; he can let her live and he can kill her in the way he deems fit. To be the master is to possess that which is nothing, to do whatever to *it* and to practise any form of what Saidiya Hartman (1997) terms 'terror making', which is the operating logic of the power vested in the master by himself and for himself. Slaves are structured by what Calvin Warren (2018) registers as 'ontological terror', which, in essence, is what haunts Aunt

Hester's existence. Ontological terror, by way of extending Hartman's 'terror making', is the infrastructure that is designed and maintained to discipline slaves who are reduced to mere flesh rather than beings with bodies, minds and souls. It is the nothingness of blacks that renders them reducible to nothing but flesh.

The flesh, according to Hartman (1997, 3), signifies the 'slave's ravaged body … the spectacular character of black suffering'. Hartman opens her text with Aunt Hester's brutal whipping and thereby punctuates the fact that to be enslaved is to be subjected to 'despotic terror'. If there is to be subject formation, this materialises for the slave as destruction, suppression, erasure, and the slave being nothing but the flesh. For Hartman, to reproduce the brutal account of Aunt Hester can be anaesthetising, and the narratives that reproduce it will go to the banal extent of rendering the pain as the thing to be transcended. Christina Sharpe (2010, 2) amplifies this argument thus: 'The anxiety that Hartman and others articulate around repeating this scene inheres in the awful configurations of power, desire, pleasure, and domination to be found not only in the original scene, but also in its transmission, transformation, and renewal, to which we in the present are equally inured. Reproducing black pain as that which is shocking and horrible, for Hartman, can create a routinised display of terror (which will then not be terror due to anesthetisation at work).'

By offering an alternative reading to Hartman's, Fred Moten (2003) asserts that the object has the capacity to resist. If such an object means the slave, for Moten slaves can resist what dehumanises them and reduces them to flesh. For Hartman, the slave is caught in the scene of subjection, whereas for Moten it is in the scene of objection. For Moten, Aunt Hester is an object that engages in the objection to its whipping – Captain Anthony's whip is resisted. While Hartman moves away from Douglass's 'primal scene', Moten focuses on it so that the crux of his intervention is the reanimation of Aunt Hester's whipping, but with a more rigorous focus on its sonic dimension. The primal scene, for Moten, cannot be avoided since such a move is illusory. Therefore, the primal scene should be reproduced. Moten also insists that in the recounting of the primal scene there is a particular function of the aesthetic signature that comes through Aunt Hester's scream. What Aunt Hester possesses, through her scream, is the 'phonic materiality' which, for Moten, is the amalgamation of blackness and sound. It is in her scream that

Moten registers both the performance of blackness and that of humanity. In fact, Moten insists on performance as the very nodal point of resistance. The content of Aunt Hester's scream, for Moten (2017, ix), is 'an alternative to representation'.

More fundamentally, however, the opposition of these possibilities faces a deadlock with Aunt Hester's flesh. The contentiousness of the primal scene seems to clearly suggest different registers. On the one hand, Moten insists on the primal scene and its radical breakdown because of the capacity of the slave to resist, or to exist. On the other hand, Hartman refuses the preoccupation with the primal scene for the very fact of it being available for reproduction that leads to its anaesthetisation. Hartman goes straight to the analytics of the flesh and the violent inscriptions that the flesh is subjected to. If performativity is to be taken as the last word, perhaps it is important to highlight the following: for Moten there is a possibility of a 'freedom drive' – the radical force that constitutes the making of the human as such. For Hartman, performativity is not the possibility but the non-recognition of Aunt Hester's humanity. It is looking for the ways in which violence veils itself – that is, 'the extreme and paradoxical condition of slavery, often mistaken for nonsense or joy' (Hartman 1997, 35). Moten (2017) argues that black performance resides where the language of ontology gets exhausted. The objects that can, do resist – or, more to the later corrective that Moten installs, performance is marked as the resistance of the object and the object engages in the remaking that will make it not be an object again. As Farley (2005, 239) amplifies: 'The slave is trained to enjoy being taken for an object. The master's will is the slave's desire.' This is sadistic; the master extracts at the level of excess to create the nothingness of the slave. If performativity is to be taken into account, it does less to account for the lacerated flesh that is subjected to Captain Anthony's brutal lashes. Aunt Hester cannot be reduced to the mercy of what Hartman refers to as the liberal extension of feelings. In performance there is a captive body.

To be the slave, as a site of enjoyment, a site of extraction, is fundamentally what it means to be captive. While the master enjoys the slave, there is no joy for the slave but pain, suffering, misery and all the existential ordeals that negate humanity. Slavery, Hartman (1997, 25) insists, is 'observing violence and conflating it with pleasure'. This means the pleasure of the master is the erasure of the slave, for the master derives pleasure from dehumanisation.

Farley (2005, 225) writes: 'Bodies are marked white-over-black.' It is this marker that justifies mastership – the master as the figure that lords over the slave on the basis of being white. Both the slaveholder and the overseer assume the same position in relation to the slave – they mean one and the same thing: master. The master is known for unleashing violence on the slave. Douglass vividly describes Captain Anthony's overseer, Mr Plummer, in this way: 'Mr Plummer was a miserable drunkard, a profane swearer, and a savage monster. He always went armed with a cowskin and a heavy cudgel. I have known him to cut and slash the women's heads so horribly, that even the master would be enraged at his cruelty, and would threaten to whip him if he did not mind himself' (Douglass [1845] 1995, 3).

From the above, it is clear that Mr Plummer, the overseer, assumes the role of the master and his conduct is as such. Even though he knows his place (he crosses boundaries at will and that 'enrage[s]' Captain Anthony), he never ceases to have the place of the master. The threat that he will be whipped by Captain Anthony is just an empty gesture. If there is something that Captain Anthony enjoys, it is the violent and sadistic character of Mr Plummer. Douglass attests that Captain Anthony is not a humane slaveholder (as if there could ever be one). Even though Captain Anthony is enraged by the barbarity of Mr Plummer, all he is worried about is that Mr Plummer should not impersonate him. But that changes nothing, in that the desire of Mr Plummer is to be a master. Indeed, Mr Plummer reigns like Captain Anthony. The slaves should not see the hierarchy of mastership - the height of the slaveholder above the overseer.

Douglass is naive to expect humanness from the slaveholder. Even an extreme degree of benevolence cannot extinguish the mastership of a slaveholder. What needs to be affirmed is that mastership cannot be separated from flesh-mongering. The barbarity of Mr Plummer does not affect Captain Anthony at the humane level. Rather, it concerns the place of being a master – the cruelty of the overseer should not be exercised more than that of the master. That is what affects Captain Anthony: the barbarity is at that level. There cannot be any feeling of compassion for the slaves that Captain Anthony tasks Mr Plummer to oversee. Also to be noted is that Captain Anthony has made Mr Plummer his extension. When the slaves see Mr Plummer, they actually see Captain Anthony.

Douglass commits an error in making a distinction between two overseers, Mr Severe and his successor, Mr Hopkins. He describes Mr Severe as a cruel man, as his name suggests, writing: 'He seemed to take pleasure in manifesting his fiendish barbarity. Added to his cruelty, he was a profane swearer' (Douglass [1845] 1995, 7). Indeed, Mr Severe is the same as Mr Plummer, both being profane swearers and notable sadists. Douglass even goes on to note that Mr Severe continues to swear even in his moment of death. Mr Severe's successor, Mr Hopkins, is regarded as the opposite of his predecessor. He is said to be less profane, not cruel and not noisy. As an overseer, he is the sovereign figure above the slave – he enslaves. 'He whipped, but seemed not to take pleasure in it. He was called by the slaves a good overseer' ([1845] 1995, 7). This is the error of seeing the good in the evil institution of slavery. The slaves who see Mr Hopkins as good do not want the end of slavery, it seems. This suggests their contentment with having an overseer who is better than his cruel predecessor. Even though Mr Hopkins is claimed not to have taken any pleasure in whipping, this might be an error on the part of Douglass. The very act of whipping is pleasure-seeking, as the one who whips is gratified by consuming the flesh of the slave. The facts that still remain with regard to Mr Plummer and Mr Hopkins are threefold: one, both are overseers and they subject slaves to the despotic terror of slavery; two, by cracking the whip on the flesh of the slaves they are the extension of their master; and three, they do not see humans, but slaves upon which they solidify dehumanisation.

Having stated that Captain Anthony was not a humane slaveholder (something that cannot be expected) it is interesting that Douglass gives another twist to his characterisation of the master. He writes:

> He was a cruel man, hardened by long years of slaveholding. He would at times seem to take great pleasure in whipping a slave. I have often been awakened at the dawn of day by the most heart-rending shrieks of an own aunt of mine, whom he used to tie up to a joist, and whip upon her naked back till she was literally covered with blood. No words, no tears, no prayers, from his gory victim, seem to move his iron heart from its bloody purpose. ([1845] 1995, 4)

Is it Aunt Hester's heartless whipping that makes Douglass question the 'humanness' of the master? At no point, of course, does Douglass claim that Captain Anthony is humane. The criticism here has to do with the paradox (master + humanness). The humane master is an oxymoron. Thus, Captain Anthony does not need to commit this act of whipping Aunt Hester to be disqualified from humaneness. The master is not humane, by virtue of being a slaveholder. The same is true of those who support slavery – there cannot be selflessness and kindness in slaveholding.

Aunt Hester's flesh does not signify an individual or an event, but the totality of slavery and its aftermath. The human question, its ethical dimension and legality, faces difficulty when the figure of the slave is introduced. The slave is not the subject, and is not the figure that is related to the world. The paradigm of difference is the one that renders Aunt Hester nothing but flesh, as she is ontologically nothing. Aunt Hester's flesh is outside the liberal discursive register of 'we are all human', by virtue of its location in relation to the question of slavery as the basis of critique. There is no humanity if there is still slavery and its aftermath. There is no humanity if race is still the organising principle of the modern colonial world. There is no humanity if the infrastructure of antiblackness still exists. There is no humanity if the despotic terror of blackness still persists. There is no humanity if structural violence, mass incarceration, police brutality and ontological exclusion are still the markers of blackness. There is no humanity if blackness is still dehumanised.

To pose questions from the site of being dehumanised has nothing to do with the claim of being human, but everything to do with ending dehumanisation. Aunt Hester's flesh cannot be seen as that which is violated by Captain Anthony, but as a conduit through which the structural position of being blackened in the antiblack world inscribes, legitimises and validates itself. In point of fact, Aunt Hester appears in order to be available for dehumanisation. So, her presence in the ontological realm is superfluous, as she is the slave. What, then, does it mean to be the human? Aunt Hester is not human, and her structural positionality as the slave renders the question meaningless, as it does not correspond with her existential misery. Aunt Hester is flesh, she is the captive figure, and her life is not her own. The human question will be relevant after the infrastructure of dehumanisation ceases to exist. This is not the effort of the master, or his generosity. Rather, the revivification of the slave from dehumanisation and the meaningful creation of the human world will bring with them other ontological possibilities. Aunt Hester's flesh serves as the cartography of this revivification.

REFERENCES

Douglass, Frederick. [1845] 1995. *Narrative of the Life of Frederick Douglass*. Mineola, NY: Dover Press.

Farley, Anthony P. 2005. 'Perfecting Slavery'. *Loyola University Chicago Law Journal* 36: 225–56.

Hartman, Saidiya V. 1997. *Scenes of Subjection: Terror, Slavery and Self-Making in Nineteenth-Century America*. New York, NY: Oxford University Press.

Mbembe, Achille. 2001. *On the Postcolony*. Translated by A.M. Berrett, Janet Roitman, Murray Last and Steven Rendall. Berkeley, CA: University of California Press.

McKittrick, Katherine. 2006. *Demonic Grounds: Black Women and the Cartographies of Struggle*. Minneapolis, MN: University of Minnesota Press.

Moten, Fred. 2003. *In the Break: The Aesthetics of the Black Radical Tradition*. Minneapolis, MN: University of Minnesota Press.

Moten, Fred. 2017. *Black and Blur.* Durham, NC: Duke University Press.

Sharpe, Christina. 2010. *Monstrous Intimacies: Making Post-Slavery Subjects*. Durham, NC: Duke University Press.

Spillers, Hortense J. 2003. *Black, White and Color: Essays on American Literature and Culture*. Chicago, IL: University of Chicago Press.

Warren, Calvin L. 2018. *Ontological Terror: Blackness, Nihilism, and Emancipation*. Durham, NC: Duke University Press.

Weheliye, Alexander G. 2014. *Habeas Viscus: Racializing Assemblages, Biopolitics, and Black Feminist Theories of the Human*. Durham, NC: Duke University Press.

8 'LANGUAGE AS BEING' IN THE POLITICS OF NGŨGĨ WA THIONG'O

BRIAN SIBANDA

Ngũgĩ wa Thiong'o's decoloniality and political philosophy of liberation are prominently represented in his struggles for the decolonisation of the mind, especially in the politics of language in literature and education. What arguably distinguishes wa Thiong'o from other African writers is his unique observation of language as being. His take on language extends to more than viewing it as a carrier of culture and a means of communication; he sees it as a means by which the dis-membered being can be re-membered. This chapter, by focusing on language as being in the politics of wa Thiong'o, as reflected in his writings, deviates from views of language as deconstruction (Orwell 1977), language as a room without a view (Kafka 1937), language as unmaking (Marquez 1982), language as disillusionment and seduction (Nabokov 1995), language as a door through which reality escapes (Robbe-Grillet 1955), language as an expression of otherness (Nganang 2001) and language as just a narrative (Brink 2007). Wa Thiong'o's unique focus on language has often been met with harsh responses. Peter Vakunta (2010, 75) argues that wa Thiong'o's 'pontifications against the use of imperial languages in African literature' are 'spurious' and a stunt that is 'simply seeking negative attention'. Vakunta is not alone in his criticism of wa Thiong'o's linguistic stance; David Cook and Michael Okenimkpe (1997) state that wa Thiong'o's thinking does not conform to any specific political, dogmatic doctrine, and Evan Mwangi (cited in Boehmer 1993) accuses wa Thiong'o of preaching Kenyan water and drinking Western wine, and of being an ideologically outdated author.

Wa Thiong'o's dedication to the struggle for liberation of the African being needs to be understood from a decolonial locus, where the colonial being has been dis-membered through the erasure of their languages, and thus re-membering can only be achieved through the return to the languages of those whose humanity has been denied or questioned. Rendering a person's language otiose is a violent decapitation of that person's humanity; it is to dis-member their being. Humanitas, the Eurocentric concept of a human being, which excluded those on the margins of modernity, justified and solidified its humaneness through the usage and nuances concentrated in language. In his activism for the revival of African languages, wa Thiong'o coined the terms dis-membering and re-membering, which Sabelo Ndlovu-Gatsheni (2015) equates with coloniality and decoloniality, respectively. Wa Thiong'o's take on linguicides and linguifams (linguistic starvation) as acts of dis-membering the African being marks him out as not just an occasional Marxist and post-colonial philosopher and novelist, as most readings of his work have mistaken him for, but as a decolonial philosopher. Wa Thiong'o argues that 'our' humanity (that is, those who exist in the zone of non-being) was denied by 'them' (those who exist in the zone of being, and give themselves the power to classify beings and non-beings), thus exposing the un-humanity of a structure of enunciation (institutions, categories of thought and languages) that built for itself an image of 'humanity' which allowed it to disqualify what did not fit its imaginary. In doing so, he moves beyond the language, culture and identity preoccupations of the post-colonialists; he has thus taken a different route from them in his disavowal of the racial imaginary of modernity upon which coloniality was erected.

Wa Thiong'o's confronting of the linguistic dis-memberment of being is a decades-long fight against linguistic Darwinism and feudalism in colonial Africa, one that can be traced from his early student years to the 1962 Makerere Conference of African Writers of English Expression, in Kampala, Uganda (Wali 1963), where he participated in the deliberations on African literature. This fight was followed by several books and essays in which wa Thiong'o chose to be faithful to his language (see wa Thiong'o 2006), despite facing opposing views from other African scholars like Chinua Achebe (1975, 1978, 1989), Léopold Sédar Senghor (1962), Wole Soyinka (1988), Gabriel Okara (1970) and Biodun Jeyifo (2018). Wa Thiong'o's call to decolonise language led him, in 1968, to become actively involved in the intellectual struggles to transform the English Department at the University of Nairobi in Kenya, a department that remained colonial in content and structure. The document 'On the Abolition of the English Department' (wa Thiong'o 1995) was a call for the 'decolonisation of the cognitive process' (wa Thiong'o 2016, 42) and of the study of so-called universal literature, which in essence was European literature. In 1977 wa Thiong'o decided to abandon writing in English and turned to his native language, Gikuyu. In pursuit of his linguistic ideology, he published his first play in Gikuyu, *Ngaahika Ndeenda*, in 1977 (wa Thiong'o and wa Mĩriĩ 1977), leading to his arrest by the Kenyan authorities. The issue of linguistic coloniality and coloniality of being has remained fundamental, and unresolved, in the era of post-colonialism. There is a need for an ongoing reassessment and reclamation of submerged and silenced languages, for the construction or rediscovery of an intelligible self.

The rejection of English and the turn to Gikuyu embody a rejection of the Western European model of being. Wa Thiong'o's several writings make it clear that language is central in dis-membering the mode of being-in-the-world-with-others. His radical but humanistic advocacy for the use of African languages in the writing of African literature needs to be understood well beyond the existing post-colonial language debates, or as just an idealistic, nativist, Third World fundamentalism or Afro-radicalism that seeks to take the Global South out of the world to some imaginary pristine authenticity of the impossible past. The advocacy for the indigenous languages should not be dismissed as reverse linguicide but understood as a decolonial call for space for, and recognition of, indigenous languages and being. Language cannot be separated from being, for languages are carried by bodies, hence how one deals with languages is how one deals with human beings (Mpofu 2019). Marginalising indigenous languages is the marginalising of the bodies that carry those languages. The advocacy to have African literature written in an African language comes from the observation that 'creative imagination is one of the greatest of re-membering practices' of a dis-membered being and of marginalised bodies (wa Thiong'o 2009, 16). Language is more than a communication system; it is a carrier of memory, a point that eluded Biodun Jeyifo (2018) in his critique of wa Thiong'o. The critique is based on issues of linguistic and communicative competence, and on 'what … a would-be African writer [should] do who wishes to write in the indigenous mother tongue but whose language neither has a writing script nor print capitalism of even an embryonic form' (Jeyifo 2018, 143). What Jeyifo exhibits is a failure to appreciate that language extends beyond the literal and economic means of communication often attached to it; it assumes metaphorical connotations aligned to life itself.

Wa Thiong'o's decolonial call for a decolonised mind, for restoration of being and dignity to the victims of coloniality, becomes the unmasking of linguicides and linguifams. His literary work is concerned with how a dis-membered people can relaunch themselves into the world that has no space for them (Thiong'o 2009). Ndlovu-Gatsheni (2015, 23) states that wa Thiong'o's decoloniality is 'ranged against imperialism, colonialism and coloniality as a constituent part of the modernist politics of dis-memberment, alienation, exploitation and alterity'. Thus for wa Thiong'o (1986), decoloniality becomes a search for a liberating perspective aimed at restoring the humanity and being of the African after centuries of suffering dis-memberment. This chapter is written in English, a colonial language, which means my mother tongue is suppressed in academia, but also that the English language should be interpreted as part of the cultural equipment I use to challenge coloniality, by using its tools of domination to lay the seeds of its defeat.

LANGUAGE AND BEING

Frantz Fanon, having experienced what it means to be voiceless, learned that 'to speak is to exist absolutely for the other' (Fanon 1963, 17) for language is essentially being. To render one language-less is to render one a non-being, for non-beings, though they might communicate, do not have a language. The ability to think, enunciate and speak is a marker of being (Mignolo 2011a, xxiv). The colonised, branded as lacking a language and letters, cannot enunciate and therefore is not a 'human' being. Language is where the identity of the people is located, for language is not what human beings have, but what human beings are (Mignolo 2011b, 139). Walter Mignolo (2009, 160) clearly states that thinking is done by a 'racially marked body in a geo-historical marked space that feels the urge or gets the call to speak, to articulate, in whatever semiotic system, the urge that makes of living organisms "human" beings'.

Wa Thiong'o (2009) discusses the mythical story of Osiris in Egypt, who was killed by his brother Set; Set then cut his body into pieces and scattered them all over Egypt. Isis re-members the scattered pieces of Osiris to life with the help of a deity. The significance of the myth lies in that a dis-membered being is re-membered to wholeness. Wa Thiong'o is the Isis of the present who seeks to re-member to wholeness beings who are dis-membered through memory loss and linguicide. Every African writer has an Isis role to play, as African writers cannot afford to be intellectual outsiders in their own land – they 'must reconnect with the buried alluvium of African memory – that must become the base for planting African memory anew in the continent and the world', and connecting with memory must mean 'a return to the base, the people, must mean at the very least the use of a language and languages that the people speak. Any further linguistic additions should be for strengthening, deepening and widening this power of the languages spoken by the people' (wa Thiong'o 2016, 76). The decades-long linguistic advocacy and activism, the call to return to the base, the resurrection of African languages by African writers, is a means of restoring the being of those who exist in the margins of modernity, an act of re-membering.

Dis-memberment captures not only physical fragmentation but also epistemological colonisation, as well as the 'cultural decapitation' that resulted in deep forms of alienation among Africans (Ndlovu-Gatsheni 2015, 25). This dis-memberment of Africa was 'simultaneously the foundation, fuel, and consequence of Europe's capitalist modernity' (wa Thiong'o 2009, 2). It is part of the 'imperial/racist reason' (Du Bois 1903) that doubted the being of the other, and is done, according to wa Thiong'o (2009), by uprooting Africans from their memory. Re-membering becomes the process of planting the memory and resisting Western modernity, as expounded by Hegel's view of Africa without history, memory or discernable being (Hegel [1837] 1944, 99).

Valentin Mudimbe (1994, xii) shares the same understanding with wa Thiong'o, in that 'the geographical expansion of Europe and its civilization ... submitted the world to its memory'. Dis-memberment meant that African bodies became 'branded with a European memory' (wa Thiong'o 2009, 10). Ndlovu-Gatsheni (2015, 25) adds that the long-term consequences of this dis-memberment process were human beings 'out of sync with their being and human beings who have lost name, language, culture and identity. At play here were broader processes of mapping, naming and owning as part of the inscription of coloniality'. The effects of linguistic erasure included looking at oneself from outside of the self or with the lenses of a stranger; and identifying with the foreign base as the starting point towards the self, that is, from another self towards one's self, rather than using the local as the starting point, from self to other selves (wa Thiong'o 2012, 38–39). The effects of linguicides and linguifams have continued to be lived after the end of colonisation.

Thus to read wa Thiong'o's advocacy for African languages from a post-colonialist perspective is flawed, as wa Thiong'o (1986) emphasised the linguistic impact of coloniality of being, as opposed to language as a mere carrier of culture and identity. Wa Thiong'o moves beyond colonisation logic that focuses on the 50 years of decolonisation and the supposed end of colonial empires, as he questions why the continent remains in a subaltern position within the global power hierarchy since the Atlantic slavery era (wa Thiong'o 1986). Coloniality is the racialised invisible power structure designed by the Euro-North American-centric modern world (Grosfoguel 2007) that hierarchises human beings according to racial ontological densities. Wa Thiong'o details the workings of coloniality as the biggest linguistic weapon, a weapon that annihilated a people's being by making them 'want to identify with that which is furthest removed from themselves; for instance, with other people's languages rather than their own. It makes them identify with that which is decadent and reactionary, all those forces which would stop their own springs of life', leading to a collective death wish (wa Thiong'o 1986, 3).

Gabriela Veronelli (2015, 108) describes coloniality of language as the 'linguistic racialization of colonised populations as communicative agents beginning in the 16th century and continuing until today'. Linguistic classification through coloniality of language, which is equivalent to colonial racial classification, led to the dehumanisation and silencing of indigenous languages and the bodies that carry those languages. Opposite racial communicators became linguistically unequal, with the languages of the colonisers valorised as 'real languages', for they could create and transmit knowledges, whereas the 'languages' of the colonised were just vulgar mumblings incapable of carrying, let alone creating, knowledge. The colonised, as inferior and non-being, could not be communicative agents as they lacked the ability to express, transmit or produce knowledge: 'The coloniality of language is an aspect of the process of dehumanizing colonized people through racialization. Because racialization is inseparable from the Eurocentric appropriation and reduction of the universe of the colonized, the relation between language and racialization is performed within a Eurocentric philosophy, ideology and politics, which include a politics of language' (Veronelli 2015, 119).

To appreciate language as being, one needs to remember the lived metaphor of Waiyaki wa Hinga, who was buried alive with his head facing downwards and not facing Mount Kenya as rituals demand, and King Hinsta, who was decapitated and his head put on display in British museums as a figure of art (wa Thiong'o 2009). The two shared the fate of physical dis-memberment, which wa Thiong'o likens to the dis-memberment of being through linguistic coloniality. The killing of these two is symbolic of the death of memory, memory that has been cut off from the head, an act that 'dis-membered the colonised from memory, turning their heads upside down and burying all the memories they carried' (wa Thiong'o 2009, 7). This memory, which is the consciousness and identity of the people, is carried through their own languages. The physical decapitation explained here is the linguistic lynching of being, as the metaphorical headless bodies are branded with European memory, a death knell of being.

The turn of the sixteenth century becomes important, as it sets the stage for the racialised linguistic hierarchy leading to the denial and dis-membering of those who embody difference, and the automatic awarding of humanity to colonisers who possessed 'languages'. Elio Antonio de Nebrija, in celebrating his invention of grammar for the Castilian language, explained to Queen Isabella the purpose his work would serve, namely to elevate the Castilian language from a vulgar status to the status of a language that could express knowledge, a language worth learning for 'many barbarians who speak outlandish tongues' (Mignolo 1995, 38; Nebrija [1492] 1946). For Nebrija, language alone distinguished human beings from other living systems, from wild animals, for language is the unique distinction of man (Mignolo 1995, 39). Any letters or other symbolic characters that the colonised used to write were described as works of the devil and not 'languages', a view articulated by Diego de Landa Calderón, a Spanish Franciscan priest and bishop of Yucatán, in regard to his encounters with Amerindians and the accompanying epistemisticides: '[they] found a great number of books in these letters, and since they contained nothing but superstitions and falsehoods of the devil we burned them all, which they took most grievously, which gave them great pain' (De Landa Calderón cited in Mignolo 1995, 71).

By being given a prescribed grammar, Castilian became a language of knowledge, since knowing meant having a language and having a language meant being able to express this knowledge. But as the racialised perspective would have it, the colonised did not have knowledge since they did not have language, and lack of language disqualified a person from humanitas. It is this context that gave birth to Oduche in Achebe's *Arrow of God* (1964), Ocol in Okot p'Bitek's *Song of Ocol* (1964) and Joseph in wa Thiong'o's *The River Between* (1965). These characters are examples of those who aspired to whiteness, to be human as defined by the racialised perspective. Wa Thiong'o's ideas are in tandem with those of Nebrija in that they both hold that language is more than just a vehicle of communication; it is a means to one's identity and to articulation of one's reality and humanity.

Coloniality of language was not a spinoff or an accompanying process of colonisation, but colonisation itself. Colonisation was a linguistic process. Coloniality reduced the colonised to inferior thing-beings, reducing their communication to infantile blabbers (Quijano 2000), thus establishing the relationship between language and being. Wa Thiong'o's advocacy and use of African languages is resistance to linguicides and erasure of being. Concerning African languages and their peripheralisation, Kwesi Wiredu (1992, 302) says that in light of the global privileging of Eurocentric knowledges, languages and coloniality in the world, in Africa 'conceptually speaking then, the maxim of the moment should be: African know thy self'. Wiredu and wa Thiong'o gesture towards epistemic disobedience that prefers a radical refusal of identifying, seeing and knowing the African being in terms of Eurocentric lenses. The motion of African self-knowledge that Wiredu points to is central to the advocacy of indigenous languages, counter to Eurocentric fictions of racialised linguistic hierarchies. Language, as argued by James Baldwin (1979), defines the other. Wa Thiong'o, by using Gikuyu in his writings and broadly advocating for the use of indigenous languages, is the 'other' who resists and refuses to be defined by a language or languages that refuse to recognise him and his humanity.

Wa Thiong'o challenges the humanity of the master's language and the perceived lack of humanity in the languages of the colonised. Through the discourse of the Anthropos (the other), he seeks to restore the humanity of those colonised through linguistic liberation without resorting to reverse linguicides and Afro-radicalism. Wa Thiong'o's linguistic shift, as evidenced in some of his literary works written in Gikuyu, is an attempt to delink from, to get outside the linguistic prison of coloniality. Coloniality defined what language is and what it is not, and in the process linguistically classified beings and thing-beings, which wa Thiong'o, through linguistic disobedience, is exposing as just the darker side of the modernity that keeps the colonised mentally and spiritually imprisoned. The dominant language, then, becomes the criterion against which the level of civilisation of the colonised will be measured, as 'the colonised is elevated above his jungle status in proportion to his adoption of the mother country's cultural standards' (Fanon 1963, 18).

WA THIONG'O GOES NAKED

The conversation between Prospero and Caliban in Shakespeare's *The Tempest* gives a better interpretation of wa Thiong'o's analysis of language and being in the age of coloniality. Caliban has no 'language', and has to be taught and given a language; therefore he is in debt to Prospero's kind human gesture, his gift of language (wa Thiong'o 2009, 2012, 2013). Language becomes a colonial tool of auto-enslavement and loss of being for 'when you did not know yourself, I gave you language' (wa Thiong'o 2009, 16), and 'I created you, but of course, in my image' (wa Thiong'o 2009, 39); 'your language was mere babble. I gave you purpose' (wa Thiong'o 2009, 29), says Prospero to Caliban. Language is the conception of one's being and that of others. This linguistic logic of conquest leads to linguicides and linguifams (wa Thiong'o 2009, 18) resulting in loss of memory and remembrance. The loss finds its epitome in *Wizard of the Crow* (wa Thiong'o 2006), where Tajirika's quest to become 'white' means losing his name and his language. Loss of one's language means a loss of being; adopting the colonising languages means achieving human status. Tajirika becomes a representation of a native dis-membered from his memory, dis-membered through language.

Language as the house of being (Heidegger 1982) is laden with identity, culture and memories of the people who use the language; George Steiner (1992, 128) emphasises this by adding that 'it is not man who determines being, but being via language [that] discloses itself to and in man'. Coloniality, as a form of dominance, remained with formerly colonised persons and communities long after flag independence, and after the arrival of what have been called post-colonial societies and experiences; maintained through coloniality of language and inferiorisation of the colonised, it kept colonial relations between the former coloniser and the former colonised intact. Language as part of the colonisation process was more than just communication of meaning; it was communication of power, not a model of signs but one of war and battle that determined power relations (Foucault 1980).

Coloniality of language dehumanises by denying the language of the colonised, by placing it in dichotomous relations that are not equal but hierarchically defined by the location of the language. Wa Thiong'o's linguistic disobedience should be understood as an act of regaining African humanity, and a refusal to surrender to the illusion of modernity and its promises to grant the peripheral Anthropos the humanitas status. Wa Thiong'o's works should be read against the logic of coloniality: he deliberately seeks to decolonise both language and being, thus opening up alternatives and possibilities for other imaginaries of language and being, expressing what Catherine Walsh (2009) calls the paradigm other, a paradigm that emerges from colonial difference. In essence, a reading of wa Thiong'o shows how the logic of coloniality manifested itself through language and denied the humanity of the other, giving rise to the call to decolonise the 'mind' (wa Thiong'o 2006) and the 'imaginary' (Gruzinski 1999), that is, knowledge and being.

Jose de Aldrete and other colonialists on a mission to civilise the barbarians established a link between linguistic behaviour, clothes and good manners, and being civilised (Mignolo 1995). Those who existed in the zone of non-being were described as lacking all markers of civility, that is, lacking a language, clothes and manners. A causal relationship was established between language and clothes; thus the lack of alphabetic writing and mastery of colonial languages relegated one to the status of a naked beast with no language, for language distinguished the beasts from those that spoke 'our' language. Wa Thiong'o, by advocating for and also writing in African languages, assumes the beast status and therefore goes naked, as he fails to adhere to the linguistic behaviour that is equated with civility. Going naked means discarding the colonial idea of being and rejecting the 'civilisation' imposed in the name of modernity, and this involves decolonising the mind. By delinking from English, wa Thiong'o delinks from the Western idea of civilisation. Colonial languages used as a form of psychological subjugation by colonisers have to be decolonised, and wa Thiong'o does so by writing in his indigenous language as a way of liberating the imprisoned being from the metaphysical empire (wa Thiong'o 2006, 16). His metaphorical nakedness is a decolonial process of re-membering. The lack of civility he enacts by writing in Gikuyu and advocating for the humanity of the African is a desire for self-definition and attainment of sovereign subjectivity. Re-membering is resistance to the objectification and dehumanisation of Africans. It is a struggle to regain lost humanity even after administrative colonialism; wa Thiong'o (2013, x) argues that 'the physical empire' has been pushed back but 'the metaphysical empire remains'.

Civility was defined by the coloniser in terms of letters and clothes. In their eyes, the indigenous people lacked letters (grammar), and lack of letters meant lack of language. Walter Mignolo (1995) establishes that in the culture of the European Renaissance, letters and civility went together and were markers of one's humanity. Christopher Columbus joined the bandwagon of those who argued for the relationship between language, nakedness and being, noting in his journal entry about the Guhanahani natives that 'God willing, when I come to leave I will bring six of them to Your Highness so that they may learn to speak' (Columbus [1492–93] 1990, 31). The indigenous Africans stood accused of walking around without any clothes, which meant that their beastly status was never in doubt: they lacked both markers of civility, that is, letters and clothes. Their nudity disqualified these colonised communicators as beings. Mignolo (1995) adds that there is an implicit connection between linguistic behaviour and good manners as signs of civility, hence speech came to be used to differentiate human beings from barbarians. By disregarding English in favour of his indigenous Gikuyu, wa Thiong'o lost civility and went around without the clothes of the master's grammar and letters. From a racialised perspective, Gikuyu has no Eurocentrically valorised expressivity. By going naked, wa Thiong'o expressed his being outside of the logic of coloniality, moving away from the monologic colonial perspective of language to a plurilogic understanding of language that is accommodating of the periphery in expressing their realities, and thus exposes the hidden workings of linguistic coloniality and its denial of being to the indigenous people.

The disobedience of writing in Gikuyu and the advocacy for indigenous languages meant 'speaking' outside the colonial linguistic boundaries and outside the racially prescribed relationship between language and being. Wa Thiong'o's seminal work, *Decolonising the Mind* (1986), clearly articulates that colonialism deprived the indigenous people of their power to 'speak', deprived them of their identity and humanity, and forced the colonial languages on them, imposing an alien identity and categorising them as non-beings unless they carried the European memory. Languaging in indigenous languages and advocating for their space and recognition is an act of re-membering, re-enacting and restoring the humanity of those bodies that carry those languages.

While Chinua Achebe, Wole Soyinka and Léopold Sédar Senghor embraced the use of English and French in their writing to speak to the empire and its victims, wa Thiong'o refuses to wear the empire's clothes, and speaks back to the empire naked in Gikuyu, as well as through his advocacy of African indigenous languages. He claims the right of those on the margin to speak, produce and transmit knowledge in their language, thus opening up alternative linguistic centres (wa Thiong'o, 2012). As a way of naming linguistic racialisation, Veronelli (2015) coined the term 'monolanguaging' as a way of capturing the linguistic hierarchy of superiority and inferiority. Monolanguaging questions the 'communicative interaction between people who perceive themselves as having a language in the full sense, and animal-like beings who are assumed to have no language but who can be trained to understand the former well enough to be able to follow their orders and do what they want' (Veronelli 2015, 124). In wa Thiong'o's literature, African languages are communal places of resisting erasure and conceptualisation of communication and communal life, outside the prison of the coloniality of language. It is through languaging that those at the receiving end of the darker side of modernity can keep their memories and their being alive. Speaking in one's languages challenges the racialised concept of monolanguaging, as one assumes the voice needed to engage in a dialogue with one's native audience.

Linguicides include colonisation of the cognitive base and also a struggle for all levels of power (wa Thiong'o 2012); Fanon (1963, 38) adds that 'colonialism is not satisfied merely with holding a people in its grip and emptying the native's brain of all form and content. By a kind of perverted logic, it turns to the past of the oppressed people and distorts, disfigures, and destroys it'. The imposition of colonial languages was a calculated erasure of memory and forced amnesia. The imposition is also evident in the geographical markers of identity, where for example Lake Namlowe became Lake Victoria, Mosi-oa-Tunya became Victoria Falls. To be included in the category of human, the colonised periphery had to adopt the universal languages, from the time of the 'discovery' of the New World to the current era of flag independence. Language continues to be a contentious issue, as was evident in the #FeesMustFall student protests of 2015–16 in South Africa which, among other things, called for the use of indigenous languages in teaching and learning in higher education. According to Nebrija ([1492] 1946), 'Indians' had to be taught the Castilian language if they wanted to climb up the ladder of humanity, for at the time of their conquest they lacked language, knowledge and manners. This also speaks to wa Thiong'o's and other Africans' experiences in school.

The teaching of colonial languages was a calculated, racialised attempt to erase the language and humanity of the colonised; Veronelli (2012, 89), like wa Thiong'o, observes that 'colonised people had to be sent to school and trained in the disciplines of linguistic docility to forget their ways of life. Only they would be inside the prison'. Francis Nyamnjoh (2012) adds that education continues to legitimise illusions of the superiority of Eurocentric knowledges and languages under the guise of abstract universalism. Education in post-colonial Africa remains a tool to lighten the darkness of the African for the 'interest of and for the gratification of colonizing and hegemonic others', including African intellectuals and elites who act as ventriloquist puppets of coloniality (Nyamnjoh 2012, 129).

Robinson Crusoe prided himself on teaching Friday how to speak (wa Thiong'o 2009, 10), attesting that 'first I let him know that his name to be Friday, which is the day I saved his life ... I likewise taught him to say "Master", and then let him know that was to say my name'. Coloniality of language and being was enforced through formal colonial education, just as 'Friday's body no longer carries any memory of previous identity to subvert the imposed identity' (wa Thiong'o 2009, 10). The type of education that the colonised student had to go through was a process of linguicides and forced memory erasure. Education was weaponised by coloniality to achieve memory loss, as observed by John Spencer (cited in Kane 1963, 21) in that education (school) is 'better than the cannon, it made conquest permanent. The cannon compels the body and the school bewitches the soul'. Formal education institutions became sites for dis-membering the African child. Through linguistic erasure and naming, Friday is denied his being and is reduced to Crusoe's property. Europe planted its memory on the African body through the vast naming system of language.

Wa Thiong'o (2000, 159) decries the dehumanisation of Africa's peoples and their languages even in a global arena like the United Nations, pointing out that 'if you look at the United Nations and all its Agencies, there is no requirement for an African language, although all the other continents are linguistically represented in the United Nations, and Europe has the lion's share of that situation'. This is true, as captured in the closing statement of the 'Asamara Declaration on African Languages and Literatures' (2000) issued at the conference titled 'Against All Odds: African Languages and Literatures into the 21st Century', held in Asmara in January 2000. Though tiptoeing around the gravity of the matter, the declaration describes the current inferior status of African languages, stating that 'we have noted with pride that despite all the odds against them, African languages as vehicles of communication and knowledge survive and have a written continuity of thousand of years. Colonialism created some of the most serious obstacles against African languages and literatures. We noted with concern the fact that these colonial obstacles still haunt independent Africa and continue to block the mind of the continent' (Against All Odds Conference 2000).

Though modest in its analysis, this international conference did agree that African languages cannot be sidelined in the struggle for Africa's humanity. Wa Thiong'o spurred on Africa's linguistic transformation, a process which, according to Ali Mazrui (2004), cannot be achieved through the master's language if genuine advancement of African languages is to be achieved. Such advancement is only possible if African people are involved 'as full and equal partners in the struggle to challenge the semantics of the dominant discourse and to inscribe new meanings and uses that a counter-hegemonic discourse has the potential to arise' (Mazrui 2004, 78). By writing in African languages, wa Thiong'o is involving those masses of African people in the advancement of their indigenous languages.

Before his turn to indigenous language, wa Thiong'o, like most of the early generations of African literary writers, adopted the use of these imposed languages. It was a case of trying to use the master's tools to dismantle the master's house (Lorde 2007) until he made his radical shift from the use of European languages to the use of an indigenous African language, as a way of fighting imperialism. This Damascene shift expressed the realisation that one cannot use the master's medium of being to resurrect the African being, which would be like whispering in the graveyard. His return to his native language is premised on the belief that his writing 'in Gikuyu language, a Kenyan language, an African language, is part and parcel of the anti-imperialist struggles of Kenyan and African peoples' (wa Thiong'o 2009, 28). The choice of language that a person uses is central to how they define themselves and how others define them. Martin Heidegger (1993, 217) states that 'those who think and those who create with words are the guardians of this home [of being]'; hence African writers are guardians of the house of being, and that house of being is language (Heidegger 1982).

As the guardians of the house of being, African writers have always been faced with a choice, either to write in their native tongues, thus reaching a limited audience, or to use a 'global' language for a global audience. When 'faced with this dilemma, African writers are forced to write in an adopted language imported through colonization, yet this allows them to champion the cause of their people on the world stage' (Bandia 2009, 15–16). Ironically, Achebe and other African writers who chose the coloniser's language over their own are, in wa Thiong'o's view, the Oduche in Achebe's *Arrow of God* (1964). In *Arrow of God*, Ezeulu, the Chief Priest, sends one of his four sons, Oduche, to learn the wisdom of the Whiteman as he will be his 'eyes there' (Achebe 1964, 189). After learning enough of the said wisdom, Oduche comes back home and imprisons the sacred python in a box. Wa Thiong'o identifies this class of African writers as the Oduches who have an incurable desire to be identified with the colonisers from whom they learned their lessons (wa Thiong'o 2009). He says that 'Oduche's story is that of all other graduates of the prison-house of European languages, they capture the python, a symbol of people's being and imprison it in a box to suffocate and possibly die' (wa Thiong'o 2009, 50). Wa Thiong'o (2009) directly calls out Senghor, a Senegalese writer, for cannibalising African languages to enrich the French language – he is the Oduche who seeks to imprison the African python in a French box. Wa Thiong'o says of Senghor that he 'hardly ever talked of enriching any African language, and the only time he showed enthusiasm for African languages was when he banned Ousmane Sembene's *Ceddo*, (a brilliant film about slavery in which the characters speak their language) because Sembene had spelt Ceddo with two d's instead of one' (wa Thiong'o 2009, 55).

Wa Thiong'o's advocacy for indigenous language has been labelled a form of nativism (Ashcroft et al. 2001) and a Third World fundamentalism that seeks to banish colonial languages and being. Wa Thiong'o does not employ this false colonial logic of banishment in the name of re-membering, for one cannot use the same exclusionary logic of coloniality to restore the humanity of those who have been dis-membered. Decolonisation of language is not the pursuit of 'othering' and the exclusion of colonial languages, but a call to decentre those languages and the accompanying racialised linguistic hierarchy. What wa Thiong'o refuses to accept is the villagising of indigenous languages and bodies, and the reduction of the indigenous to mere local specificities with no impact on the universal canon of humanity. Asserting the humanity of the dehumanised cannot be done by sanitising the linguistic wound, but through languaging in indigenous tongues. This is not a philosophical contradiction for writers who have weaponised and domesticated colonial languages in the struggle for decolonisation, but rather an alternative way of unmasking the racist linguistic hierarchies.

It should be noted that through his philosophical journey, wa Thiong'o has come to clarify the place of colonial languages in challenging the empire and its idea of the human (wa Thiong'o 2012), as he continues to write in English. His advocacy for indigenous languages is not a call to erase the colonial languages and the bodies that carry those languages; it is part of the decolonial struggle which Gayatri Spivak (1996) calls strategic essentialism as opposed to Third World fundamentalism and Afro-radicalism, although vigilance should be exercised to avoid strategic essentialism declining into the essential (Mpofu 2019). The writing in a colonial language by wa Thiong'o seems to be a *contradictio in adjecto*, but Boaventura de Sousa Santos (2014, 238) sums up this perceived contradiction as an enabling one:

> The fertility of a contradiction does not lie in imagining ways of escaping it but rather in ways of working with and through it ... An enabling contradiction is a contradiction that recognizes the limits of thinking or action in a given period or context but refuses to view them at a distance or with reverence, as is typical of conformist thinking and action. An enabling contradiction is inflexible with the limits and rather comes as close as possible to them and explores their own contradictions as much as possible.

Wa Thiong'o's language as being is not about revenge or erasure of colonial languages, but rather a practice of decentring colonial languages as the only real languages and the Eurocentric idea of humanity as the only humanity. The future imagined by wa Thiong'o is one of co-existence of languages, where all languages are equal in their differences. In his *Globalectics: Theory and Politics of Knowing* (2012), there is delinking from the colonial centre to cultivate pluriversal centres, as exemplified by the concept of 'globalectics', which is derived from the shape of the globe. Aimé Césaire (1972) agrees that there is no one centre, and any point is equally a centre. Wa Thiong'o (2012) calls for a globalectical existence that embraces wholeness, interconnectedness, equity of potentiality of parts, tension and motion. In a globalectical existence, languages and cultures are a network not in terms of a racialised hierarchy, but on an equal level without doubting the humanity of the other, thus moving away from the Eurocentric linguistic and cultural universe.

Writing in indigenous language and advocating for their use is wa Thiong'o's practice of strategic essentialism, one that articulates the 'discourse of the Anthropos'; it is a 'body politics of the Anthropos which forces humanitas to think through exteriority, to localise and contextualise itself in its historical and geopolitical determination' (Luisetti 2012, 50). It is a refusal to surrender to the racialised linguistic hierarchy, a refusal to put on the metaphorical clothes of civility. Wa Thiong'o challenges the silencing and criminalisation of indigenous languages and bodies, and calls for a new humanity built on differences and on respecting multiple local particularities.

CONCLUSION

Wa Thiong'o's narration of the story of a farmer who brought up an eagle among the chickens (2009, 97–98) is a befitting conclusion to this discussion. The eagle was raised as a chicken and could not remember its eagle-ness. It knew the language of chickens, hence it assumed the being of a chicken and could not fly, nor dare to try. It took a hunter to make the eagle re-member its being. The eagle only starts to fly after it re-members its wings. Wa Thiong'o assumes the role of the hunter, who through the use and advocacy of African languages reconnects Africans with their being, re-members their memory and reminds them how to fly. Through the concepts of dis-memberment (coloniality) and re-membering (decoloniality), and by practising epistemic disobedience, he consistently challenges linguistic feudalism and argues for the collapsing of a racialised linguistic hierarchy, so that there is no one universal linguistic centre that uses language to assign the status of being and non-being. By engaging in linguistic disobedience, wa Thiong'o excludes himself from the 'magic of the Western idea of modernity' and its 'ideals of humanity' (Mignolo 2011a, 161). His lack of patience with 'feeble' African men of letters (wa Thiong'o 1986, 1997) who have rushed to defend the language of the centre, and appropriated it as their own at the expense of indigenous language, speaks of his disappointment with the African community's keepers of identity and knowledge.

REFERENCES

Achebe, Chinua. 1964. *Arrow of God.* London: Heinemann.

Achebe, Chinua. 1975. *Morning Yet on Creation Day*. New York, NY: Anchor.

Achebe, Chinua. 1978. 'The Role of the Writer in a New Nation'. In *African Writers on African Writing*, edited by Douglas G. Killam, 7–13. London: Heinemann.

Achebe, Chinua. 1989. *Hopes and Impediments: Selected Essays*. London: Doubleday.

Against All Odds Conference. 2000. 'The Asmara Declaration on African Languages and Literatures'. Accessed 24 June 2020. https://www.culturalsurvival.org/publications/cultural-survival-quarterly/asmara-declaration-african-languages-and-literatures.

Ashcroft Bill, Griffiths, Gareth and Tiffin, Helen. 2001. *Post-Colonial Studies: Key Concepts*. London: Routledge.

Baldwin, James. 1979. 'If Black English Isn't a Language, Then Tell Me, What Is?' *New York Times* 29 July.

Bandía, Paul. 2009. 'Translation Matters: Linguistic and Cultural Representation'. In *Translation Studies in Africa*, edited by Judith Inggs and Libby Meintjes, 1–20. London: Continuum.

Boehmer, Elleke. 1993. 'Review of *Moving the Centre: The Struggle for Cultural Freedoms*, by Ngũgĩ wa Thiong'o'. *Wasafiri* 18: 67–68.

Brink, André. 2007. 'Languages of the Novel: A Lover's Reflections'. In *African Literature: An Anthology of Criticism and Theory*, edited by Olaniyan Tejumola and Olaniyan Ato, 333–39. Oxford: Wiley-Blackwell.

Césaire, Aimé. 1972. *Discourse on Colonialism*. Translated by Joan Pinkham. New York, NY: Monthly Review Press.

Columbus, C. [1492-93] 1990. *Journal of the First Voyage*. Translated by Barry Ife. Warminster: Aris and Phillips.

Cook, David and Okenimkpe, Michael. 1997. *Ngũgĩ wa Thiong'o: An Exploration of His Writings*. Oxford: James Currey.

Du Bois, W.E.B. [William Edward Burghardt]. 1903. *The Souls of Black Folk*. Chicago, IL: A.C. McClurg.

Fanon, Frantz. 1963. *The Wretched of the Earth*. Translated by Constance Farrington. New York, NY: Grove Press.

Foucault, Michel. 1980. *Power/Knowledge: Selected Interviews and Other Writings 1972–1977*. Translated by Colin Gordon, Leo Marshall, John Mepham and Kate Soper. New York, NY: Pantheon Books.

Grosfoguel, Ramón. 2007. 'The Epistemic Decolonial Turn: Beyond Political-Economy Paradigms'. *Cultural Studies* 21(2–3): 211–23.

Gruzinski, Serge. 1999. *La Pensée Métisse*. Paris: Fayard.

Hegel, Georg W.F. [1837] 1944. *The Philosophy of History*. Translated by J. Sibee. New York, NY: Wiley.

Heidegger, Martin. 1982. *A Dialogue on Language*. Translated by Peter Hertz. Oxford: Harper One.

Heidegger, Martin. 1993. *Basic Writings: From Being and Time (1927) to The Task of Thinking (1964)*. Translated and edited by David Farrell Krell. San Francisco, CA: Harper San Francisco.

Jeyifo, Biodun. 2018. 'English is an African language – Ka Dupe! [For and against Ngugi]'. *Journal of African Cultural Studies* 30(2): 133–47.

Kafka, Franz. 1937. *The Trial*. Translated by Edwin and Wilma Muir. New York, NY: A.A. Knopf.

Kane, Cheikh H. 1963. *Ambiguous Adventure*. Portsmouth, NH: Heinemann.

Lorde, Audre. 2007. *Sister Outsider: Essays and Speeches*. Berkeley, CA: Crossing Press.

Luisetti, Frederico. 2012. 'The Savage Decolonialist'. *Comparative Studies in Modernism* 1: 29–53.

Marquez, Gabriel G. 1982. *One Hundred Years of Solitude*. Translated by Gregory Rabassa. New York, NY: Limited Editions Club.

Mazrui, Ali A. 2004. *English in Africa: After the Cold War*. Clevedon: Multilingual Matters.

Mignolo, Walter D. 1995. *The Darker Side of the Renaissance: Literacy, Territoriality, and Colonization*. Ann Arbor, MI: University of Michigan Press.

Mignolo, Walter D. 2009. 'Epistemic Disobedience, Independent Thought and Decolonial Freedom'. *Theory, Culture and Society* 26(7–8): 159–81.

Mignolo, Walter D. 2011a. *The Darker Side of Western Modernity: Global Futures, Decolonial Options*. Durham, NC: Duke University Press.

Mignolo, Walter D. 2011b. 'Geopolitics of Sensing and Knowing: On (De)coloniality, Border Thinking and Epistemic Disobedience'. *Postcolonial Studies* 14(3): 273–83.

Mpofu, William J. 2019. 'Doing Decoloniality in the Westernized University in Africa: A Philosophy of Liberation Take'. Paper presented at the Decolonisation Colloquium of the Centre for Teaching and Learning, University of the Free State, Bloemfontein, 23 August.

Mudimbe, Valentin Y. 1994. *The Idea of Africa*. Bloomington, IN: Indiana University Press.

Nabokov, Vladimir V. 1995. *Lolita*. Paris: Olympia Press.

Ndlovu-Gatsheni, Sabelo J. 2015. 'Genealogies of Coloniality and Implications for Africa's Development'. *Africa Development* 40: 13–40.

Nebrija, Antonio D. [1492] 1946. *Gramática de la lengua castellana*, edited by Romeo Galindo and Munoz Ortiz. Madrid: Edición de la Junta del Centenario.

Nganang, Patrice. 2001. *Dog Days*. Charlottesville, VA: University of Virginia Press.

Nyamnjoh, Francis B. 2012. '"Potted Plants in Greenhouses": A Critical Reflection on the Resilience of Colonial Education in Africa'. *Journal of Asian and African Studies* 47(2): 129–54.

Okara, Gabriel. 1970. *The Voice*. Oxford: Heinemann Educational Publishers.

Orwell, George. 1977. *1984*. London: Penguin Books.

p'Bitek, Okot. 1964. *Song of Ocol*. London: Heinemann.

Quijano, Aníbal. 2000. 'The Coloniality of Power and Social Classification'. *Journal of World-Systems Research* 6(2): 342–86.

Robbe-Grillet, Alain. 1955. *Le Voyeur*. Paris: Editions de Minuit.

Santos, Boaventura de Sousa. 2014. *Epistemologies of the South: Justice against Epistemicide*. Boulder, CO: Paradigm Publishers.

Senghor, Léopold S. 1962. Le Français, langue de culture. *Esprit* 11: 837–44.

Soyinka, Wole. 1988. *Art, Dialogue and Outrage*. Ibadan: New Horn Press.

Spivak, Gayatri. C. 1996. 'Subaltern Studies: Deconstructing Historiography?' In *The Spivak Reader*, edited by Donna Landry and Gerald MacLean, 203–37. London: Routledge.

Steiner, George. 1992. *After Babel: Aspects of Language and Translation*. Oxford: Oxford University Press.

Vakunta, Peter W. 2010. 'Aporia: Ngũgĩ's Fatalistic Logic on the Position of Indigenous Languages in African Literature'. *Journal of the African Literature Association* 5(2): 74–82.

Veronelli, Gabriela A. 2012. 'Una América Compuesta: The Coloniality of Language in the Americas and Decolonial Alternatives'. PhD diss., Binghamton University, New York, NY.

Veronelli, Gabriela A. 2015. 'The Coloniality of Language: Race, Expressivity, Power, and the Darker Side of Modernity'. *Wagadu* 13: 108–34.

Wali, Obiajunwa. 1963. 'The Dead End of African Literature?' *Transition* 10: 13–15.

Walsh, Catherine. 2009. *Multiculturalism, State, and Society: Struggles (De)colonial of Our Time*. Quito: Universidad Andina Simón Bolívar.

Wa Thiong'o, Ngũgĩ. 1965. *The River Between*. London: Heinemann.

Wa Thiong'o, Ngũgĩ. 1986. *Decolonising the Mind: The Politics of Language in African Literature*. Oxford: James Currey.

Wa Thiong'o, Ngũgĩ. 1995. 'On the Abolition of the English Department'. In *The Post-Colonial Studies Reader*, edited by Bill Ashcroft, Gareth Griffiths and Helen Tiffin, 438–42. London: Routledge.

Wa Thiong'o, Ngũgĩ. 1997. *Writers in Politics: A Re-Engagement with Issues of Literature and Society*. Oxford: James Currey.

Wa Thiong'o, Ngũgĩ. 2000. 'African Languages and Global Culture in the 21st Century'. In *African Visions: Literary Images, Political Change, and Social Struggle in Contemporary Africa*, edited by Cheryl B. Mwaria, Silvia Federici and Joseph MacLaren, 155–62. Westport, CT: Greenwood Press.

Wa Thiong'o, Ngũgĩ. 2006. *Wizard of the Crow – Mũrogi wa Kagogo*. New York, NY: Pantheon Books.

Wa Thiong'o, Ngũgĩ. 2009. *Something Torn and New: An African Renaissance*. New York, NY: Basic Civitas Books.

Wa Thiong'o, Ngũgĩ. 2012. *Globalectics: Theory and the Politics of Knowing*. New York, NY: Columbia University Press.

Wa Thiong'o, Ngũgĩ. 2013. *In the Name of the Mother: Reflections on Writers and Empire*. Nairobi and London: East African Educational Publishers and James Currey.

Wa Thiong'o, Ngũgĩ. 2016. *Secure the Base: Making Africa Visible in the Globe*. Chicago, IL: University of Chicago Press.

Wa Thiong'o, Ngũgĩ and Wa Mĩriĩ, Ngũgĩ. 1977. *Ngaahika Ndeenda*. Nairobi: Heinemann.

Wiredu, Kwesi. 1992. 'Formulating Modern Thoughts in African Languages: Some Theoretical Considerations'. In *The Surreptitious Speech: Présence Africaine and the Politics of Otherness, 1947–1948*, edited by Valentin Mudimbe, 301–32. Chicago, IL: University of Chicago Press.

9 THE UNDERSIDE OF MODERN KNOWLEDGE: AN EPISTEMIC BREAK FROM WESTERN SCIENCE

NOKUTHULA HLABANGANE

Boaventura de Sousa Santos (2007) argues that Western science is implicated in the power dynamics of the world. For this reason, if Western science is linked to modernity, it must also be linked to coloniality. Western science and modernity are premised on a number of basic principles, one of which is an emphasis on knowledge that issues from the mind, which is divorced from the body. In other words, thinking is the product of a 'rational man' who is unencumbered by 'body-politics' that speak to the thinking being's social and geographical positioning. As such, because the thinking being is not restricted by positioning and location, their knowledge is not only universal, it is also apolitical. Further, the importance that is placed on the (thinking) mind, as opposed to the (feeling) body, introduces a hierarchy and opposition between the mind and the body. Therefore, positioning such knowledge as apolitical and a-contextual hides its inherent discriminations and hierarchies, naturalising them and allowing them to escape deconstruction. Anibal Quijano (2007) attributes this propensity to assume a privileged place among other knowledge systems to the cloaking of Western knowledge in mystery, making it the exclusive province of a privileged few. It is thus made seductive by being coupled with power. In this regard, then, Euro-North American modernity has assumed an almost automatic right to dominate thinking, and now underpins all aspects of life, what Ramón Grosfoguel (2007), Nelson Maldonado-Torres (2007) and Walter Mignolo (2007) call coloniality. Therefore, the assertion by Western science that it is 'objective' and thus beyond contextual considerations masks its historical situatedness, its provincialism, and its complicity in universalising intersubjective relations that encompass even African subjects.

This chapter seeks to denaturalise Western science by placing it under a decolonial lens so as to unmask its situatedness and highlight its context-dependence. Decolonial thinking, as posited by decolonial scholars such as Grosfoguel, Mignolo, Maldonado-Torres, Santos, Quijano, Enrique Dussel (2014), Sabelo Ndlovu-Gatsheni (2015), Sylvia Wynter (1991) and others points to an intricate relationship between Western expansionism, capital, knowledge and coloniality. That is to say, modernity has two sides: one that was always intended to benefit the West, and a darker side that effected violence in order to enable the benefits enjoyed by the West. Modern science is characterised by solipsism – a monologue internal to the subject, informed by the maxim *I conquer therefore I am*, the predecessor of Descartes's *cogito ergo sum, I think therefore I am* – which gives epistemic privilege to the Western man (Grosfoguel 2013). While Western modernity is conceptualised and written about to give the impression that it was a singular event, it was in fact multiple in its manifestations and impacts. 'Modernity' is used in this way to underscore a particular point: the centring of the Enlightenment philosophy underpinning modern rationality that was to inform colonialism. The possibility of dialogic thinking is closed off, as other knowledge systems are systematically denigrated and condemned to a marginal status.

In this chapter I will argue that while Western science has pushed for and assumed a universal status it is, in fact, a provincial view of the world – a knowledge system that, like any other, vies for and underpins a particular perspective on the world. I begin by giving a definition of decoloniality, and then explore the concepts of modernity and coloniality, showing how one is dependent on the other. Finally, I will subject the practical example of HIV/Aids (human immunodeficiency virus/acquired immune deficiency syndrome) to a decolonial critique, and show how the epidemic was imagined and accounted for by dominant discourses which constructed a particular subject/object while they simultaneously constructed the Self/Other dichotomy. These questions are important to us, because they are a window on how knowledge production continues to underpin relations of domination.

COLONIALITY OF KNOWLEDGE, POWER AND BEING

Decolonial thinking is an invitation to unmask and to deconstruct received knowledge about many aspects of our naturalised life. Central to decolonial epistemic perspectives is to shift the geography of reason away from the fundamentals of Eurocentric thinking to include other knowledge systems. The fundamentals of Eurocentric knowledge are based on a binary system that excludes certain knowledge systems, while elevating others. This is not a simple and innocent matter of knowledge systems vying for ascendancy in a world order just for the sake of it. On the contrary, the site of knowledge production and vetting has been a subject of and basis for violence, discrimination and domination. The repression and imposition of knowledge speak to one's legitimate place in the world order. Knowledge is thus a mechanism that justifies domination and conquest. From this point of view, knowledge is an important place to start in order to understand relations of differently positioned people, nations and continents in the current world order.

The prisms through which people are understood, the rewriting of their cultures, knowledge systems and ways of being, all amount to what Grosfoguel (2007), Maldonado-Torres (2007) and Mignolo (2007) call coloniality of knowledge. This means that the primacy of place that is accorded Western ways of knowing and being, which are then imposed in understanding other knowledges and ways of being, constitutes coloniality of knowledge. These other ways of knowing and being are rendered unintelligible when filtered through Western sensibilities that, for example, set greater store by the mind in juxtaposition with and preference to the body and spirit, that prioritise instrumental/rational pursuits such as profit which lead to individualism, and that conceive of nature and culture as dichotomous entities with culture gaining mastery over nature. While these ways of being and knowing have been exalted to represent the epitome of evolution, so to speak, they are in fact particular to a certain way of thinking. More than that, they undergird a particular sociopolitical agenda.

Decolonial thinking points to an intricate relationship between Western expansion, capital, knowledge and coloniality. As posited by decolonial epistemic perspectives, the coloniality/modernity dialectic points to how modernity co-exists with coloniality. Coloniality is the relations of domination that continue even after colonialism has ceased. While colonialism had physical structures that perpetuated its existence, such as Christian missionary schools, trading enclaves and manufacturing plants, as well as government structures wholly run by colonists, coloniality is ubiquitous; its footprints are found in every aspect of life and are not dependent on the physical presence of the colonial administration. Coloniality has proved to be more enduring than colonialism. This is in some part due to the knowledge systems with which it conceives of and engages with the world. The idea *I think, therefore I am* is central to Western science (Grosfoguel 2008, 2012) and its implications spill over into other facets of life. Informed by this maxim, Western ways of knowing are instrumental in effecting a violent world system that is, first and foremost, true to the spirit of conquest, subjugation and appropriation (Maldonado-Torres 2008). By espousing a hierarchical opposition between the mind and the body, nature and culture, black and white, men and women, work and play, public and private, Western knowledge follows the logic of maximum accumulation at whatever cost, neatly expressed by Darwin's notion of the 'survival of the fittest'.

I make two related arguments here. First, Western science cannot be thought of as outside the aspirations of modernity; it is premised on modernity – they are two sides of the same coin, so to speak. Western science, which is characterised by a mathematical, logocentric understanding of the world that informs the bullying tendencies mentioned above, presupposes knowledge that is universal and a knower who is not situated. Related to this is the way in which, by systematically hiding its locus of enunciation, it accords itself a 'god-eye view of the world' (Grosfoguel 2008, 4). The boundedness and embeddedness of Western science in a particular, prescribed context are systematically hidden, enabling it to catapult itself to an omnipotent, omniscient and omnipresent status. Like a god, it purports to exist at a distance from the sociopolitical mess of everyday living and the power dynamics that bear on this. Dussel (2014) argues that had Descartes, the propagator of the Cartesian thinking that became the bedrock of Western science, acknowledged the relationship between the body and the mind, he would have been forced to put a price on slavery. By systematically minimising this relationship, slavery could be morally justified as the enslaved were thought of as bodies without souls and, like the beasts of burden, they could be exploited with impunity. Therefore Western science, as a product of Cartesian thinking that hides the locus of enunciation as well as the enunciator, is systematically, strategically and wilfully blind to sociality and power dynamics. It hides the beneficiaries of the world order espoused by the science, and naturalises the suffering of those who are imagined through its prisms. In this way, it privileges the enunciated and obscures the identity of the enunciator. This is a strategic lever of power that needs to be unmasked. That is to say, in a way, Western science not only perpetuates modern aspirations of conquest, silencing, discrimination and domination, but also naturalises these aspirations in that it purports to espouse a natural, apolitical view of the world. It is wilfully ignorant of the suffering perpetuated by the modernity/coloniality dialectic, as it thrives on a reductionist model of the world.

MODERNITY/COLONIALITY

The modernity/coloniality dialectic is important in decolonial thinking. Central to coloniality is the logic that produces the Other and the institutions that uphold it, including institutions that reproduce modern conceptions of being, power and knowledge. These conceptions are rooted in linear and dualistic thinking informed first and fundamentally by the Cartesian system of thought. This world view, predicated on particular notions of being that divorce the body from the soul, gives rise to dualistic and teleological thinking that presupposes a linear trajectory of development. This forms the basis of modernity.

Central to this thinking is that an evolved being is Christian-centric, has gravitated towards 'civilisation' and is a master over 'nature'. The idea of a teleological scale of development that encapsulates modern thinking is the basis for coloniality; it is the essence of Othering, which is informed by the *I think, therefore I am* world view that privileges individualism, reductionist and binary thinking, hierarchies and rational thinking devoid of emotion. This kind of thinking displaces other knowledge systems and ways of engaging with the world that emphasise communality, a complex understanding of the world and how people and things interrelate, and thinking that is mediated by one's location and positionality. Moreover, it precludes the possibility of historical conversations by postulating an *in situ* view of the world. In this sense, the above-mentioned knowledge systems can be viewed as mechanical and instrumental, on the one hand, and humanistic, on the other.

The Euro-North American tendency to universalise its knowledge is intricately linked to coloniality which is, in turn, linked to colonialism premised on subjection and subjugation of those thought of as the empire's Other.

This idea of the Other follows from the arguments made above – the hierarchisation of knowledge and thus of people. Grosfoguel (2008) argues that racism is the idea that some people are less human than others, and as such, also have inferior knowledge and thus inferior intelligence compared to 'real humans'. Furthermore, the idea of the Other is a direct consequence of the modernity/coloniality dialectic. The Other is one conquered by the Self, and thus becomes colonised by the Self. In the quest for conquest, the Other is vanquished and made in the inverse image of the Self, in order to fortify the Self. Therefore, the other side of modernity is coloniality. Maldonado-Torres (2008) reflects on the modern subjectivity as a consciousness born out of the radical unevenness between the European and the native. He argues that modernity is thus born in the moment when Western civilisation takes the place of God and defines its mission as an expansionist one, rendering every Other a slave by means of 'naturalising war'. This state of war that characterises relations between Europe and the native is 'the radical suspension or displacement of ethical and political relationships in favour of the propagation of a particular death ethic that renders massacre and different forms of genocide as natural' (Maldonado-Torres 2008, xi). The conquest and the colony are quotidian exercises in which 'imperial God and imperial man become immediate proofs of the existence of each other' (2008, xi).

In the same way that abyssal thinking (Santos 2007) presupposes that recognition can only be possible between coloniser and colonised, the modernity/coloniality complex highlights their interdependence – as subject and object. The European expansionist impulse, birthed since 1492, paved the way for a dynamic constitution of different aspects of life in the empire and its Other. Following from this, Mignolo (2011) argues that to understand the local, one must simultaneously understand Europe's relation with its Other. And according to Dussell (2014, 12), the development theory which promises modernity is, in fact, a fallacy as it envisions each country and each nation as an entity in itself, with unhindered ability to 'develop'. On the contrary, decolonial perspectives argue against the growth path envisioned by development theory. According to decolonial epistemic perspectives, empire and its colony are implicated in the reproduction of each other. The universalising tendency of Western knowledge systems is wilfully blind to this dialectic. Dussel (2014) asserts that while some scholars criticise modern rationality as an instrument of terror, he criticises it for concealing its own irrational myth about its universality, its 'zero sum' and 'god-eye view' of the world. That is, an all-knowing point of view that is independent of time and place and devoid of human interference, and is thus universal and wilfully ignorant of the pain it perpetuates by negating the ways of being and knowing of its Other.

Further and related assertions of the decolonial epistemic perspective are that Western science functions by, firstly, separating units of the world into boxes, whereas we are all constituted in dialectical relations – this puts paid to the notion that some people are yet to progress towards modernity. The fact is that we are all in modernity, but are experiencing different aspects of it. The possibility of experiencing modernity positively rests on the possibility of the Other experiencing it negatively. These are the two inextricably related sides of modernity. Secondly, difference is organised into hierarchy; and thirdly, these orientations are naturalised. Finally, Western science intervenes in the production of inequalities in that the creation of the Other justifies their exploitation and differential treatment. In this way, we see a link between racism and capitalism, and how racism powerfully enables capitalism. Because Western science is blind to the dialectic of modernity/coloniality, it automatically buys into the dualism inherent in evolutionary thinking – progressive versus primitive, science versus folklore, us versus them, here versus there, and so on.

MODERNITY/COLONIALITY AND SOCIAL EVOLUTION

The above characteristics imply a hierarchy of being, which can be summed up by historically fraught questions such as *Do you have a God? Do you have a soul? Do you have knowledge?* (Grosfoguel 2013). This logic, characteristic of the modern world view, not only informed and resulted in inequalities and violent encounters between the peoples of the world, but also sought to justify them. These questions, which are informed by the modernity paradigm that espouses a developmentalist view of the world, imply a need for some nations to be always catching up with Western ideals of modernity.

It is from this point of view that we can understand Santos's (2007) argument about an abyssal line informed by abyssal thinking, characterised by binary logics of 'us' versus 'them', where one cannot recognise the Other. The distance between the two is thought to be deep and infinite. More than that, in theory, the distance needs to be closed at whatever cost and, ostensibly, for the benefit of the people who are seen to be lagging behind. Grosfoguel (2008, 4) sums up the West's attitude in this regard thus: 'Develop or I will kill you';

'Transform or I will kill you'; 'Democratise or I will kill you.' From this point of view, knowledge becomes less a matter of surviving and thriving on one's own terms and in one's own context than a primary site for international relations of domination and conquest. For this reason, Maldonado-Torres (2008) characterises modernity as a paradigm of war.

Characterising knowledge systems and people in a hierarchical manner is problematic on a number of fronts. Firstly, the universalising principle does not take into account contextual factors. This tendency precludes the possibility of envisioning pluriversal knowledge systems representative of a pluriversal world with a plurality of experiences and values. By espousing an omnipotent, omniscient and omnipresent god-eye-view knowledge system, the possibility of dialogic thinking is closed off. This essentially deprived Africans and other marginalised people of the world of legitimacy and recognition in the global cultural order dominated by Eurocentric presumptions. The former were thought of as 'body' – a thing without knowledge and the consciousness to assume an equal place in the world order, or understand and frame their plight in terms of that which questions their position in the political economy of the world.

The purported value-free nature of Western science does not necessarily mean absence of biases. As argued above, the biases are seen in the perpetuation of a particular world view and relationship. This is the crux of the matter, and can be transposed to all aspects of life – what Quijano (2000, cited in Grosfoguel 2008, 6), calls the 'colonial power matrix' that involves the economy, education, health and wellbeing, religion, social organisation, the legal system, politics and all other aspects of life. Grosfoguel (2008, 4) calls this a Western-centric, Euro-North American-centric, capitalist, sexist, patriarchal, Christocentric, liberal dispensation. Anything outside of this matrix of power is denigrated as inferior and deficient. At the core of relations of domination is a deep-seated doubt about the very humanity of the Other, expressed in the question: are you really human? This gives rise to radical alterity, the reification of difference, with strategic outcomes that will be alluded to when the example of so-called African sexuality and HIV/Aids is considered later in this chapter. In this vein, I argue for thinking by metonymy – that is to say, how HIV/Aids was understood encapsulates and points to bigger issues, such as cultural racism and racial capitalism.

Quijano (2007, 542) discounts the notion that Europeans are the exclusive bearers, creators and protagonists of modernity. How then do we account for this long-standing fallacy? In response, Grosfoguel (2008), for instance, would argue that knowledge systems from other parts of the world were subjected to epistemicide in a quest to have the West prevail over other nations. In essence, what is being argued here is that what has come to be known as Western science also has its roots in other parts of the world. While acknowledging and foregrounding this important insight, I start from the premise that has taken root which purports a unique Western science, whose motivations and use were coupled with the sinister project of Western expansionism and its concomitant characteristics. Following Thomas Kuhn (1962), it can be argued that Western science is functioning from within a particular paradigm. Kuhn argues that all scientific inquiries occur within paradigms that dictate the parameters of inquiry and interpretation. As a result, scientific inquiries are designed to explore the applicability of the accepted paradigms to an expanding range of data. They do so in order to affirm the validity of the paradigm, rather than to challenge it.

THE PRIMACY OF WESTERN SCIENCE: HISTORY AND CONTEXT

The point made above – that all knowledge systems represent a way of seeing, perceiving and thus engaging with the world – behoves underscoring. Furthermore, all knowledge systems represent a political view. In the case of Western science, this view can be summed up in the statement *I think, therefore I am*, thereby privileging the thinking subject involved with himself to the exclusion of others. This assertion simultaneously calls for a suspension of any other way of perceiving and engaging with the world and advocates for the domination of a particular way of seeing and engaging with it. History is replete with examples of warfare waged on the knowledge front. Indeed, the idea of coloniality that encapsulates being, knowledge and power speaks to this in a fundamental way. The maxim *I conquer, therefore I am* – the precursor of *I think, therefore I am* – is accompanied by epistemicides associated with actual genocides. Sylvia Wynter (1991) attributes this genocidal impulse of the West to the belief that the world was given to whites – the Imperial man – by God to conquer – *propter nos* (for our sake). This belief, based on the understanding that God resides in and favours places of the world where there is enlightenment, was the driving force of the founding fathers of Europe. This view is captured by the observation that places unoccupied by Europeans are in a state of nature, where life is barbaric, nasty and short. Therefore, these places need Western civilisation. Moreover, this civilisation will be imposed by hook or by crook if need be for, according to the logic of *propter nos,* beyond the equator one can sin no more (anything and everything is allowed at the behest of God and by His will). Maldonado-Torres (2008) argues that 1492 signalled a radical change in how difference was perceived. Seduced by the possibility of wealth, European voyagers and explorers conceived of the idea of *propter nos* that gave them carte blanche to steal, plunder and pillage with impunity. He argues that whereas the guiding principle heretofore was the 'love of God', this radically changed to the 'love of gold'. By questioning the humanity of the people they encountered on their so-called voyages of discovery, the European voyagers could absolve themselves of any moral obligation towards them.

Grosfoguel (2008) argues strongly for linking European colonial expansion to the subsequent intellectual division of labour whereby the West became the producer of knowledge thought of as credible and the referee in deciding what was credible knowledge. He sketches a picture of bloodshed en masse in these epistemic wars that sought to hierarchise knowledge, rendering some knowledge as credible while discounting other knowledge systems. He argues that these hierarchical tendencies are the basis for the Western-centric, racist, patriarchal and sexist knowledge that enjoys epistemic privilege today. This knowledge is based on Eurocentric assumptions that give impetus to practices of Othering which not only recognise and give primacy to difference, but also put such difference in a hierarchy that speaks to the very fundamental question: are you human? These universalising binaries – human versus sub-human, exterior versus interior, progressive versus backward, universal versus local – underscore this implied question. Such universalising schemas undergird and are undergirded by power dynamics. Knowledge and power thus go together and, as such, coloniality of knowledge is equal to coloniality of power and coloniality of being.

In an insightful piece that traces the factors that might have influenced Descartes's *cogito ergo sum,* Dussel (2014) argues that Descartes needed to conceive of a science without people, so to speak, to come to this conclusion. By conceiving of a science that divorced the body from the soul, Descartes closed himself off from the external world opened up to us by our feelings, imagination and passions. In this way, the purportedly pure machine of science is blind to race, gender and class. These important sociological indicators would not be primary sites and pillars of analysis – they would be incidental to analysis. From this point of view, 'the quantitative indeterminacy of any quality will only be the beginning of all illusory abstractions about the "zero point" of modern philosophical subjectivity' (Dussel 2014, 10). This is part of a long history of the Christian world founded on the idea of the primacy of the soul above the body. The body was and could be nothing but an object of knowledge. From the Eurocentric perspective, certain races are condemned as inferior for not being rational subjects. They are objects of study, consequently bodies closer to nature. In a sense, they become dominatable and exploitable: Cartesian thinking is able to ignore and naturalise the modernity/coloniality dialectic by disregarding the union of the body and the soul. The thinking individual, who stands above their experiences and thus in a particular locus of being and enunciation, is essentially independent of both intersubjective and social relations: 'First in that supposition, the "subject" is a category referring to the isolated individual because it constitutes itself in itself, in its discourse and its capacity of reflection. The Cartesian *cogito ergo sum* means exactly that' (Quijano 2013, 26). Therefore, knowledge flowing from such a standpoint denies intersubjectivity and social totality as the sites of production of all knowledge. The 'object' to be studied is not independent of a given field of relations either. Furthermore, the idea that the subject is the bearer of 'reason', while the 'object' is not only external to it, but is of a different nature, is a falsehood founded on Euro-North American abyssal thinking. Cartesian thinking thus emphasises difference and not inequality. Where inequality is considered, it is thought to be of nature – only European culture is rational, and can contain subjects; the rest are irrational, they can only be objects of study (Quijano 2007, 174).

This falsehood is sustained by violence and by ideologies that supposedly reflect a reality. By denying intersubjectivity, the Other is made absent in the conversations that take place following the logic of *cogito ergo sum*, except as an object of Eurocentric knowledge. As such, 'the radical absence of the other not only postulates an atomistic image of social existence in general, but also denies the idea of a social totality, which led to adopting a reductionist vision of reality' (Quijano 2007, 173). Descartes's posture and considerations were geared towards upholding relations of domination between empire and its Other. This is in view of the argument that knowledge is not so much a relation between an individual and something, but rather a relation between people for the purpose of something. Acknowledging the union of the body and the soul would have meant putting a quantifiable price on slavery (Dussel 2014).

The knowledge that flows from the premise of *ergo et sum* is thus used to hide relations of domination by hiding the union of the soul and the body. From this point of view, such knowledge can only be instrumentalist. It cannot respond to the fundamentals of inequality. Knowledge informed by the prescripts of *cogito ergo sum* is thus about privileging a certain understanding of the world that is silent on the relationship between the individual and society, and between empire and its Other. It is thus not far-fetched to argue that Euro-North American knowledge is decadent in that it seems unable to respond to the challenges that it spawns. Tied to capitalism, Western science purports to have similar values of mastery and survival of the fittest. As such, it has wrought much unnecessary pain and cannot seem to be able to correct itself, as evidenced by increasing inequalities, exclusion of the majority of humanity, degradation of the planet and climate change. This assertion provides a response to the question of whether coloniality is abstract or concrete. The coupling of difference and hierarchy results in the same outcome of violence. Therefore, coloniality or modernity not only produces identities and categories, but also the experiences of people. Modernity thus ignores its own decadence by always producing the same narrative – a reductionist view of the world produced by supposedly pure observation that isolates variables in a mechanical model of that world. It is caught in its original objectives of effecting an unequal world order and expanding its global domination. It is from this point of view that I argue that Euro-North American knowledge cannot go far in resolving the many challenges that beset the world.

THE NATURE OF SCIENCE

Western science has bypassed any real scrutiny and criticism by shrouding itself in mystery. Instead, critique has largely centred on what have been called 'epistemologies of equilibrium' (Ndlovu-Gatsheni 2015), which advance a modernist critique of modernity, and thus do not fundamentally challenge its precepts but rather serve the perverse role of obfuscation. Western science is supported by 'institutions, vocabulary, scholarship, imagery, doctrines, even colonial bureaucracies and colonial styles' (Said, cited in Smith 1999, 2) that bolster its clout. It erected an abyssal line between itself and other knowledge systems, casting itself as a superior kind of knowledge, while castigating these other systems. The abyssal line denotes both vertical and horizontal hierarchies. Vertically, other knowledge systems are relegated to an inferior position. Horizontally, the line defines its purported characteristics and, by so doing, marks its inclusionary and exclusionary criteria. Western science fashions itself as universal, objective, logocentric, apolitical and impartial, effectively casting itself as having a god-eye view of the world, outside and above world power dynamics and other worldly concerns, except to add to knowledge in aid of human civilisation and progress.

By implication, other knowledge systems are thought of as local, intuitive, subjective and partial, and thus fraught with human frailties such as emotions, politics and the attendant short-sightedness. An example is the notion of a 'scientific West' and an 'intuitive East', with antithetical pairs of attributes, namely scientific versus intuitive, theoretical versus practical, causal versus correlative thinking, adversarial versus irenic or geometric versus algebraic. Furthermore, Western science has remained valid across historical periods, geographic locales, social strata, gender identifications, and economic and technological differentials. However, Sander Gilman (1985) asserts that science works differently in the real world. Paula Treichler (1991) argues that when cultural differences among human communities are taken into account, they tend to be enlisted in the service of this reality, but their status remains utilitarian. Western science has assumed the role of both player and arbiter, in that it prescribes a particular view of the world. Also, it imposes its view of what constitutes credible and worthy knowledge. It is a master signifier – the alpha and the omega of knowledge systems. As such, the methodologies associated with Western science emphasise distance of the observer, purporting to be concerned with pure observation without interpretation, thereby concealing their human qualities and interests. In a continuing vein, it assumes a static and mute object of study (atoms that have no subjectivity of their own), which thus unproblematically fits within knowledge parameters informed by Eurocentric imaginations.

This approach has led to an intellectual division of labour in which the West's Other is used as raw material, and as human species are processed through Western knowledge and lenses in order to vindicate the primacy of place of this knowledge in the world and in epistemology. My contention here is not so much about the usefulness of the knowledge derived from Western science, but rather about that of any knowledge system: such a knowledge system is necessarily incomplete, perspectival and, as such, has to be put on the same analytical plane as any other knowledge systems. In the next section of the chapter I use the example of how HIV/Aids has been studied to underscore the points I have made above.

HIV/AIDS AS AN *ÜBER* OTHERING SITE

While Western science is but a particular and provincial view of the world, its epistemological primacy of place is tied to Western capital and modern thinking. In this context, this section of the chapter reflects on the matrix of hierarchies implicated in knowledge production, power and being as a form of soft oppression in the realm of sexuality. Sexuality, while a site of soft oppression, is very much at the centre of questions about one's humanity and one's conception of Africa, the continent that has always borne the brunt of and suffered the consequences of the Western gaze. What does each have to do with the other? In considering this question, I will speak about the relationship between these seemingly unconnected aspects of life, and show how inequalities are perpetuated and justified by this complex matrix, using the example of 'African Aids' as a prime and contemporary site of Othering. I will argue that the HIV/Aids epidemic has been a site that has strengthened abyssal thinking, recentring the West and its knowledge systems, while excluding and silencing others. Against a Eurocentric norm, knowledge of others as sub-human, and as raw material to be analysed through prisms that essentially question their humanity, drove and informed impulses and practices that are central to how HIV/Aids has been conceived of and approached. The advent of HIV/Aids became the site for rationalising the study of the exotic Other, a curiosity that invited the unidirectional Western gaze that ultimately makes objects of subjects.

Jean Comaroff and John Comaroff (1992) remark on the unjust conclusions that conventional scientific methods reach regarding people who are thought of as the Other of the researcher. They caution against the difference-making tendencies of such methodologies, which emphasise a speaking individual who is not based and rooted in any context. From this point of view, the speaking individual is taken at face value. Such an apprehension of the speaking individual ignores a number of issues that relate to science. Firstly, that individual utterances, while representing a particular world view, are also partial and perspectival. This is not least a result of the fact that the speaking individual speaks into a constraining and already prescribed mould, as directed by the questions they are asked and which reflect the researcher's point of view and interests. Secondly, that the spoken, in an interview, is a snapshot that precludes historical conversations. Thirdly, that, taken out of context, data collected through conventional methods are open to being exoticised by a researcher who presumes distance between himself or herself and those researched. Lastly, that for research to achieve justice, data collected through conventional methods should not be read and interpreted in and of itself; it should also be restored to a world of meaningful interconnectedness. The above considerations also, and perhaps mostly, apply to surveys and other closed-ended ways of collecting data, which, by virtue of controlling for 'extraneous variables' and thus painting a pure rendition of 'results', are given higher scientific value.

Other important points are made in the Comaroffs' *Ethnography and the Historical Imagination* (1992) that could be used to support my assertion about how the HIV/Aids epidemic is a contemporary and prime site of Othering. In particular, they highlight the Othering tendencies of conventional research. These are manifested in the assertions made above that Western science, in particular, is premised on abyssal thinking, which purports to uphold a distance between the researcher (holder of knowledge) and the researched (objects to be subjected to the researcher's knowledge). This distance is such that the researcher and the researched cannot recognise each other. In this vein, Comaroff and Comaroff argue that the interview encounter becomes more like an interview between strangers who lack any sort of entanglement, whereas an interview is not so much an encounter between strangers as a meeting of people who are implicated in each other. It is this posture and understanding of the world that informed the mass movement of scholars and researchers from the North to study what became known as 'African Aids', ostensibly perpetuated by an 'African sexuality' to which the high prevalence rate of HIV/Aids in Africa was attributed. The curiosity of these scholars and researchers was informed by the apparently exotic nature of this African sexuality which, according to them, is characterised by practices such as polygyny, dry sex, wife inheritance, promiscuity, the virgin cleansing myth and intergenerational sexual relations. This view of Africa is informed by a belief that the continent is not only different from the USA, for instance, but that the difference is hierarchical. African sexuality is seen to be informed by 'African culture', which has yet to evolve from what Hobbes observed many years ago about 'man in the state of nature' – unbridled sexuality that is animal-like and does not show a higher consciousness (Lloyd and Sreedhar 2019).

As an example of this, Treichler (1991) argues that early medical observers constructed the medical evidence they were observing to fit pre-existing assumptions about African sexuality and disease. This corroborates Gilman's (1985) assertion that the actual may not mimic closely the ideal of science. Contrary to being objective and neutral, Gilman argues that the association of Africans with sexuality and the tendency to link African sexuality with disease have a long history in Western thought and, as such, may influence how science is carried out and the resultant conclusions. Treichler (1991, 189) asserts that a view is entrenched that 'in dealing with Aids, we are not just dealing with sex, we are dealing with life ways and complex cultural patterns', which further cements the view that Africans are promiscuous by nature and are culturally resistant to modifying their sexual behaviour. She postulates that, for example, Edward Green, a prominent anthropologist who plies his trade in Africa during his sojourns there from abroad, holds the view that 'changes in behaviour which promote[s] the spread of Aids will go against social and cultural norms and values in Africa and against deeply ingrained behavioural patterns' (Packard and Epstein 1991, 356). In this way, 'traditions' are reified as historically static. This type of cultural essentialism leads to exoticism, which entrenches the view that Africans are not people with problems, they are the problem. Deconstructing the specific case of 'African Aids', Paul Farmer (2001) points to the epistemic injustice perpetuated by the systematic conflation of structural violence with culture. He attributes this tendency to Western ideas about an exotic Other and its epistemological tools that confirm the Other's 'backwardness'.

Western ideas of the world compartmentalise aspects of life such that sexuality and social reproduction are thought of as 'local', while the economy, for instance, is thought of as 'global'. So, while Africa is in intricate relationships with the rest of the world at the level of the economy, somehow social reproduction in Africa is divorced from these relations (Fassin 2007).

Therefore, contrary to the purported status of science as a perfect knowledge of things (Dussel 2014, 15), research on HIV/Aids in Africa, informed by this abyssal thinking, has played into the usual tendencies of Othering and thus silencing. Mark Hunter (2010) argues that without addressing the structural reasons why women and men have more than one sexual partner, for instance, any behavioural intervention campaign is unable to provide a major breakthrough. Remarking on a different topic altogether, Grosfoguel (2008, 1) makes a point that is general to knowledge production: 'With few exceptions, [Western "experts"] produced studies about the subaltern rather than studies with and from a subaltern perspective; theory was still located in the North, while the subjects to be studied are located in the South.' HIV/Aids was a classic site where such tendencies were repeated with little, if any, reflexivity. Critical thinking would have awakened researchers to the fact, stated by Hunter (2010), for example, that the most celebrated Zulu 'traditions' today emerged in the colonial period.

Believing in their expert status and superior knowledge, researchers from the North conceived studies about an imagined Africa that went on to prove their preconceived ideas about the continent. Decolonial epistemic perspectives can help us understand why this was possible in the first place. In the first instance, views about Africa informed what could be said to be coloniality of knowledge, of power and being. Coloniality of knowledge can be seen in the imposition of a particular world view on the understanding of HIV/Aids. Firstly, drawing on colonial views of Africa, the advent of HIV/Aids resurrected notions of the Other, who is not only different, but also inferior. Secondly, the reductionist, compartmentalised view of the world led to the obscuring of root causes for the disproportionate prevalence of HIV/Aids in Africa. The history of epidemics is thus an integral part of the history of racial segregation in South Africa (Hunter 2010). This obscuring led to the silencing of inequalities and structural violence against people who are most vulnerable. Instead, the victims of such structural violence were blamed. Malkki (1995, 17, cited in Fassin 2007, xv) asserts that this is 'anthropological culturalism' which, by essentialising difference, produces 'subtly de-historicising, dehumanizing effects'. Behavioural and culturalist interpretations that have been used to explain the dramatic spread of the disease are as ineffective as they are unjust.

Commenting specifically on the injustices of Aids research in South Africa in particular, Didier Fassin (2007) goes on to say that causing suffering and ignoring the effects of that suffering are a contemporary reality. He asks a moral question: what is a just society? He responds that it is one that remembers, because ignoring the past not only harms understanding of the present, but also compromises present action. The solutions advanced from the premises of biomedical medicine, for instance, are just as reductionist as behavioural and culturalist interpretations, focusing on fighting the disease while ignoring the factors that make victims vulnerable to disease, and not offering any long-term solutions to the extent that, should there be another global epidemic, the very same sub-alternised groups that have been imagined through the Euro-North American prism will be as vulnerable as they are now to HIV/Aids.

The site of intervention was the individual and their behaviour, and solutions were effected at that level. Other points of view were systematically silenced. For instance, research has shown that communities most affected by HIV/Aids display more than average knowledge of how HIV is transmitted and how it could be prevented (Farmer 2001). However, this knowledge fails to translate into health-affirming practices. Audrey Pettifor et al. (2004) and Lisa Arai (2008) argue further that while the structural determinants of sexual ills are apparent, policy approaches prioritise changing motivations such as choice, rather than changing the determinants themselves. Giving a concrete example of a place characterised by premature death on a large scale, Hunter (2010) argues that places are power-laden and formed in relation to other places; he emphasises that the participants in his study attributed their heightened vulnerability to *isimo* – the way they understood things to be (conspiring against them). Such conversations were precluded by a unilateral understanding of HIV/Aids as an illness perpetuated by a set of factors that are internal to the individual (their behaviour) or group (their culture).

Tuhiwai Smith (1999, 2) highlights 'ways in which the pursuit of knowledge is deeply embedded in the multiple layers of imperial and colonial practices'. She says that for indigenous communities, research is a dirty word due its objectifying tendencies. Informed by the logic of individualism, proposed interventions to counter the spread of HIV/Aids have favoured the market economy. These include buying expensive pharmaceutical drugs and other products, while leaving the contextual structural issues that increase vulnerability intact. The logic of wanting to have and construct the Other is closely linked to capitalism. In the widespread disregard of death in capitalist societies and the advancing of solutions that do not question and undermine capitalism's premises, we see glimpses of how reductionist and thus racist solutions (that blame the victim's behaviour and culture as deviant) powerfully enable capitalism. In this vein, then, the dominant approach to understanding and responding to the HIV/Aids epidemic has ignored the modernity/coloniality complex that perpetuates a dialectical relationship between development and underdevelopment.

By imposing a world view on mute Others, the West sought to effect indirect rule over Africa, using HIV/Aids as a means to achieve this aim. Treichler (1991), amongst others, argues that the Aids epidemic was the site on which power relations of domination already in place were reproduced. In this sense, both Smith (1999) and Treichler (1991) argue that narratives, too, perform a function of domination and subjugation: 'Information does not simply exist; it issues from and, in turn, sustains a way of looking and behaving towards the world' (Treichler 1991, 124). As such, issues of power and representation loom large in the perpetuation of an unjust order. Furthermore, the question of Aids in Africa cannot be fully understood unless issues of racial exploitation, subjugation and discrimination are simultaneously considered. These factors, more than the purported different and thus regressive cultural and sexual mores of Africans, go a long way towards accounting for the disproportionate HIV/Aids vulnerability amongst individuals, groups and nations on the continent.

CONCLUSION

In this chapter I have argued for the simultaneous reading of modernity and coloniality. I have reasoned that, contrary to the view that Western-derived knowledge is apolitical and acontextual, it is strategically political and can be implicated in sustaining an unequal world order. I have used the precepts of decolonial thinking to argue that the disembodied and unlocated neutrality of the ego-politics of knowledge is a Western myth that works to perpetuate its dominant position in world politics. Informed by and flowing from Cartesian thinking, Western knowledge that privileges modern conceptions of being, knowledge and power is wilfully and strategically ignorant of the dialectic of modernity/coloniality that pursues coloniality of knowledge, power and being. I have sought to show the relationship between these seemingly disparate loci of understanding.

At the core of domination is the logic that produces the Other while simultaneously defining and recentring the Self. By adopting a narrow view of the world, Western science or knowledge precludes the possibility of historical conversations about the relationship between the empire and its subaltern. As such, Western knowledge silences views from its periphery while it valorises itself as universal. HIV/Aids, as I have shown, is a classic and contemporary site on which these power dynamics have been elaborated and entrenched in Africa.

REFERENCES

Arai, Lisa. 2008. 'Low Expectations, Sexual Attitudes and Knowledge: Explaining Teenage Pregnancy and Fertility in English Communities: Insights from Qualitative Research'. *Sociological Review* 5(2): 199–217.

Comaroff, Jean and Comaroff, John. 1992. *Ethnography and the Historical Imagination*. Boulder, CO: Westview Press.

Dussel, Enrique. 2014. 'Anti-Cartesian Meditations: On the Origin of the Philosophical Anti-Discourse of Modernity'. Translated by George Ciccariello-Maher. *Journal of Cultural and Religious Theory* 13(1): 1–53.

Farmer, Paul. 2001. *Infections and Inequalities: The Modern Plagues*. Berkeley, CA: University of California Press.

Fassin, Didier. 2007. *When Bodies Remember: Experiences and Politics of AIDS in South Africa*. Berkeley, CA: University of California Press.

Gilman, Sander. 1985. *Difference and Pathology: Stereotypes of Sexuality, Race and Madness*. New York, NY: Cornell University Press.

Grosfoguel, Ramón. 2007. 'The Epistemic Decolonial Turn: Beyond Political Economy Paradigms'. *Cultural Studies* 21(2–3): 211–23.

Grosfoguel, Ramón. 2008. 'Transmodernity, Border Thinking and Global Coloniality. Decolonizing Political Economy and Postcolonial Studies'. Accessed 23 June 2020. https://www.ikn-network.de/lib/exe/fetch.php/themen/grosfoguel_2008_transmodernity.pdf.

Grosfoguel, Ramón. 2012. 'Decolonizing Western Uni-versalisms: Decolonial Pluri-versalism from Aimé Césaire to the Zapatistas'. *Transmodernity: Journal of Peripheral Cultural Production of the Luso-Hispanic World* 13: 1–17.

Grosfoguel, Ramón. 2013. 'The Structure of Knowledge in Westernized Universities: Epistemic Racism/Sexism and the Four Genocides/Epistemicides of the Long 16th Century'. *Human Architecture: Journal of the Sociology of Self-knowledge* 11(1): 73–90.

Hunter, Mark. 2010. *Love in the Time of AIDS: Inequality, Gender and Rights in South Africa*. Indianapolis, IN: University of Indiana Press.

Kuhn, Thomas. 1962. *The Structure of Scientific Revolutions*. Chicago, IL: University of Chicago Press.

Lloyd, Sharon A. and Sreedhar, Susanne. 2019. 'Hobbes's Moral and Political Philosophy'. In *The Stanford Encyclopedia of Philosophy*, Spring 2019 edition, edited by Edward N. Zalta. Accessed 23 June 2020. https://plato.stanford.edu/archives/spr2019/entries/hobbes-moral/.

Maldonado-Torres, Nelson. 2007. 'On the Coloniality of Being: Contributions to the Development of a Concept'. *Cultural Studies* 21(2–3): 240–70.

Maldonado-Torres, Nelson. 2008. *Against War: Views from the Underside of Modernity*. Durham, NC: Duke University Press.

Mignolo, Walter D. 2007. 'Delinking: The Rhetoric of Modernity, the Logic of Coloniality and the Grammar of De-Coloniality'. *Cultural Studies* 21(2–3): 449–514.

Mignolo, Walter D. 2011. *The Darker Side of Western Modernity: Global Futures/Decolonial Options*. Durham, NC: Duke University Press.

Ndlovu-Gatsheni, Sabelo J. 2015. 'Decoloniality as the Future of Africa'. *History Compass* 13(10): 485–96.

Packard, Randall M. and Epstein, Paul. 1991. 'Medical Research on AIDS in Africa: A Historical Perspective'. In *AIDS: The Making of a Chronic Disease*, edited by Elizabeth Fee and Daniel Fox, 346–76. Oakland, CA: University of California Press.

Pettifor, Audrey, Rees, Helen V., Steffenson, Annie, Hlongwa-Madikizela, Lindiwe, McPhail, Catherine, Vermaak, Kerry and Kleinschmidt, Immo. 2004. 'HIV and Sexual Behaviour Among Young South Africans: A National Survey of 15–24 Year Olds'. Johannesburg: University of the Witwatersrand Reproductive Health and HIV Research Unit.

Quijano, Anibal. 2007. 'Coloniality and Modernity/Rationality'. *Cultural Studies* 21(2–3): 168–78.

Quijano, Anibal. 2013. 'Coloniality and Modernity/Rationality'. In *Globalization and the Decolonial Option*, edited by Walter D. Mignolo and Arturo Escobar, 22–32. London and New York: Routledge.

Santos, Boaventura de Sousa. 2007. 'Beyond Abyssal Thinking: From Global Lines to Ecologies of Knowledge'. *Review* 30(1): 45–89.

Smith, Linda Tuhiwai. 1999. *Decolonizing Methodologies: Research and Indigenous Peoples*. Dunedin: University of Otago Press.

Treichler, Paula. 1991. 'AIDS and HIV Infection in the Third World: A First World Chronicle'. In *AIDS: The Making of a Chronic Disease*, edited by Elizabeth Fee and Daniel Fox, 377–412. Berkeley, CA: University of California Press.

Wynter, Sylvia. 1991. 'Columbus and the Poetics of the *Propter Nos*'. *Annals of Scholarship* 2(8): 251–86.

10 THE FICTION OF THE JURISTIC PERSON: REASSESSING PERSONHOOD IN RELATION TO PEOPLE

C.D. SAMARADIWAKERA-WIJESUNDARA

When we reflect on the role of the company in modern society, its pervasiveness in every element of our existence as human beings is conspicuous. It is evident in the food that we consume, the water we drink, clothes we wear, pharmaceuticals we depend on and jobs that provide us with the income that enables us to acquire these resources to sustain life (O'Connell 2010, 202). It is particularly striking that these functions are accomplished by an entity that has neither body nor soul nor will (Dewey 1926, 655). That said, a company is not merely the aggregate of a group of people; it has, by definition, a personality of its own that is recognised by the law.

What then is the nature of the juristic person that is a company, and what are the implications of this for natural persons (of flesh and blood)? The law may posit a technical answer to this question, namely that a company is an association of natural persons authorised by the state, in terms of its charter or memorandum of incorporation, to undertake a specified business and in doing so be empowered to act as a natural person. Penington (1931, 36) defines a company's being as 'an artificial being existing only in contemplation of law', as an entity that has properties conferred upon it by 'the charter of its creation'. The most important properties, according to Penington, are those of immortality and individuality.

Pennington's definition is particularly useful as it extends beyond a description of the functioning of a company into the purpose of its recognition as a legal person, namely the immortal ownership of property. This on its own may still not provide clarity as to the relationship between the juristic person of a company and natural persons, but it implores us to interrogate the normative underpinnings of the concept of the company. In this chapter I propose to do this by considering the historical development of the recognition of the juristic person, specifically within the context of imperialism and colonialism. I will argue that the juristic person occupies a place in the zone of existence while simultaneously maintaining some natural persons in the Fanonian 'zone of non-being' (Fanon 1967, 82). And I will anchor this conceptual exploration in the context of South Africa, not only because of the relevance to the country of the colonial elements of the company in the form of the Dutch East India Company (DEIC), but also because of the contemporary implications of the South African Constitution (Republic of South Africa 1996b) for the relationship between natural and juristic persons in this society.

In undertaking this exploration I am not suggesting that the concept of a company (or commercial juristic persons) is homogeneous or without exception. Nor am I attempting to demonstrate a genetic linear growth from early imperial enterprises such as the DEIC to the modern company, such as those incorporated in South Africa today. There is, however, a significant normative underpinning within their conceptual similarity of design and purpose which this chapter seeks to expose. Colonial oppression has been described as systemic. The modern company, as a constituent institution, remains an apparatus for control over land. Furthermore, this control is ideologically racialised and manifests itself in the poverty of those relegated to the zone of non-being.

What is significant about such a contention is that it may lead us to a more honest engagement with the elastic and mystifying nature of the company, in turn facilitating a more deliberate engagement with the power dynamics that a company enables – and the concomitant accountability of the natural persons behind the company. This may prompt us to reassess the suitability of the current discourse on the human rights obligations of the company (which remain controversial), to the extent that this discourse entrenches the power dynamics that enable this juristic person to violate human rights for the benefit of natural persons who are veiled from accountability's gaze. A more apt approach to concerns about the ways in which the company violates natural persons may be to reassess the legitimacy of the current form of an institution that facilitates such violations with relative impunity. That is, this may compel us to interrogate the cause rather than the symptom of the company's deleterious power over natural persons.

UNPACKING THE NATURE AND PURPOSE OF JURISTIC PERSONALITY

According to Judith Katzew (2011), the idea of the company was initially designed to provide for the consolidation of capital from various sources to support the entrepreneurial ventures of individuals or groups of individuals. In the context of the joint-stock or share-based company, this means separate ownership (of those who invested in the company, thereby bearing the risk of losing that investment in exchange for the potential growth of the investment) and control (of those whose investment was not at stake, but who stood to gain from the beneficiation of the company that would be achieved through their effective management of resources) (Katzew 2011, 694). The incentive of the shareholders to invest was presumably the limitation of risk to the extent of the initial investment (notwithstanding what liabilities might be engendered by those charged with growing the investment) and the additional potential for its growth (Katzew 2011, 694).

The notion that 'the business of business is business' has been credited to economist Milton Friedman and justifies the proposition that the purpose of a company is to maximise profits (Friedman 1962, 112). This had the effect of delegitimising activities of the corporation outside of making money, or related to spending that was not specifically geared towards making more money. The shareholder value doctrine (advocating for the primacy of shareholder interests) has become conventional wisdom and dictates the approach taken by corporations in several jurisdictions. It exonerates the company from obligations other than the making of profit, as the interests of the juristic person are presented as exclusively profit maximisation (Denning 2013). The furtherance of these interests has been widely regarded as being subject only to the rules of the game – the game being the operation of the free market and the prohibition of deliberate acts designed to circumvent its functioning (Baird and Henderson 2008). The fiction of the company has therefore provided a vehicle for the avoidance of liability of the investors and the entrepreneurs that it seeks to invite with the prospect of gain relative to diluted risk (Bilchitz 2008, 754).

The *Salamon* case is the classic authority for the distinct legal personality of a juristic person (Salomon Case 1896). The characteristics of legal personality are the ability to have an identity (and a name), own property in that name (which then forms part of a patrimonial estate), have standing before a court to sue and be sued, and have the entitlement to rights. With this descriptive account in mind, it is pertinent to consider some of the theories that seek to explain the nature of the company as a juristic person.

The origins of the modern corporation have been attributed to Roman law. The early fictional theory of juristic personality is credited to Pope Innocent IV (who was incidentally also a champion of the divine right to conquest, which will be visited later in this chapter), in the context of ecclesiastic corporate bodies being immune to criminal or civil sanction on account of having no body to be punished nor any will to be condemned (Dewey 1926, 655). It is from this that the theory of the corporation as an immortal fictional person is said to have arisen. The recognition of this fiction was later developed, as the concept of the nation state rose to prominence, into the theory that the state alone could grant recognition of personhood (Dewey 1926, 666–69). This came to be known as the concession theory, on the basis that the recognition of capacity of the juristic person was a concession by the state, as the presiding authority over social relations (Dewey 1926, 666–69). This, John Dewey argues, was done in an attempt to entrench power and simultaneously exercise that power to prevent the collective power of ecclesiastical and business groupings from encroaching on the power of the state (Dewey 1926, 667).

Alternatively, the will theory suggests an interpretation of a fictional person as nuancedly distinct from an artificial person. This employs the concession theory to hold that the juristic person is artificially constructed by, and given content through, legal recognition (Dewey 1926, 670–73). The will theory suggests that a fictional being comes into existence in the formation of a juristic person. The will theory presents the collective volitions of the members or shareholders (particularly the majority of them) as culminating in the distinct volition of the company (Dewey 1926, 670–73).

In a similar vein, the group personality theory relies on Frederic William Maitland's conception of the company as an aggregation of groups collecting to pursue specific interests which culminate in 'psychic organisms, possessing not fictitious but real psychic personality' (Dewey 1926, 670). An alternative take, borrowed from Friedrich Carl von Savigny's conception of the state, is that a company functions in a distributive rather than a collective manner.

This is particularly so in the context of the contestations for power within the various collectives that constitute the company, and which pursue contrary interests at times. As such, the company displays its own will and consists of various groupings, but is essentially psychically distinct from these groupings (Dewey 1926, 670). The problem with the elasticity of these theories is that, due simply to a legal construct, juristic personality conveniently facilitates the pursuit of individualist interests without the burden of concomitant liability (Dewey 1926, 668).

The representative theory centres on the separation of ownership and control (Deiser 1909a, 228–29), in terms of which collective ownership is represented in shareholding/stakeholding. The shareholders'/members' rights are indivisible and their individuality is irrelevant. They operate within a nexus of association. This theory requires acceptance either that rights are held by a non-existent (unreal) entity, or that the collection of rights loses the properties of each individual right and is aggregated into the will of the majority. This would have the effect of excluding minority or dissenting shareholders/stakeholders from the nexus of association. In terms of this theory, technically minorities should not be entitled to interfere with the will of the majority, but this is not the case as justiciable minority shareholders'/stakeholders' protections are granted in several jurisdictions (Deiser 1909a, 228–29). The representation theory proves contradictory, in that the legitimacy of juristic personality is founded in the representation of constituent rights-bearing individuals acting collectively; however, when acting in association, each individual necessarily loses individuality as rights attach to the share/stake.

A solution to this tension appears in the idea of collective holding of rights, contained in George Deiser's suggestion that property ownership can be either individual or collective (Deiser 1909a, 229–33). Therefore, the juristic person is symbolic and merely serves as an administrative device for collective property ownership. Interests in the property are not distinct, but exist for the purpose of common benefit. This recognises that the ultimate rights holders and beneficiaries of the juristic person are always natural persons. Rights existing only in the abstract and never engaging in the real world of natural persons have no content. As such, the rights attributed to the juristic person belong to the natural persons who constitute it, albeit in different capacities than would be the case if those rights were directly held (Deiser 1909a, 229–33).

The binary of juristic and natural persons originally departed from the premise that natural persons have inviolable rights by virtue of being human. However, this practical distinction was eroded over time, as juristic persons were granted rights by virtue of interpretation of what it meant to be persons for legal purposes endowed with the authority to act as a natural person would, to the extent possible (Dewey 1926, 669). The movement from the recognition of juristic persons as properly artificial entities, with no inherent rights, to persons in the equal sense as natural persons, has generated immortal persons (Chomsky 1999, 97). Furthermore, as the concept of distinct personality grew, specificity about purpose stated in the charter or memorandum of incorporation became less determinative (Chomsky 1999, 97).

Dewey suggests that the aim of theories of juristic personality is to make sense of the recognition of an entity through which natural persons can act with limited liability for the consequences of their actions (Dewey 1926, 673). This is in the context of an individualistic age concerned primarily with the right to private property. The fiction is employed as a way of deflecting accountability of natural persons that would be of moral character, while the concession theory grants legitimacy to the fiction. Due to the elasticity of the concept of a fiction, the company is able to derive benefits for natural persons while simultaneously shielding them from reproach. In this way, 'persons' may come to represent any content that the law attributes to the concept, including being a 'right-and-duty bearing unit' as classically described by Maitland (Maitland 1905, 193; see also Dewey 1926, 673).

On the other hand, Deiser suggests that the theory of juristic personality exists to establish a conceptual foundation for understanding and solving corporate problems, and not 'to furnish the doctors of jurisprudence with a cadaver that might serve for dissecting purposes' (Deiser 1909a, 305). As such, the nature of juristic personality is important only to the extent that it determines the parameters of the rights and obligations of the juristic person. The fiction generated around collective activity and the recognition of legal personality creates the illusion of a robust concept in the law (Deiser 1909b, 308). This is however misleading, as the content of the fiction is dependent on the intricacies of the jurisdictions within which the fiction applies (Deiser 1909b, 308). The absence of acknowledgement of this fact results in the elasticity of the concept being used to mean what is beneficial for those who employ the fiction at a given place and time. Ultimately '"[p]erson" signifies what the law makes it signify' (Dewey 1926, 655).

Reading Dewey's and Deiser's suggestions together, we may conclude that the relevance of the nature of juristic personality can be situated in the purpose that the construction enables. Fundamentally, whether the fictional theory, which the *Dadoo* case (Dadoo Case 1920) has shown to have taken precedence in our law in close association with the concession theory, or the collective rights theory is seen as the basis for the existence of a legal personality, a common thread can be drawn. This thread is the ownership of property for the end benefit of natural persons who are invested in the company, with no correlate risk in that property or in the activities associated therewith.

Not surprisingly, the converse of the limitation of liability of the natural persons who are invested in the juristic person is the displacement of liability that would ordinarily rest in those persons, were they to carry on business in their own name. This displaced liability is theoretically situated in the distinct juristic person. However, as this is a fictional person, the extent of its liability is limited against the assets it holds. The complexities of the interrelations between natural persons and any moral character of the potential impact of activities of the juristic person are, in essence, lost.

The *Salamon* case set the tone for recognition of instances where the distinction between the juristic person and the natural persons behind it could be disregarded, but this was limited to instances where the construct was employed to commit fraud. Consequently, there are very limited instances where the veil between the juristic person and its shareholders/members will be pierced. This is necessarily so, as we have established that limitation of liability is a fundament of the construct of the juristic person. The lack of accountability is exacerbated by the fact that a juristic person may comprise members or shareholders who are numerous and disparate in space and time, and may themselves be juristic persons. It becomes difficult to deconstruct the fragments of natural personality that constitute the juristic personality in order to secure accountability and limit harm (Deiser 1909a, 220). This may be conceded to as part of the objectives of the fiction, but must be recognised as problematic when it facilitates the subversion of duties that natural persons might have in relation to one another.

The theories of juristic personality do not provide very much content. Recognising the sustaining notion of the company as a 'construct' may not provide universal content, but is useful in confronting the reality that corporate personality is what the law allows it to be, and as such the law is empowered, if not compelled, to dictate the parameters of action and the means of attaching accountability to such action. Meaningful accountability would see those natural persons who benefit from the juristic person being accountable for the detriment to others that may be caused by the existence and power granted to that juristic person.

In confronting the elasticity of the concept of the fiction or construct of the juristic person, which veils the natural persons that animate it, it is necessary to recognise that '[a] corporation cannot be for one purpose, so many men, for another purpose a person, and for another purpose a fiction' (Deiser 1908, 135). We may accept Deiser's conclusion that central to the nature of the juristic person is the matter of property (1909b, 305). As such, the proposition that juristic persons are conduits for collective property holding becomes compelling.

SIMILARITY OF DESIGN AND PURPOSE: AN IDEOLOGICAL GOLDEN THREAD

Venkat Rao argues that the company as a juristic person emerged from the mercantilist approach to economic power (Rao 2011). This pivoted on imperial expansion and control of landed property as the literal foundation of power. Conquest of South Africa is conventionally ascribed to the Dutch (Rao 2011), while in practice this was done through activities incidental to the commercial endeavours of the DEIC (Rao 2011). This demonstrates the inextricable symbiotic relationship between commercial and political expansion endeavours that has occurred locally and globally (Callinicos 2009, 136). Companies have justified the appropriation of land in the furtherance of commercial pursuits in contexts ranging from unapologetic and theologically motivated conquest, to variations on the theme of a crusade for democracy in territories where barriers to entry by companies into markets were perceived to exist (Chomsky 1999, 65–68).

Philip Stern argues that the English East India Company (EEIC) and the DEIC (collectively EICs) were the originators of the modern multinational (Stern 2016, 428). His argument is premised on their legal personality and corporate structure (separating ownership in joint transferrable stock/shares and management control). Furthermore, he asserts that the EICs are historical reference points for globalisation, capitalism and international trade law. Specifically, he sees these companies as the points at which medieval collective commercial endeavours turned to more intricate capitalist principles and practices (Stern 2016, 429).

Stern criticises comparisons between the EICs and the modern company on the basis that instances of juristic persons do not follow a pattern of linear development, but are rather generated from the peculiarities of social and political contexts (Stern 2016, 431–32). A second reason for his opposition to this analogy has been the sovereign dimensions of the EICs (Stern 2016, 433): both companies maintained armies and amassed territories, which fell ostensibly under their control. It may be contended, however, that variations in the configurations and exercise of power between the EICs and the modern company should not discount the purpose-made design of the control of land (and consequently labour) that applies in both cases.

Due to the anchoring of this chapter in South Africa, I will focus on the DEIC as a reference point. The philosophy of the jurist Hugo Grotius motivated the DEIC's stance in respect of both the entitlement to trade as well as that of conquest (Stern 2016, 436). Grotius specifically extended recognition of personhood to juristic persons when expounding on the right of persons to carry on war and assume dominium over conquered territories and peoples (Stern 2016, 437). He also influenced the proposition that the DEIC could legitimately be a sovereign and a subject simultaneously (Stern 2016, 438). This ideological context, Stern (2016, 444) notes, explains the mutually reinforcing character of the nation state and the company. The fact of both these institutions being juristic persons draws into focus the at times artificial distinction between public and private power (especially to the extent that the distinction is used to justify the absence of obligation to act in protection of the interests of disempowered natural persons).

The DEIC operated as a private company but was inherently a national enterprise (Geen 1946, 7). The Dutch government had substantial shareholding in it, and the steward of the early Dutch Republic was the chairman of the DEIC. Shareholding was limited to Dutch subjects, and small shareholders were encouraged. It was granted status as a legal person by a charter granted by the States General of Holland empowering the Council of XVII, which required a payment to the government over 21 years that was ostensibly reinvested into the operations of the DEIC. The Council of XVII was empowered to conduct trade, amass colonial possessions, maintain an army and make treaties with foreign powers (Geen 1946, 7).

Colonial occupation of the Cape took place in 1652, led by Jan van Riebeeck who was the ship surgeon and commander of the DEIC mission to set up a refreshment station for Dutch ships bound for the East (Geen 1946, 8–9). In 1660 he was promoted to the rank of governor, swearing obedience to the governor general at Batavia, and used his authority as commander of the DEIC and governor to constitute a Council of Policy. This Council notably included a law officer (who established a high court of justice), senior merchants, a chief salesman, bookkeeper, treasurer and two military officers (Geen 1946, 8–9). In effect, the DEIC had established itself as a monopoly and sovereign over the Cape.

The DEIC exercised control over the Cape, and introduced and maintained a deliberate social order consisting of four main groups: DEIC servants (employees), free burghers (employees who had been relieved of service and contracted to hold land in exchange to sustain farming operations), slaves and the Khoi (Lucas 2004, 32). Of these groups, the employees and free burghers were mostly white, with the exception of some employees and manumitted slaves who were referred to as 'free blacks', some of whom originated from other Dutch colonies. The DEIC also shaped the emerging society through the creation of a culture of materialism (Lucas 2004, 28). Some of the more superficial similarities between the DEIC in the Cape and modern corporations include the purchase carried by corporate identity and its signage and attendant symbols, including a company logo carried on all manner of objects ranging from packages to dinner plates (Lucas 2004, 28). As the DEIC operations in the Cape grew more self-sufficient they expanded territorially. Wars were instigated with indigenous communities to remove perceived threats to DEIC control (Lucas 2004, 72).

Notwithstanding the attainment of political independence, liberated colonies tend to nonetheless retain the residual economic, legal, political and cultural institutions of the colonial era – the normative underpinnings of which often go without interrogation (Sibanda 2011, 495). This is evidenced in the South African case. The significance of the shift in relationship of the indigenous persons to the DEIC, as a company, may be argued to be both physical and ontological; they shifted from being independent free agents to becoming dependent utilities whose occupation of space was now dictated by European settlers through the instrument of a company. Of further significance was the fact that the DEIC utilised this labour (without reward) on terms of its own making. Those terms, established by the DEIC, formed the foundation of mercantile law and labour relations in South Africa while overshadowing and reconstituting indigenous governance systems. To this effect the divine right of conquest utilised the law as an instrument for control (Ramose 2007, 313). This was the same law that was constitutive of and constituted by the company as a juristic person.

COLONIALISM AND THE COMPANY'S PARTICIPATION IN ZONES OF BEING

This reflection on the DEIC and the beginning of colonial occupation of South Africa warrants the reassessment, prompted by Anibal Quijano, of the perception of history as a sequence of events where slavery and serfdom are presented as pre-capital occurrences (Quijano 2000, 550). Power relations set up by Europeans in the course of their conquest of the Global South, as seen in South Africa, were centrally based on racial classification and perceptions of European superiority. Central to this project were the ideas that modernity and progress were linear and in the sole preserve of Europeans (Quijano 2000, 552–53). Processes such as modernisation, corporatisation and globalisation have been championed in the name of development, and have served to both legitimate themselves and to put themselves beyond question (Tully 2008, 478). This circular logic pervaded colonial institutions, including companies used as instruments in various colonial contexts. Slavery was a deliberate commodification of human labour and was utilised to produce goods for consumption by the world market in the service of capitalism. Race was used as a social classification of the world's population and justified conquest, displacement and subjugation. The European Enlightenment brought with it conceptions of the identity of the European as central and superior, while others were essentialised into homogenised, inferior identities (Quijano 2000, 550–51).

The approach adopted by the DEIC in the Cape demonstrates that racial classification was strategic in facilitating the domination that justified exploitation. According to the Eurocentric conception of being, the body was the object of reason (Quijano 2000, 555). The distinction between body and reason (stemming from soul) enabled the theorisation of racial hierarchy.

Furthermore it allowed for the viewing of the bodies classified as certain races as mere objects, and thus inherently inferior to reasoned subjects.

Frantz Fanon refers to the recognition of the Hegelian 'I and other' that animated the conception of the Eurocentric (and patriarchal) conception of the human self (Fanon 1967, 82). He suggests that there is no black other, as the other, albeit distinct from the self, is still human. He thus presents blackness as existing in the zone of non-being, below the 'other' (Gordon 2007, 11). People in the zone of being are recognised socially as human beings and thus reap the fruits of humanity, including rights and access to resources (Gordon 2007, 8). The sub-human or non-human exists in a zone of contested humanity or negation (Fanon 1967, 82). The zone of non-being is characterised by violence and inconsequentiality; it is a zone where social practices and convention normalise arbitrary death and the non-human status of those who exist in this zone (Gordon 2007, 11). For the black person, any attempt to alter this condition is necessarily an act of violence. Gordon (2007, 11) explains that this is because change necessitates visibility, which is violent when that visibility is of an existence that is supposedly illegitimate.

To this effect Ramón Grosfoguel (2016, 10) propounds that racism is 'a global hierarchy of superiority and inferiority along the line of the human that have been politically, culturally and economically produced and reproduced for centuries by the institutions of the "capitalist/patriarchal western-centric/ Christian-centric modern/colonial world-system"'. As such, racism, according to Grosfoguel's definition, is primarily but not necessarily reliant on race as a signifier. Therefore race is relevant to understanding the relationship between juristic persons and natural persons, especially in a context where some of the first companies (such as the DEIC) would relegate persons to the zone of non-being on the basis of race, as a justification for their dispossession and exploitation.

Race as a focal point is justified on the basis of the understanding of race as the dividing line between the zones of being and non-being (Grosfoguel 2016, 11). It assumes that relations such as class, sexual orientation and gender operate as factors within the zones, and therefore manifest as forms of oppression that are experienced differently in the zone of being than in the zone of non-being. According to Grosfoguel's taxonomy, therefore, racism is a structural, hierarchy-related recognition of humanity. The racist violence of dispossession within colonialism, which would be unjustifiable if exercised against human beings, is justified as it involves the dispossession of objects (Grosfoguel 2016, 14). In this way the company as a juristic person occupies the zone of being, while possessing the property of those that occupy the zone of non-being, as well their efforts. This is enabled by virtue of the company being recognised as a juristic person in the conceptualisation of natural persons who inhabitant of the zone of being.

THE MODERN COMPANY: (POST)-COLONIAL SOUTH AFRICA AND THE CONSTITUTION

In South Africa, the common law definitions of natural and juristic persons prevail for the purposes of the contemporary Companies Act (No. 71 of 2008), as the terms are not specifically defined there or in other South African legislation. Section 7 of the Companies Act does, however, make specific reference to the purpose of promoting the rights set out in the Bill of Rights that forms chapter 2 of the Constitution of the Republic of South Africa (Republic of South Africa 1996b) in the application of company law. While this may suggest an inclination towards a respect for human rights that would break from the conception of a company as being an instrument for exploitation, as outlined above, further examination suggests that a commitment to rights may be more an inclination towards the preservation of privilege and subjugation.

The Constitution itself has been contested as being a product of unconvincing consent, given the nature of the compromise secured by the Convention for a Democratic South Africa negotiated settlement (More 2011, 170). James Tully argues that this is the nature of legal consent, as it is produced gradually through a shift from sanction for non-compliance to buy-in by habit and rules that appear natural in social, political and economic life (Tully 2008, 472). Mabogo More (2011, 178) posits that the Constitution reaffirms the entitlement of the bearers of the fruits of the divine right of conquest. This is because of its resort to the language of South Africa belonging to all those who live in it, without tangible regard to the violence of displacement that gave birth to the country; it therefore assists in perpetuating a convenient historical amnesia. More argues further that the latest transfer of political power, resulting from compromises secured in the negotiated settlement, has maintained economic power in the hands of white people and secured the original project of white supremacy. This occurrence is not unique to South Africa, as the situation of economic and military power outside the control of the sovereign states in the former colonies has made their political power appear tokenistic (Tully 2008, 477).

If this line of reasoning is adopted, then it is not surprising that Section 8 (2) and Section 8 (4) of the Constitution, respectively, provide '[a] provision of the Bill of Rights [that] binds a natural or a juristic person if, and to the extent that, it is applicable, taking into account the nature of the right and the nature of any duty imposed by the right' and that 'a juristic person is entitled to the rights in the Bill of Rights to the extent required by the nature of the rights and the nature of that juristic person' (Republic of South Africa 1996a). This begs the question: what entitles a juristic person to rights generally regarded as 'human rights'? (Interestingly, the only right in the Bill of Rights qualified as 'human' is dignity.)

Adopting the collective theory of juristic personality, it may be argued that the collective rights of the individuals that constitute a juristic person converge into the rights of the juristic person. This is, however, problematic on several accounts. The first is that it assumes that there would not be competing interests and rights of those within the juristic person, and that the exercise of a right to a specific end would be possible. Even if it did amount to a convergence of rights, this would be problematic as it would amount to the persons whose rights the juristic person is drawing from effectively receiving a duplicate set of rights in addition to their own right that contributes to the collective right (and effectively is no longer equal to others who do not possess the same). As I have noted, this is avoided by the argument that the juristic person is an entity distinct from its constituent natural persons. However, that takes us in circular fashion back to the question of why a juristic person would be entitled to rights.

Perhaps a more pertinent question would be what the purpose of conferral of rights on juristic persons is. There we may conject that the answer, in terms of More's (2011) reasoning about the Constitution being a compromise document, would be that the entitlement to property rights would secure the property of the juristic person amongst other rights, such as the right to privacy (which would secure the non-transparency of the juristic person) and the right to free speech (which would secure the right of the juristic person to influence policy). An example of this would be the financing of election campaigns (Brown 2015, 161).

In this way, securing the property rights of the juristic person secures rights in land that entrench white control of most of the land in South Africa. This statement must be situated historically. We may depart from the point of the Natives' Land Act (No. 27 of 1913). This Act facilitated legal displacement of the country's black inhabitants, and thereby established a 'captive labour force' and set the tone for formal apartheid (More 2011, 179). It is relevant to note that this Act was repealed only in 1991. The Natives' Land Act prohibited natives (classed as all black peoples including 'Africans', 'Coloureds' and 'Indians') from owning or buying land anywhere except in native reserves. Factually, even in these spaces title was generally granted in terms of long leases by the municipality.

Fanon describes colonialism as the combination of the conquest of territory and the oppression of people (Fanon 1967, 81–83). The politics of liberation was therefore necessarily a politics of land restitution (Fanon 1967, 82). Land is quite literally the foundation of life. It is material in the sense that it is the source of shelter and food, but it is also representative of dignity in the sense of the right to life and to agency (More 2011, 179). Colonialism created conditions for the majority of the colonised to be condemned to poverty and consequently death (More 2011, 179).

Lost land and lost sovereignty (in the form of displacement and deprivation of freedom) for masses of indigenous peoples are a legacy of colonialism (More 2011, 179). The distinction between freedom and liberty is important to note for the purposes of understanding the manner in which the company is utilised to continue subordinating persons and restricting them to the zone of non-being (More 2011, 175). Although potentially free of constraints and physical bondage, liberated persons are not free to determine what a meaningful existence would amount to. Instead, for survival and literally for the entitlement to occupy space, someone else's space, people must sell their labour on terms over which they have little or no power (Ramose 2007, 319).

The matter of survival of those who occupy the zone of non-being requires further scrutiny. Poverty is a function of the structure of economic relations and not a natural and inevitable phenomenon (O'Connell 2010, 205). What has been described as epistemic fundamentalism dressed in the garb of universality and neutrality perpetuates the thinking that solutions to problems will be found by addressing the symptoms rather than the cause of systemic inadequacies (Ndlovu and Makoni 2014, 505). The reality of the zero-sum nature of the current economic system, which incorporates basic goods and services and forces them onto a global scale, make it natural, if not necessary, that some are deprived while others enjoy excess (O'Connell 2010, 204).

The limitations of regarding the world as (post-)colonial are evident when one examines the remaining institutions that operate on and perpetuate power relations that closely resemble those evident under colonial rule. Morgan Ndlovu and Eric Makoni refer to the emergence of the idea of coloniality as an understanding of the ways in which colonialisms have continued to exist, notwithstanding the dismantling of the overt political and judicial administrations of colonial governments (2013, 47–48). Coloniality, as the more nefarious and subtler operation of Western modernity and development, maintains the zones of being and non-being (Mignolo 2009, 39). The role of structures and institutions in perpetuating colonial power dynamics does not always capture our attention to the extent that its potential consequences should compel us to recognise.

The idea that juristic persons in their current form are essential for development, and create employment, plays into notions of the trickle-down effect that have somehow not been deterred by evidence of increasing inequality and the absence of broad-based redistribution of wealth globally, and in South Africa in particular (Ndlovu and Makoni 2014, 506). Morgan Ndlovu and Eric Makoni draw attention to the way in which trickle-down thinking that idealises international investment and job creation simply perpetuates inequalities, as indigenous people generally operate as cheap labour dependent on others who own the means of production (Ndlovu and Makoni 2014, 511). To this end, globalisation is not an objective and organic process but rather a construct informed by a specific underpinning ideology (O'Connell 2010, 204).

Ndlovu, reflecting on the Marikana massacre that took place in August 2012, when 34 human beings employed as miners were killed in the course of demanding a living wage, questions whether state actors can fathom an economic system different to that which enabled the conditions that facilitated the massacre (Ndlovu 2013, 56). He notes that for as long as exploitation continues, resistance to it make the occurrence of violent suppression inevitable. Part of the project of coloniality is the undermining of the rationality of the perspective of the oppressed, in the context of a reference point that is positioned as neutral but is nonetheless Eurocentric. The conditions that prevail for the majority of black South Africans occupying the zone of non-being are violent and inhumane (Ndlovu 2013, 56–57). Most sectors of the economy remain dominated by white people (in the form of ownership or control) and black people are relegated to being cheap labour. Perhaps the most disturbing aspect of this dynamic is the purported neutrality with which poverty is viewed. The conduct of the state that facilitates and perpetuates inequality cannot be dismissed without, again, turning our attention to the historical context that informs the very formation of states in (post-)colonial countries. We are reminded that juristic persons with commercial interests were at the helm of the dissection of Africa into nation states at the 1884 Berlin Conference (Ndlovu 2013, 57).

LIMITATIONS OF HUMAN RIGHTS: SERVING THE ZONE OF BEING

The South African Constitution is heralded as the solution to the ills of injustice and inequality; however, its abstract ideals are not reconciled with the concrete experiences of poverty (Modiri 2015, 224–5). The ways in which the law produces the subjects it seeks to protect, and the necessity of the adoption of that victim subjectivity in order to benefit from such protection, are co-constitutive (Brown 2000, 231). Those who do not have the means to enforce their rights must appeal to the benevolence of others to act on their behalf, or alternatively be satisfied with remaining in the zone of non-existence. The net effect is an attempt to mitigate the effects of poverty rather than to eradicate its causes or even envision a society where poverty is intolerable.

Joel Malesela Modiri exposes a contradiction in the recourse to rights as a remedy to end poverty (Modiri 2015, 255). Fundamentally, using these rights to secure the institutions and systems that generate poverty contradicts the effect of appeals to rights to create carve outs (specific instances in which transgressions are deemed unacceptable and for which symptomatic relief is provided) in respect of deviant conduct; these appeals are attempts to mitigate the harmful effects of institutions, rather than ways to call into question the legitimacy of those very institutions and of the power they have to cause harm. Appeals to these rights also frame harm as sensational instances that offend conceptions of what is permissible, but do not require accountability of actors in the scheme of social power dynamics and the ways in which dynamics of subordination and control are maintained (Modiri 2015, 255). To this effect, Sanele Sibanda questions whether the liberal democratic constitutional paradigm is conducive to bringing about the structural change that is necessary to free impoverished people from the status of dependent non-beings (Sibanda 2011, 497). Rights, in their current context, require an appeal to power without questioning the legitimacy of that power.

Tshepo Madlingozi also refers to the Marikana massacre of miners who were essentially contesting their location in the zone of non-being, where they were expected to accept the terms of an existence as objects to be acted upon, or as mere functionaries in a system (Madlingozi 2016, 138–39). He argues that colonial apartheid creates an ontology of being where being white, equated to being human, is greater than being black, which is equated to being sub-human (Madlingozi 2016, 124). He argues that the transition to a constitutional democracy represented merely a transition in phases of coloniality and not liberation in the sense of restored ontological and material humanity (Madlingozi 2016, 129). Liberation is understood in terms of restored dignity and land, as well as agency over that land, including the conditions of subsistence on that land (Madlingozi 2016, 135). To this end he argues that human rights discourse extends the discourse of determination of who is human and who is not, and the pursuit of the recognition of human rights translates into the aspiration towards being white and Western, as a prerequisite for existence in the zone of being.

In the context of the company, this manifests as recourse to finding and enforcing human rights obligations of juristic persons in response to violations of the rights of natural persons. It involves balancing the rights of juristic persons against those of human beings in a context that purports to make use of an even scale – as opposed to re-imagining the acceptable parameters of activity or even legitimate purposes of juristic persons in society, having recognised the fictional and at best artificial nature of corporates. Recourse to rights to mitigate the plight of those relegated to the zone of non-being neglects the manner in which rights entrench the system that created the conditions for relegation into that zone in the first instance. That is, the paradoxical operation of rights is neglected (Brown 2000, 234).

Rights are premised on a liberal individualism. They formulate power as a zero-sum game that requires, at best, a balancing act that maintains political and social order. Wendy Brown cautions that '[w]e must take into account what rights discourse does not avow about itself' (2000, 237–38). She argues that we must be critical of an approach that incrementally solves or mitigates problems with a view to a later solution to the extent that our energies and attentions are occupied with alleviating the symptoms of injustice, rather than addressing its causes. One of the paradoxes of rights that she identifies is that they regulate by circumscribing the category that they serve to protect and simultaneously dismantle. They are presented as protections that persons simply ' cannot not want ', notwithstanding their limiting effect on systemic solutions (Brown 2000, 237–38). This paradox stems from the resolvability of the challenge to a system that, in seeking to modify the system, appeals to that very system to be more accommodating, thereby necessarily legitimating it (Brown 2000, 238).

It has been argued that oppression is contextual, and as such the remedy for it must address its context. Brown (2004, 460) asks: '[y]es the abuse must be stopped but by whom, with what techniques, with what unintended effects, and above all unfolding what possible futures?' Frustrations with human rights do not necessarily stem from a conceptual rejection of rights, but rather a rejection of the ways in which rights discourse is used to patronise those with lived experiences of poverty and injustice in the face of the rights-based protection of those institutions that perpetuate these experiences.

POSSIBILITIES OF THE FICTION/CONSTRUCT: POWER AND RESPONSIBILITY OF THE STATE TO GOVERN

It is prudent, finally, to contemplate the fundamental question of what the source of power of one person over another is. Deiser submits that control is ultimately a function of the power of the strong over the weak, and that inevitably some persons are able to exert force over others and as such influence those others to act in accordance with their own will and for their own benefit (Deiser 1908, 135). While a detailed exposition and contestation of the operation of power is beyond the scope of this chapter, as are the implications of the juristic personality of the state itself, it may be argued that this authority to enforce power operates centrally at the state level. The classic social contract theory suggests that the state's authority to govern is derived from the consent of the governed (Deiser 1909a, 226–27). Theoretically, with this authority comes the expectation that the state will regulate relations between persons in a manner that is just, using the power and authority entrusted to it.

Natural persons have utilised the construct of the juristic person and the amorality of profit-seeking to exert control without personal accountability (Stephens 2002, 46). This has been exacerbated by the potentially nebulous control structures that the fiction enables, which at times make identification of the persons behind the fiction itself a nearly impossible task. This is evidenced by the manner in which persons have profited from the oppression enacted by companies in the form of dispossession, slavery and genocide (Stephens 2002, 46). The fiction of the juristic person has thus far been employed to effect the imposition of the interests of the strong over the person of the weak or weakened, including the interest of maintaining a relative position of strength. The fiction has operated, largely unquestioned, within a colonial frame of reference.

In order to extend decolonisation beyond the tokenistic into the tangible transformation of power relations, the reality and consequences of dispossession must be interrogated (Tuck and Yang 2012, 7). Therefore, the systemic nature of poverty and the manner in which the company operates as an instrument in this system are relevant. So too is the manner in which this construct has operated to obscure the racialised relations between natural persons and the dehumanising operation of coloniality. The golden thread of control of land is significant against the backdrop of the company's role in historical and continuing dispossession. The occupation by the juristic person of the zone of being, at the expense of persons consigned thereby to the zone of non-being, is central in this process of questioning. The manner in which the construct of the juristic person empowers the inequitable control of land and the generation of captive labour is central to this.

The contention that coloniality imposes an epistemological paradigm that proclaims itself inevitable and absolute may explain the lack of interrogation of the role that juristic personality plays in maintaining colonial relations of power. A hesitation about re-imagining this paradigm supports Ramose's argument that colonialism was not only genocidal but epistemicidal, in that indigenous epistemologies were discredited and replaced with a Eurocentric monopoly on reason (Ramose 2007, 313). This has extended to the purportedly neutral principles that have informed and animated institutions such as the company. The utility and desirability of the legal construct of the company as a juristic person can and must be interrogated by the state, which in theory confers upon the construct its very existence. In this process the epistemic points of reference must be consciously situated when populating the construct of the company, bearing in mind the real consequences that the construct has had and continues to have on persons of flesh and blood.

REFERENCES

Baird, Douglas G. and Henderson M. Todd. 2008. 'Other People's Money'. *Stanford Law Review* 60(1): 1309–43.

Bilchitz, David. 2008. 'Corporate Law and the Constitution: Towards Binding Human Rights Responsibilities for Corporations'. *South African Law Journal* 125(4): 754–89.

Brown, Wendy. 2000. 'Suffering Rights as Paradoxes'. *Constellations* 7(2): 230–41.

Brown, Wendy. 2004. '"The Most We Can Hope For": Human Rights and the Politics of Fatalism'. *South Atlantic Quarterly* 103(2–3): 451–463.

Brown, Wendy. 2015. *Undoing the Demos: Neoliberalism's Stealth Revolution*. New York, NY: MIT Press.

Callinicos, Alex. 2009. *Imperialism and Global Political Economy*. Cambridge: Polity Press.

Chomsky, Noam. 1999. *Profit over People: Neoliberalism and Global Political Order*. New York, NY: Seven Stories Press.

Dadoo Case. 1920. *Dadoo Ltd and Other Appellants v Krugersdorp Municipal Council Respondents*. 1920 AD 530.

Deiser, George F. 1908. 'The Juristic Person I'. *University of Pennsylvania Law Review and American Law Register* 57(3): 131–42.

Deiser, George F. 1909a. 'The Juristic Person II'. *University of Pennsylvania Law Review and American Law Register* 57(4): 216–35.

Deiser, George F. 1909b. 'The Juristic Person III'. *University of Pennsylvania Law Review and American Law Register* 57(5): 300–314.

Denning, Steve. 2013. 'The Origin of "The World's Dumbest Idea": Milton Friedman'. *Forbes* 26 June. Accessed 24 June 2020. https://www.forbes.com/sites/stevedenning/2013/06/26/the-origin-of-the-worlds-dumbest-idea-milton-friedman/#514888ce870e/.

Dewey, John. 1926. 'The Historic Background of Corporate Legal Personality'. *Yale Law Journal* 35(6): 655–73.

Fanon, Frantz. 1967. *Black Skin, White Masks*. Translated by Charles Lam Markmann. New York, NY: Grove Press.

Friedman, Milton. 1962. *Capitalism and Freedom*. Chicago, IL: University of Chicago Press.

Geen, M.S. 1946. *The Making of the Union of South Africa*. London: Longmans, Green and Co.

Gordon, Lewis R. 2007. 'Through the Hellish Zone of Nonbeing: Thinking through Fanon, Disaster, and the Damned of the Earth'. *Journal of the Sociology of Self-Knowledge* 5(3): 5–11.

Grosfoguel, Ramón. 2016. 'What is Racism?'*Journal of World-Systems Research* 22(1): 9–15.

Katzew, Judith. 2011. 'Crossing the Divide between the Business of the Corporation and the Imperatives of Human Rights: The Impact of Section 7 of the Companies Act 71 of 2008'. *South African Law Journal* 128: 686–711.

Lucas, Gavin. 2004. *An Archaeology of Colonial Identity: Power and Material Culture in the Dwars Valley, South Africa*. New York, NY: Kluwer Academic/Plenum Publishers.

Madlingozi, Tshepo. 2016. 'Social Justice in a Time of Neo-Apartheid Constitutionalism: Critiquing the Anti-Black Economy of Recognition, Incorporation and Distribution'. *Stellenbosch Law Review* 2016(1): 123–47.

Maitland, Frederic William. 1905. 'Moral Personality and Legal Personality'. *Journal of the Society of Comparative Legislation* 6(2): 192–200.

Mignolo, Walter D. 2009. 'Coloniality: The Darker Side of Modernity'. In *Modernologies. Contemporary Artists Researching Modernity and Modernism. Catalog of the Exhibit at the Museum of Modern Art, Barcelona, Spain*, edited by C.S. Breitwisser, 39–49. Barcelona: Museum of Modern Art.

Modiri, Joel Malesela. 2015. 'Law's Poverty'. *Potchefstroom Electronic Law Journal* 18(2): 224–74.

More, Mabogo P. 2011. 'Fanon and the Land Question in (Post) Apartheid South Africa'. In *Living Fanon: Global Perspectives*, edited by Nigel C. Gibson, 173–86. New York, NY: Palgrave Macmillan.

Ndlovu, Morgan. 2013. 'Living in the Marikana World: The State, Capital and Society'. *International Journal of African Renaissance Studies* 8(1): 46–58.

Ndlovu, Morgan and Makoni, Eric N. 2014. 'The Globality of the Local? A Decolonial Perspective on Local Economic Development in South Africa'. *Local Economy* 29(4–5): 505–18.

O'Connell, Paul. 2010. 'Brave New World? Human Rights in the Era of Globalisation'. In *International Human Rights Law: Six Decades after the UDHR and Beyond*, edited by Manisuli Ssenyonjo and Mashood A. Baderin, 195–212. Farnham: Ashgate.

Penington, R. 1931. 'Origin of Corporations'. *Corporate Practice Review* 2: 33–37.

Quijano, Anibal. 2000. 'Coloniality of Power, Eurocentrism, and Latin America'. *Nepantla: Views from the South* 1(3): 533–80.

Ramose, Mogobe Bertrand. 2007. 'In Memoriam: Sovereignty and the "New" South Africa'. *Griffith Law Review* 16(2): 310–29.

Rao, Venkat. 2011. *A Brief History of the Corporation 1600–2100*. Accessed October 2016. http://www.ribbonfarm.com/2011/06/08/a-brief-history-of-the-corporation-1600-to-2100/.

Republic of South Africa. 1996a. *Bill of Rights of the Constitution of the Republic of South Africa*. Pretoria: Republic of South Africa.

Republic of South Africa. 1996b. *Constitution of the Republic of South Africa*. Pretoria: Republic of South Africa.

Salamon Case. 1896. *Salomon v Salomon & Co Ltd*. 1896 UKHL [United Kingdom House of Lords] 1.

Sibanda, Sanele. 2011. 'Not Purpose Made! Transformative Constitutionalism, Post-Independence Constitutionalism and the Struggle to Eradicate Poverty'. *Stellenbosch Law Review* 3: 482–500.

Stephens, Beth. 2002. 'The Amorality of Profit: Transnational Corporations and Human Rights'. *Berkeley Journal of International Law* 20(1): 45–90.

Stern, Philip J. 2016. 'The English East India Company and the Modern Corporation: Legacies, Lessons and Limitations'. *Seattle University Law Review* 39: 423–45.

Tuck, Eve and Yang, K. Wayne. 2012. 'Decolonisation is Not a Metaphor'. *Decolonisation: Indigeneity, Education and Society* 1(1): 1–40.

Tully, James. 2008. 'Modern Constitutional Democracy and Imperialism'. *Osgoode Hall Law Journal* 46: 461–93.

1 THE CULTURAL VILLAGE AND ITS IDEA OF THE 'HUMAN'

MORGAN NDLOVU

The business of cultural tourism naturally depends on the idea of cultural differences. However, in the context of the present modern/colonial world order, where being human is no longer a natural endowment but is affirmed or negated by a system that creates a hierarchy between 'superior' and 'inferior' beings, cultural tourism has also become a site of denying the common humanity of modern subjects. Thus, on the one hand, there are those whose humanity is affirmed by the presence of the cultural tourism business, and on the other hand, there are those whose humanity is negated by the same business. In such a situation, the business of cultural tourism becomes a microcosm of the very modern/colonial world order in which the subject of being human is characterised by a tussle between affirmation and negation, rather than being something taken for granted. In the case of South Africa, the staging of the cultural village tourism business is underpinned by a struggle between the experiences that affirm and those that negate the humanity of the subjects involved, along the lines of race, class, gender, sexuality, religion and ethnic classification.

In this chapter, I develop a two-pronged approach to the idea of the 'human' in the staging of cultural villages in South Africa. The first is a genealogical approach that historicises the constraining structural conditions that permeate the idea of cultural villages in South Africa, and their conceptions of what constitutes being human or non-human. This is a situation that cannot be conceived of outside an understanding of the construction of the modern/colonial world system – a system in which the global tourism industry in general and cultural villages in particular are steeped. The second, phenomenological approach focuses on how the historically rooted structural conditions that still exist in South Africa produce particular ideas and practices about being human and not being human within the cultural village tourism industry. I will argue that while cultural village tourism in the country primarily seeks to maximise profit from the booming cultural tourism business, this happens at the expense of the humanity of the subjects who are on the dominated side of the colonial power differential. In combining these two approaches, I aim to address the limitations of both 'present-ism' and 'historicism' as ways of understanding the making of cultural villages and their idea of humanity.

THE MODERN WORLD SYSTEM AND THE INVENTION OF THE SUB-HUMAN

The structure of cultural village tourism in South Africa is undeniably a hierarchically organised one, with the capitalist class that owns the cultural villages at the top, and at the bottom an impoverished working class that provides labour for the villages. However, what is quite intriguing about the manner in which this structure is constructed is the idea that it is sustained through the coerced participation of those at the bottom of the hierarchy, who are its victims. Thus, in her definition of what cultural villages are, Elizabeth Jansen van Veuren (2001, 139) describes them as 'purpose-built complexes intended, with the help of cultural workers, as a simulation of aspects of the way of life of a cultural grouping, as it was at a specific period (or over several periods) of time'. This definition is quite perplexing, because apart from the idea it presents that these villages reproduce colonial myths about being a non-Western 'Other', the poor working-class people from indigenous communities who are employed there not only experience 'harsh exploitation and [other] demeaning work situations' (Jansen van Veuren 2001, 143) but are coerced to participate in staging the same cultural villages. This model of the relationship between superior and inferior beings in the cultural village is reflective of the normative relationship between superior and inferior beings in the whole modern/colonial world system, whose dehumanising structure is capable of inducing non-voluntary actions among subaltern communities in ways that may make these actions appear as though they are voluntary.

In general, the modern world system is predicated on the dominance and hegemony of a Western-centred modernity. This is a modernity/

coloniality whose origins are traceable to Europe's usurpation of world history (Ndlovu-Gatsheni 2013), beginning with the 'voyages of discovery' by figures such as Christopher Columbus and Vasco Da Gama in the fifteenth century. These voyagers ventured outside Europe to encounter the indigenous peoples of the non-Western world – peoples whose humanity they doubted on the basis of the fact that they practised traditions and cultures that were different from those of the Western subject.

These early encounters between Western and non-Western subjects are important to our understanding of the present conceptions of humanity that exist, even in cultural tourism projects such as that of the cultural village in South Africa, precisely because they marked the beginning of a system that would question the humanness of the non-Western subject and has continued to do so up to the present. Thus, for instance, as soon as Christopher Columbus stepped off the ship onto American soil in October 1492, the difference that he encountered in the cultures and religions of the indigenous peoples of the 'New World' made him preoccupied with the question of whether the non-Western subject had a soul. This question inaugurated the discourse of a 'people without souls' (Grosfoguel 2013) – a discourse that has justified the negation of the humanity of the non-Western subject ever since. However, the significance of the idea of a 'soul-less' people, a myth on which the modern/colonial world was founded, lies not only in the production of superior and inferior beings but also in the inauguration of a hierarchical world system within which modern/colonial subjects are classified. At the apex of the hierarchy is a Western subject and at the bottom is a non-Western, colonial one. In their locations at these two polar opposite positions, the modern/colonial subjects have contrasting tales of what it means to be human, precisely because being at the apex means that one's humanity is excessively affirmed, while being at the bottom means that one struggles to be recognised as human.

In terms of the sequence of events that unfolded after Columbus's 'discovery' of the Americas, the inauguration of the discourse of a 'people without souls' was followed by processes of dehumanisation that included the enslavement of indigenous peoples and direct and indirect forms of colonisation, all of which signified the radical nature of the doubt that existed about the humanity of the non-Western subject in the eyes of the imperial Western subject. This radical doubt was accompanied by what Ramón Grosfoguel describes as multiple hierarchies of power or 'heterarchies of power' (Grosfoguel 2007, 217) that cannot be accommodated in the reductionist analyses of the Marxist political economy and cultural studies paradigms, since they had sexual, political, epistemic, economic, spiritual, linguistic and racial dimensions. In other words, the architecture of the modern world system that came into being after the voyages of discovery of 1492 resembles a 'historical-structural heterogeneous totality' of sexual, gender, spiritual, epistemic, economic, political, linguistic, aesthetic, pedagogical and racial/ethnic hierarchies (Grosfoguel 2007), many of which are visible in the cultural village tourism of South Africa. Thus, as I will elaborate later in this chapter, the dehumanised subject involved in cultural village tourism experiences various forms of negation of humanity along the lines of race, gender, class and spirituality, to name but a few.

In general, the modern world system predicated on a Western-centred modernity is a synchronic, heterogeneous structural system that reproduces itself even in the face of anti-systemic movements and change. Thus, even though we live in a world that is 'post-colonial' in nature, there is no doubt that colonial tendencies and practices of the past are still present and intact, except for the juridical-administrative colonialism that collapsed with the demise of white settler governments across the non-Western world.

The answer to the question of why the modern world system remains, reproducing itself and reifying inequalities even in moments characterised as instances of change, lies in making sense of the difference between a 'world system' and a 'world order' (Ndlovu 2014). The former is more resistant to change, as it is sustained by the latter. Thus, in the face of anti-systemic movements such as the anti-colonial liberation struggles, the world system produces a series of world orders for survival, concealment, reform and continuity. This means that the demise of juridical-administrative colonialism in formerly colonised regions such as Africa did not inaugurate a new world system, but only served to produce a new world order that concealed the synchrony of the continuing modern world system. In other words, world orders represent a series of diachronic movements within a singular synchronic structural modern world system that is resistant to change – a process that leads to 'repetition without change' (Fanon 1963, 23) in liberation efforts to decolonise the world. However, the modern world system's ability to resist change is also derived from the failure by anti-systemic agencies to comprehend the historical-structural totality of the system, thereby waging isolated struggles that focus on singular components of the entanglement in such a way that the idea of a concerted effort is negated. Thus, for instance, a feminist discourse that privileges the challenging of patriarchy within the modern world system at the expense of racism, xenophobia, tribalism and capitalism, to name but a few other hierarchies of oppression, negates the liberation struggle against colonial modernity as a whole.

The modern world system, from its very inception, has always been constitutive of a modernity/coloniality project that produces beneficiaries of the structure on its 'brighter side', who are Western subjects, and victims of the structure, found on its 'darker side', who form the identity category of the non-Western subject (Mignolo 2011). In the context of understanding meanings of humanness as projected in activities such as those of the cultural village tourism industry in South Africa, the interdependent parts of the modernity/coloniality project that sustains the modern world system can also be characterised in the Fanonian terms of the 'zone of being' and the 'zone of non-being' (Fanon 1967, 10). The zone of being is in essence the brighter side of the modernity/coloniality project, and the zone of non-being is the darker side of this dichotomous system. This characterisation is useful in that it helps us to understand that, by its very nature, the structure of the modern world system produces subjects who are considered 'human', or the '*humanitas*', and those who languish at its bottom and fall into the category of the 'non-human' or the 'anthropos' (Mignolo 2009). In the cultural village tourism industry of South Africa, it is interesting to note that the anthropos is constituted by members of a racial, class, gender, ethnic, spiritual and sex category. This therefore makes the idea of deracialisation different from that of decolonisation, as the former merely replaces white bodies with black bodies without changing the colonial logics of domination and subjugation of one group of people by another.

THE MODERN WORLD SYSTEM AND THE POLITICS OF KNOWING

That the humanity of those in the zone of non-being, whose existence is equivalent to that of objects and sub-ontological beings, is negated cannot easily make sense to those in the zone of being, unless the subject who exists in this zone of being is able to 'shift the geography of reason' (Gordon 2011, 96) or jurisdiction and think from the position of being a dominated subject in the scheme of the 'colonial differential' (Mignolo 2005, 381). This is simply because the modern world system as a structure sustains itself through a colonial politics of knowing that privileges the world views of the dominant subjects. Thus, even though there is always a pretence of neutrality, our knowledges are always situated (Grosfoguel 2007; Haraway 1988), hence we always speak from a particular epistemic location in the existing power structures. This means that 'nobody escapes the class, sexual, gender, spiritual, linguistic, geographical and racial hierarchies of the modern/colonial/capitalist/patriarchal world-system' (Grosfoguel 2007, 213) when producing knowledge about a particular phenomenon.

In the context of examining how and why the idea of humanness in the cultural village tourism industry in South Africa is produced in the manner in which the villages have done, it is important to be open about one's 'geo-politics', 'ego-politics', 'body-politics' and 'theo-politics of knowledge' (Grosfoguel 2007). Such openness about one's epistemic standpoint is intended to undermine the common myth in Western philosophy that it is possible to produce objective and universal truths that are acceptable across different socio-historical experiences. This myth conceals the coloniality present in knowledge production by attempting to deny the fact that all knowledges are partial, hence even those that assume to be a 'god's-eye-view' (Castro-Gomez 2003, n.p.) are just points of view that pretend to be without points of view (Grosfoguel 2007). In this analysis of the idea of the human in the South African cultural village tourism industry, I speak from the epistemic position of a dehumanised subject in the power structure of the colonial differential, rather than from the position of a dominant subject such as the owner of a cultural village or a tourist.

While my approach is to present a perspective about how the cultural villages in South Africa produce particular meanings about humanness during the conduct of their tourism business, by attempting to write *from* a position of the oppressed subjects and not merely *about* the oppressed (Grosfoguel 2007), thereby shifting the geography of reason (Gordon 2011), it is important to highlight that social locations do not always correspond with the epistemic location of the subject that speaks. This is more pronounced in formerly colonised contexts, where the colonisation effect works at the epistemic level by successfully deploying the myths of objectivity and universal truths to make the subjects who are socially located on the dominated side of the colonial power differential speak from the position of the dominant subject. This decoupling of epistemic location from social location has led to a situation where the oppressed are hoodwinked into participating even in projects that perpetuate their own oppression. Awareness of this arms a research exercise of this nature with a road map for understanding how technologies of subjection such as the colonisation of knowledge, power, subjectivity and imagination produce colonial subjects, even in the absence of a visible juridical-administrative colonial system. This can only be reversed through some form of 'epistemic rebellion' and 'disobedience' (Mignolo 2009, 159) that can open a door towards knowing that which was meant to be concealed and remain unknown.

THE 'BRIGHTER SIDE' AND 'DARKER SIDE' OF CULTURAL VILLAGE TOURISM IN SOUTH AFRICA

The cultural village tourism industry of South Africa, like the modern world system that it mirrors, is constituted by an interdependent hierarchical structure of modernity/coloniality. Thus, it is made up of participants who occupy the 'brighter side' of the cultural village tourism project and those who languish on its 'darker side'. Those on the brighter side of the staging of the cultural villages include the owners of the villages, who reap the lion's share of the tourism income (Jansen van Veuren 2003) and tourists who enjoy the gaze, while on the darker side of the enterprise are the exploited employees who provide cheap labour as well as the performers of culture, whose impoverished circumstances force them to re-enact negative myths and racial stereotypes about who they are (see Ndlovu 2014, 105).

In order to understand all the nuances of the interdependent structure of modernity/coloniality in the construction of cultural villages, as well as its effects on the idea of humanity, it is important to briefly examine their location in time and space, the nature of their political economy, the profiles of their participants and the cultural content of their displays, all of which reveal their imbrication in and entanglement with the modernity/coloniality project of the modern world system. The first initiative to construct a cultural village in South Africa was undertaken in 1965 by a white entrepreneur (Jansen van Veuren 2003). This was at the height of the apartheid era in which the indigenous subject constituted by the black race was subjected to crude forms of colonial oppression and segregation. The timing of the construction of the first cultural village in South Africa, by a subject whose race category was in the process expressing radical doubt about the humanity of the indigenous black subject, must thus be viewed with suspicion, as it could not then have been possible to deviate from the dominant discourse about what it means to be a black African, seen from the point of view of the coloniser. It is, therefore, not surprising that after the physical erection of this first cultural village by an individual white entrepreneur, the apartheid government through its provincial arm – the then Transvaal Provincial Administration – followed suit by constructing its own cultural villages, in 1975 and 1984. This was simply because the idea of a cultural village did not deviate from the broader apartheid project of denying co-humanness of white South Africans with the indigenous black people of South Africa; hence the idea was supported and promoted at state level. Thus, for instance, the idea of cultural villages dovetailed well with the apartheid regime's divide-and-rule ideology, as these villages would fuel tribalism of the kind that was already being promoted through the adoption of 'Bantustan' policies.

After the demise of apartheid at the juridical-administrative level in 1994 the construction of cultural villages continued, but under the control of various stakeholders such as white and black entrepreneurs, as well as the democratic government and community-based organisations. While this time around there were many stakeholders involved in these activities, the cultural content of the villages did not depart from the colonial script of what it meant to be an indigenous black African subject. Thus, for instance, because of their displays of what are supposedly the 'cultures' of indigenous black Africans, the villages continued to be accused of representing 'myths instead of culture' (Tomaselli and Wang 2001, 23); of presenting cultural practices in a romantic, superficial and ahistorical manner, frozen in time; of reproducing stereotypes, generated by the West's desire for exoticism and imaginings of the primitive 'Other' (Craik 1997, 118; Jansen van Veuren 2003, 150) and of treating tourists as if they were for the most part uncritical, passive consumers who enjoyed such representations because they confirmed their preconceived stereotypes (Marschall 2003, 110). This clearly shows that even though the idea of cultural villages later came to be implemented by different stakeholders, including victims of coloniality, they remained a dehumanising project that inferiorised the non-Western 'Other'. It also shows that deracialisation of the structures of modernity/coloniality is not tantamount to their decolonisation, since the aim of decolonisation is to dismantle the hierarchies of colonial oppression that reproduce these structures in terms of a differently ordered racial composition.

The criticisms levelled against the cultural content of the villages are not without merit, when one looks at what is on display during the performance of what is supposedly culture before the tourist audience. Thus, for instance, themes of primitivism, barbarism, female nudity and cannibalism, among other demeaning cultural displays, dominate the cultural content of many of the villages. At the cultural village of PheZulu Safari Park, bare-breasted women perform what one can interpret as 'female nudity' and as a sign of promiscuity, while the warrior images presented by male performers can be read as seeking to sustain the myth of black Africans as 'bloodthirsty savages' (Ndlovu 2014, 85–86). This is not to dispute the fact that the performers have their own positive interpretations of the performances, such as that of displaying 'purity' and 'virginity', or the celebration of heroic exploits by the Zulu king, Shaka Zulu; it is merely to emphasise that a counter-hegemonic discourse that is steeped in themes that were popularised by coloniality is in itself limited in its subversive content.

Indeed, by the end of the nineteenth century, the notion of a savage, with its various connotations, had become a routine concept in descriptions of black Africans. According to Jan Pieterse (1992, 35), the nineteenth-century 'savage' is characterised by *absences* such as clothing, and other attributes of lack of civilisation. Moreover, 'savages' are associated with raw nature, and 'in addition to representations of Africans *as* animals there are representations of Africans *and* animals, brought together in a single picture' (Pieterse 1992, 43). At PheZulu Safari Park, the cultural village performances take place in a safari park, a nature reserve, alongside the viewing of wild animals, for example crocodiles and snakes. This spectacle of 'authenticity' about being a black African or a Zulu is further amplified by a display of craft objects at the entrance to the cultural village that depict nude images of what are supposedly typical African people, armed with traditional weapons and living in the midst of wild animals. This makes it clear that a cultural village such as that of PheZulu Safari Park is steeped in Eurocentric discourses that characterise Africans either as animals or as living together with animals – a development that is reminiscent of how the European iconography of the nineteenth century depicted Africans and the peoples of the non-Western world in general.

By and large, cultural villages such as PheZulu Safari Park are a mirror of the colonial exhibitions of the 1890s in Europe, where non-Western peoples were featured to rehearse what were supposedly their cultural identities before their European spectators. According to Annie Coombes (1994), almost all of the public displays of non-Western communities in exhibitionary narratives between 1890 and 1930 were underlined by a rhetoric of 'objectivity' and 'authenticity', and as such, had a number of different implications for the construction of racial stereotypes. During this time, Zulu people featured in the drama *Briton, Boer and Black*, where they were inhabitants of the 'Zulu Kraal' and were validated by Henry Morgan Stanley as 'real savages' in this way: 'Your "savages" are real African natives, their dresses and dances, equipment and actions are also very real and when I heard their songs I almost fancied myself among the Mazamboni near Lake Albert once again' (Coombes 1994, 88).

Such evidence of the structure of the colonial discourse that informs the content of many of the cultural villages indicates that these villages continue to project the cultural identities of black Africans in a dehumanising manner, even in the age dubbed 'post-apartheid' in South Africa.

The themes of witchcraft and black magic in the cultural content of many of the villages such as PheZulu Safari Park represent a Christian-centric imagery about being a non-Western subject. According to Sabine Marschall, 'a brief appearance of the Zulu traditional diviner or *sangoma* is also a standard at Phezulu (and at most other cultural villages), catering for those Westerners who are fascinated by "witchdoctors" and "black magic" in the dark continent' (Marschall 2003, 113).

The figure of a traditional healer is found across almost all cultural villages and is used to sustain the myth of 'witchdoctor', but what needs to be noted is that in the idea of the witchdoctor there is a discourse of lack of civilisation and of the darkness of the continent that justifies the imposition of Western civilisation, which is assumed to be the bringer of a necessary light. This celebration of Western civilisation as the source of light is projected through the theme of witchdoctors without noticing the contradiction in the term itself, as one cannot be a 'witch' and a 'doctor' at the same time.

The dehumanising effect of cultural villages is primarily enabled by a discourse and a process that colonise space and time. Firstly, all the cultural villages are situated outside urban centres such as Pretoria, Johannesburg and

Durban, among others. Lesedi cultural village is located just outside Pretoria, and PheZulu Safari Park is located in the proximity of Durban. This is not just a coincidence but is meant to project being an indigenous and authentic black African subject as being outside modernity in terms of the 'here and now'. In the logic of the Western imaginary, cities and urban centres are signs of a flourishing modernity. This is in contrast to the rural and semi-rural settings that are characterised as wilderness – a spatio-historical temporality that is associated with the original 'dark continent' of Africa and its 'backward' indigenous communities of the past. In other words, the urban represents the fullness of modernity, whereas the semi-urban or the rural is the antipode of this fullness. In this way, the cultural villages emerge as relics of the past, which existed in a state of backwardness; hence, by revealing an instance of a lack of human qualities they are a source of celebration of the triumphalism of Western civilisation.

The false salvationist rhetoric of modernity/coloniality is also discernible in the political economy of the cultural villages. Thus, despite the fact that they are presented as pro-poor projects, these villages are generally sites of economic exploitation and, in some instances, racial subjugation. For example, in the typical instance of a white-owned cultural village, the stereotypical colonial racial roles of the black people as workers and entertainers, and the white people as managers, owners of the means of production and spectators are perpetuated. There is not yet a single instance of a cultural village in which these roles are reversed. Instead, even in instances where black people are the managers, owners and spectators, the workers and performers are always black. This is a development that one can characterise in Etienne Balibar's terms as 'racism without races' (Balibar 2007, 85) – a development that reinforces the myth of whiteness as the normal state of humanity and blackness as an antipode and a sign of the lack of humanity.

In general, the idea that the cultural villages of South Africa are neither a salvationist intervention to address the plight of the oppressed, nor innocent of colonial matrices of power within the spatio-historical temporality dubbed 'post-apartheid', means that we need to redefine their significance. This cannot be achieved merely by focusing on what these villages are, based on their physical appearance, but must involve seeking an answer to the question of what they fundamentally stand for within the structure of modernity/coloniality. This is a question that requires a decolonial observer to analyse how the concept of the 'cultural village' was coined in the first place. Thus, for instance, what can be deduced in the idea of a cultural village is that it is made complete by linking two concepts that, in their totality, question the humanity of the indigenous subject. The first concept is that of 'culture', which develops out of the ontological question of being a non-Western subject. The second concept is that of a 'village', which emanates from the developmental question that doubts the modernity of the indigenous subject. The totality of the meanings of the two nouns 'culture' and 'village' results in a rhetoric that mirrors the 'backwardness' of indigenous people.

Cultural villages as a dehumanising project can also be characterised as aimed at revealing more about the achievement of the project of modernity/coloniality than about the backwardness of the indigenous subject. As Walter Mignolo (2007, 470) observes, 'the colonization of time and the institution of the temporal colonial difference were crucial for the narratives of modernity as salvation, emancipation and progress'. After observing the staging of the cultural village, an observer is meant to be convinced that the triumphalism of Western civilisation was, indeed, a justified project which brought 'development' to the indigenous people, as the indigenous subject was in a state of 'pre-modern' stagnation. The concepts of development and under-development are deliberately evoked, albeit indirectly, because these concepts serve as 'new versions of the rhetoric of modernity insofar as both concepts were invented to re-organize the temporal and spatial colonial difference' (Mignolo 2007, 472). The cultural village is, therefore, a site where the anthropological discourse of being and the development discourse of linear development meet each other to define the 'authenticity' of an indigenous subject as being backward and outside of modernity. This is why cultural villages are staged outside spaces where modernity flourishes, so as to pronounce eloquently that the authenticity of the indigenous people of South Africa lies in being part of the wilderness – a representation of temporal and spatial colonial difference.

Cultural villages can also be characterised as a sign of racial and colonial woundedness. They are a social space where the colonial subaltern that carries the burden of colonial difference faces a crisis of lack of options to avoid the threat of suffering a racialised colonial wound. This colonial subaltern is the black subject whom Fanon (1963) describes as the wretched of the earth, who not only suffers damnation, but is also coerced to legitimise their oppression by feigning voluntary participation in the restructuration of the structure of modernity/coloniality. In the whole of the non-Western world, the pain of colonial wounds varies across time and space, but cultural villages rank among the sources of the deepest wounds, since, in addition to the already visible pain of losing valuable resources such as land, the oppressed are required to mock themselves to appease the very powers that are a source of their misery. In other words, cultural villages represent misery within misery, as those who are the object of the project of epistemic death under the auspices of modernity/coloniality are not only forced to carry the cross on which they are being crucified, but are also required to entertain the crucifier as they suffer the pains of death.

CONCLUSION

In conclusion, it needs to be emphasised that the problem with the idea of the human today is a challenge produced by a dehumanising global structure. This means that projects such as cultural villages are not dehumanising in their own right, but merely reflect what is wrong with the modern world system and the world order in which we find ourselves today. In other words, there is no way that projects such as the cultural village can be transformed, or have a transformative effect on society, without a restructuring and re-ordering of the world which they merely reflect. In the context of a post-colonial world order, the cultural villages are a sign of its myth; hence they need to be read as a phenomenon that reveals rather than hides the dehumanising project of modernity/coloniality.

REFERENCES

Balibar, Etienne. 2007. 'Is There a Neo-Racism?' In *Race and Racialization: Essential Readings*, edited by Tania Das Gupta, Carl E. James, Roger C.A. Maaka, Grace-Edward Galabuzi and Chris Andersen, 85–88. Toronto: Canadian Scholars' Press.

Castro-Gómez, Santiago. 2003. 'La Hybris del Punto Cero: Biopolíticas imperiales y colonialidad del poder en la Nueva Granada (1750–1810)'. Unpublished manuscript. Bogotá: Instituto Pensar, Universidad Javeriana.

Coombes, Annie E. 1994. *Reinventing Africa: Museums, Material Culture, and Popular Imagination in Late Victorian and Edwardian England.* New Haven, CT: Yale University Press.

Craik, Jennifer. 1997. 'The Culture of Tourism. Touring Cultures: Transformations of Travel and Theory'. In *Touring Cultures*, edited by Chris Rojek and John Urry, 114–136. Canadian Scholars' Press.

Fanon, Frantz. 1963. *The Wretched of the Earth*. Translated by Constance Farrington. New York, NY: Grove Press.

Fanon, Frantz. 1967. *Black Skin, White Masks*. Translated by Charles Lam Markmann. New York, NY: Grove Press.

Gordon, Lewis R. 2011. 'Shifting the Geography of Reason in an Age of Disciplinary Decadence'. *Transmodernity: Journal of Peripheral Cultural Production of the Luso-Hispanic World* 1(2): 95–103.

Grosfoguel, Ramón. 2007. 'The Epistemic Decolonial Turn: Beyond Political-Economy Paradigms'. *Cultural Studies* 21(2–3): 211–23.

Grosfoguel, Ramón. 2013. 'The Structure of Knowledge in Westernized Universities: Epistemic Racism/Sexism and the Four Genocides/Epistemicides of the Long 16th Century'. *Human Architecture: Journal of the Sociology of Self-Knowledge* 11(1): 73–90.

Haraway, Donna. 1988. 'Situated Knowledges: The Science Question in Feminism and the Privilege of Partial Perspective'. *Feminist Studies* 14(3): 575–99.

Jansen van Veuren, Elizabeth. 2001. 'Transforming Cultural Villages in the Spatial Development Initiatives of South Africa'. *South African Geographical Journal* 83(2): 137–48.

Jansen van Veuren, Elizabeth. 2003. 'Capitalising on Indigenous Cultures: Cultural Village Tourism in South Africa'. *Africa Insight* 33(1/2): 69–77.

Marschall, Sabine. 2003. 'Mind the Difference: A Comparative Analysis of Zulu Cultural Villages in KwaZulu-Natal'. *Southern African Humanities* 15(1): 109–27.

Mignolo, Walter D. 2005. 'On Subalterns and Other Agencies'. *Postcolonial Studies* 8(4): 381–407.

Mignolo, Walter D. 2007. 'Delinking: The Rhetoric of Modernity, the Logic of Coloniality and the Grammar of De-Coloniality'. *Cultural Studies* 21(2–3): 449–514.

Mignolo, Walter D. 2009. 'Epistemic Disobedience, Independent Thought and Decolonial Freedom'. *Theory, Culture and Society* 26(7–8): 159–81.

Mignolo, Walter D. 2011. *The Darker Side of Western Modernity: Global Futures, Decolonial Options*. Durham, NC: Duke University Press.

Ndlovu, Morgan. 2014. 'Cultural Villages in Post-Apartheid South Africa: A Decolonial Perspective'. PhD diss., Monash University.

Ndlovu-Gatsheni, Sabelo J. 2013. 'The Entrapment of Africa Within the Global Colonial Matrices of Power: Eurocentrism, Coloniality, and Deimperialization in the Twenty-First Century'. *Journal of Developing Societies* 29(4): 331–53.

Pieterse, Jan Nederveen. 1992. *White on Black: Images of Africa and Blacks in Western Popular Culture*. New Haven, CT: Yale University Press.

Tomaselli, Keyan G. and Wang, Caleb. 2001. 'Selling Myths, not Culture: Authenticity and Cultural Tourism'. *Tourism Forum Southern Africa* 1(1): 23–33.

12 A FRAGMENTED HUMANITY AND MONOLOGUES: TOWARDS A DIVERSAL HUMANISM

SIPHAMANDLA ZONDI

Built on the dark underbelly of slavery and colonial imperialism, modernity required the drawing of a line between one part of humanity, considered by the colonial powers to be a superior race, and another part considered as inferior, thus making human co-existence impossible. But, as Aimé Césaire (1972, 2) shows, this division of humanity into ideal modern humans and 'the Negro', haunted by contradictory and unreconciled ideas, did not just brutalise the conquered, who remain dominated in many ways, but also dehumanised the conquerors, the dominant race to this day. This led W.E.B. Du Bois ([1903] 2012) to conclude that the problem of the twentieth century (and of the modern world generally) was the colour line, a line that sustains deep-seated wounds by perpetuating global racism and its ramifications for the humanity of those viewed as the 'other'. To deal with the challenges faced by Africa and other regions on the periphery of the modern world system, society first needs to recognise the fact of this division of humanity.

The colour line is of principal significance in considering what happened to the constitution of the human, the humanity of peoples. But it is only one of many lines on which Western modernity as a civilisation is based, including the line between Western culture as superior and other cultures as inferior, the gender line that places the male above the female in a globalised patriarchy, the line between Christianity and other religions, the line between Eurocentrism as the source of rationality and other ways of knowing as mere traditions and cultures, the line between rich and poor on a global scale, and so forth. This chapter critically meditates upon the subject of humanism today and how it impacts on the quality of global dialogues, in order to propose where we might begin to shift understanding of the concept towards a decolonial humanism so that diversal global dialogues become possible. I use the term diversal in this chapter to imply an ontological, epistemological and political position that is contrary to the hegemonic idea of the universal. This is because while the universal enabled an imposed homogeneity of phenomena, a diversal position enables heterogeneity to thrive.

THE HUMAN LINE AND HUMANISM OF A COLONIAL NATURE

The lines of division that run through Western modernity militate against the ideal of a common humanity based on shared human values, ethics, interests and pursuits. The human line, which often takes the form of the myth of race, leaves a large part of humanity with no true self-consciousness until they rebel against the norm of modernity. It leaves 'the Negro' and others – the indigenous people, the poor and the oppressed – with a double consciousness by forcing them to see themselves through what W.E.B. Du Bois refers to as the veil of racism (Du Bois [1903] 2012), placing them in a condition where they see themselves through the gaze of others. They end up with conflicting ideals, dreams, identities and personas, and are thus unable to say definitively what it means to be human and how to 'do human' in their circumstances. In these conditions, they are left with the burden of having to shout that they too are human, and that they need to breathe, claiming back that very basic human activity. This is what campaigns like #BlackLivesMatter in the USA in 2016 symbolise (Lebron 2017). The Black Lives Matter movement emerged, like the #FeesMustFall and #RhodesMustFall movements in South Africa (Ndlovu 2017), out of the cries of 'I can't breathe' by the black poor, and are a reminder that modernity, its capitalist world system and its omnipresent imperial man suffocate others, threatening to cast them into a zone of social death so that they become dead while alive. They become a death-bound people, living with the constant possibility of their arbitrary deaths as a necessary part of the world system (JanMohamed 2005).

The idea of humans and how they are organised is a major underlying problem here. The paradigm of humanism, upon which the modern world system is founded, organises all aspects of society on the basis of hierarchies of beings and non-beings rather than circles of human beings. Hierarchies define who is below and who is above, whereas circles define whom we relate to in the journey of life. The hierarchy creates competition among people, cultures, civilisations, races and families for a spot at the top as a necessary logic of success. This logic creates conditions that lead Du Bois ([1903] 2012) to decry being black as being like the seventh-born child in the human family – born behind the veil, made obscure as if one represents a shame in the midst of other members of this family. In fact, colonial or imperialist versions of humanism advance the humanity of the people of modern Europe and its diaspora at the expense of other peoples, leading to what Frantz Fanon (1963) describes as a zone of being and a hellish zone of non-being. This results in what Lewis Gordon (2007, 7) terms 'people hidden in plain sight'; these are 'people who are submerged' and, as a consequence, supposedly 'do not exist'. This fact of invisible people leads to their dispensability; they are subject to everything from the questioning of their humanity to demonisation, exploitation, enslavement, colonisation, epistemicides, cultural death and genocides. Such people exist as a problem, a conundrum, an inconvenience, as Du Bois ([1903] 2012) concluded.

In the paradigm of colonial humanism, progress is understood as moving from a low stage of being to a higher stage, where the latter is defined in relation to whiteness. As a result, those who are at the lower stage are thought to be unsuccessful. While there is room for solidarity in this kind of civilisation, the overwhelmingly dominant view is that one must first climb up to a position of having achieved success, and then pull others up from below or who were moving in the opposite direction to oneself. This is why philanthropy is largely the work of the rich who have a kind heart: they give a little out of the plenty they have towards relief for those struggling below them. The poor receive gratefully the crumbs that the rich gracefully allow to fall from their table of abundance.

In the capitalist world system, economic progress among countries is thought to be about moving through successive phases from low to higher forms of production, so that feudal societies are classified as backward and capitalist ones as advanced; in the case of socialist systems, the socialist phase is deemed the most advanced phase of society, one still to come (Mignolo and Escobar 2010). Both capitalist and socialist paradigms see economic development in terms influenced by the logic of hierarchies, in essence taking the European experience as universal and also justifying its universalisation through means that have included brutal processes of enslavement and slave trade, imperialist expansion of the European nation state, colonial conquest and rule, and neocolonial arrangements introduced in the post-1945 period that continue up to the present day. In their rise from a low state to a higher one, countries might have to undertake crude exploitation of the environment and of the poor, using the latter as a labour force with which to leapfrog over other states. The necessity of competition means that each country must think about how to grow at the lowest possible cost, and even at the expense of others. This capitalist logic, born from the colonial version of humanism of the post-European Enlightenment period, reinforces the division of humans into zones of being and non-being, indispensable and dispensable peoples, people who live in affluence through the labour of other people who must live in squalor, near or on dump sites, collecting garbage thrown away by the affluent to whom they sell their labour for a minimal wage. Super-exploitation is the experience of people in the zone of non-being.

This is a humanism that makes the will to power, the desire to climb up above others, critical for progress, at the expense of the will to co-exist with others in conditions of peace, love and justice (Ndlovu-Gatsheni 2016). Countries as political entities are organised in terms of the same principle of hierarchy. The logic of international politics is therefore that countries must acquire more of the currency of political power than other countries if they want to have greater influence over decisions made in the international arena that will affect them (Bull 1977). This made possible the colonial enterprise that helped give European countries an advantage in relation to other countries, one which continues today. It has enabled them to exert greater influence in regard to international negotiations about the global economy, the natural environment and climate change, energy resources, commodity prices, intellectual property rights and other major issues that are currently subject to international negotiations and decision-making.

In the experiences of the peoples of the Global South (hereafter referred to as the South), the powerful and dominant countries in the international system have paid lip service to the need for securing the common good, pursuing shared human aspirations and finding universal purposes of being, shared norms and values, and therefore common legality and legitimacy for all in the world (Chimni 2006). As far as their experiences go, the dominant powers do everything to frustrate fundamental transformations that must happen in order to produce a more equal human society and an equitable distribution of global power. They resist giving all countries equal access to world markets. They undermine the fight against the destruction of the environment in order to protect their multinationals so that these entities can maximise their profits. They shirk the responsibility to reverse the scourges of climate change and poverty. They claim that they want to do much, but not that which could equalise their societies with those of poorer countries. There is plenty of evidence of such roles and positions taken by the so-called developed countries (which are mainly the former colonial powers, with the USA and Japan joining this group in the twentieth century) on matters that are critical for the prosperity of developing countries, including access to markets, levelling the playing field of international trade, ample space to develop their own policies free of outside interference, eradication of heavy external debt burdens on poorer countries, reparations for past exploitation and oppression, and other such issues (Acharya 2014).

At the very base of all these problems, I suggest, is the form of humanism that was born in processes involving imperialism, slavery and colonialism as the dark underbelly of the modern world. This was a humanism that is under-theorised and neglected in discussions about the making of the modern world, especially in the literature on international relations and world history. It is a humanism that was necessary for the construction of what James Blaut calls a coloniser's model of the world (Blaut 1993). It is an understanding of human order that accepts the drawing of lines between some humans and other humans based on the assumption of a naturally unequal distribution of power, an acceptance of unequal power relations (Quijano 2007). In this configuration of power, human architecture and the intersubjective space of thought, the conditions of unequal status, opportunities and power among humans that follow class, race, gender and other divisive lines, are made to seem natural. This is a humanism that permits the dehumanisation of portions of human society whose humanity is presented as a disaster, an anomaly, an aberration and a series of questions (Gordon 2007). It is a form of humanism that, while masquerading as recognition of the humanity of many, permits the violation of the humanity of others. It is natural, in this orientation of humanism, that violence, theft of others' land and resources, the destruction of the cultures of indigenous peoples outside the West and the silencing of their voices, and the denigration and erasure of the history of others should be justified as part of the project of making humanity better – the so-called civilising mission (Césaire 1972). So, for Euro-North American modernity's construction of the human to thrive, the existence of monsters who would export violence and racism to the whole world is necessary, as a threat to be used to defend its imposition of a global humanism of its own making. This is a humanism that is rooted in a Euro-North American consciousness of itself, perceived as beginning with the abandonment of the terrible period of the Dark Ages and the entry into the era of rationality and secular modernity. Seen from the underside of modernity, it becomes obvious that the birth of this humanism coincided with the inception of the colonial project, so that Europe's discovery of itself became simultaneously the 'discovery of the other' (Scott 2000, 119). The enlightenment of Europe and its view of humanity required the invention of the darker other, in order for this other to be subject to methods designed to eliminate it as an option for how to be human. This is why this humanism emerging out of the European Renaissance was a rebirth of a sense of being human for Europeans, and a violent end to other ways and styles of being human. It was a humanism experienced in the South as what Fanon (1963, 312) calls a 'succession of negations of man and an avalanche of murders'.

Today, the inequality that exists between the nations of the West and other nations is not limited to unequal economic development but extends to other areas of human society. Western knowledge has been exalted to the point where it is hegemonic in the world. But we know that the enslavement and colonisation processes entailed the destruction of other knowledges indigenous to colonised territories, almost two thirds of the world in land area. The actually provincial Western culture has been made global to the point where it seems naturally so, when in fact the process of imposing it on others was accompanied by genocides and other forms of violence. Western technologies have been made hegemonic to the point that we can hardly remember that there are many civilisations and different cultures that created various technologies for human progress over a long period of time (Grosfoguel 2013). Western civilisation, like all other major civilisations before it, has given much to the world that could have transformed the world for the better, had it allowed the plethora of other civilisations and cultures to contribute to the diversity of human society and its progress. If it were not based on the logic of hierarchy which makes domination necessary, Western civilisation would not have wasted so much energy on dominating and destroying other civilisations in its search for complete control over the whole world.

As I have said above, fundamental to the construction of modernity in all its appearances and hidden forms is the construction of the human in terms of hierarchies and dichotomies. These have made it possible for forces of modernity to naturalise the domination of specific humans by a specific, generally self-conscious group of other humans. On this basis, space and time were reorganised in order to produce the modern world and the category of the modern human from which others were excluded, thus making permanent the invented categories of race, class, gender, religion and so forth (Quijano 2007). The resultant paradigm of the human is haunted by the fact of the questioned legitimacy of others in the construction of the world for the West, the Euro-North American modern world, the world of the whites, the rich, the male and heterosexual Christian. It is a co-existence of humans with inhumanity, for while some appropriate the privilege of being human, others are consigned to exist in conditions of bare life, living with questioned legitimacy in naturalised zones of non-being, in damnation and with disaster (Sithole 2016). 'Such people,' Gordon (2011, 97) argues, 'are treated by dominant organizations of knowledge as problems instead of people who face problems. Their problem status is a function of the presupposed legitimacy of the systems that generate them.'

This condition leads to false dialogues between categories of the human family, because the lines of ontological distinction drawn elevate some into what Sylvia Wynter (1976, 82) calls the 'omnipotent imperial men'. True dialogue happens among human beings or human communities, but under the spell of the colonial model of the world, dialogue turns into a monologue where the European man speaks and others have to mimic; he exists while others survive. According to the narrative of Euro-North American modernity, the European man invented everything, including the very names of others, the names of the places they live in, world history, and even the modern world itself. Jack Goody's point (Goody 2006) is precisely this, that the making of the modern entails the theft of the history of others and the installation of the European narrative as the master story in, of and about the world. It is a monologue of a stolen history. This obviously leads to a monologue about the past, the present and the future. As John Headley (2007) shows, the Euro-North

American modern's story is that all key modern ideas, systems and regimes on which the world today is founded are European. There is no question about the existence of these creations, but only about how they can be managed and improved. So, in this view, there is no fundamental debate about the story of the modern world. This means that if the global dialogues today are about the challenges and prospects of democracy, the state of human rights and freedoms, the questions of natural resources and wealth, the environment and human disasters, the global economic crises and so forth, this is not global dialogue in the true sense of the word, but a series of monologues in which Africans, Asians, Arabs, Latin Americans, peoples of the Pacific and so forth participate in mimicry rather than as sovereign voices. The discourse, the concepts and the language are Euro-North American, so Euro-North Americans speak, and others speak through the veil of Euro-North American rationality.

Today's big global dialogues about shared sovereignty, world peace, international justice, the world economy, global cosmopolitanism, global commons, international obligations and the diffusion of norms and values in the twenty-first century come across as just such monologues. As Sabelo Ndlovu-Gatsheni (2015) shows, global dialogues are conducted on the assumption that there is a clash of cultures, a clash of civilisations, often because of the resistance of what must be backward cultures to the necessary spread of the superior Western culture to other cultural zones.

AN ALTERNATIVE HUMANISM IS POSSIBLE: THE WILL TO CO-EXIST IS NECESSARY

I have said that the first thing we need to do is to discuss the problem frankly and understand where we are as the world of humanity, and why. The second task we need to undertake is to develop a new basis for the construction of an alternative humanism in order to make possible the equal recognition of human beings and diversal dialogues among equals, so that no part of the human family feels the need to assert and defend the legitimacy of its claim to humanity and to demand recognition as humans. A diversal dialogue is horizontal, vertical and inclusive – in essence, a conversation among equals – in which diversity, even if this includes fundamental differences, is not only tolerated and understood, but welcomed and encouraged as a necessary part of being human. This project entails the destruction of the pillars on which colonial humanism is built, at least in two areas.

The first is the line of distinction by means of which human beings have been divided into categories that are assumed to be superior and inferior. This human line leads to death for a large part of the human family, what Orlando Patterson (1982, 105) calls 'social death', and pushes the human project on a world scale to a dead-end. It also renders the world civilisation being imposed on all humans as decadent, in that it produces and reproduces permanent problems (such as wars, poverty, inequality, racism and sexism) that it cannot solve, to paraphrase Césaire (1972). If this process 'de-civilises' the dominant while brutalising the dominated, then it is a civilisation unto death that we are talking about, one which must be transcended through the making of a decolonial humanism on the basis of conversations or diversal dialogues across cultures and civilisations, with a view to bringing about a pluriversal world, a world for all. While colonial humanism led to a universal world, a world where others have to die to themselves, their cultures, their context and their aspirations in order to fit in, what is desirable is a pluriversal world where the presence of a diversity of cultures, civilisations, ways of knowing, models and modes of powers is necessary. To this end we must develop, encourage and entrench new ethics of life, ethics of peace and justice. These ethics must be designed to decommission the basis of colonial humanism. The new humanism will be premised on a decolonial understanding of humanism in which all humans are assumed to be equal.

The second necessary measure is to acccept that the new humanism has to be anti-bourgeois, anti-colonial, anti-imperial and anti-globalisation as we know it. This is not to argue for a mere response to these tendencies within the existing framework of global humanism, but for transcending them in the process of transforming human relations in fundamental ways. This involves a transformation of the very notions and models of power and space, which have so far been conceived according to the Cartesian principles of hierarchy and lines of distinction whereby the global village is the footstool for Western powers. It must be fashioned on the basis of what Ngũgĩ wa Thiong'o (2012) describes as 'globalectics': the ability to view and conceive of things from equally different, unique and diverse perspectives, thus collapsing the hierarchies of beings, of cultures, of languages, of knowledges and powers. It is about levelling the playing field so that difference does not equal inequality, and diversity does not imply inferiority and superiority.

There are three related organising concepts that have come from various parts of the dominated world which I want to propose as essential for the fashioning of a new paradigm of humanity, the paradigm of equality, shared dignity and solidarity. The first of these relates to the will that drives humans towards peaceful and mutually enriching co-existence rather than domination. Enrique Dussel (2008, 13) puts forward the idea of the 'will to live' as an alternative to the 'will to power' that epitomises the coloniality of power in the modern. Friederich Nietzsche ([1906] 2017) coined the latter phrase to describe what is believed to be the main driving force of humans, the force behind the pursuit of the highest position in life. It takes as granted that the human wants to rise above others to occupy the apex of a hierarchy, which also makes necessary the domination of some by others. Thus, this will to power underpins the colonial logic of dominating others to prove one's worth, exploiting others to amass one's wealth, subordinating others to establish one's power. On the other hand, for Dussel, the will to live is premised on the fact that the originary desire of humans is to live rather than to dominate. It is the desire to avoid death and extinction. This makes humans collective beings by virtue of their origin. The will to live is the positive force and capacity to move, to restrain and to promote. At its most basic level, this will drives humans to avoid death, to postpone it and to remain within human life. It leads to the constitution of political power as obedience of leaders to the collective will of the community, the consensus of the people based on their shared will to live.

This means that at the global level, achieving consensus must involve reconciling the will to live of the small island society of Fiji with that of the bigger society of the United Kingdom, rather than being based on the current reality where the former is expected to make sacrifices in the interest of the latter, because the dominant always have their way. Lasting and true consensus cannot be imposed by violence or other acts of domination driven by the will to power over others. This can only create a momentary quietness as the oppressed think about how next to express their will to live – by revolutionary violence, subversion or other, subtler ways of fighting.

The second, related concept involves a paradigm of wholeness and equality that gives rise to another view of ways of doing globalisation, described in terms of Wa Thiong'o's (2012) globalectics. The concept is derived from the shape of the globe and the interface between various points on its surface, as an alternative conception to that of the global world in Eurocentric thinking, in which various points on the surface all intersect with one crucial centre, forming the shape of a hub and spokes. The single centre point produces homogenising forces, universalising impulses and centralising tendencies, so that globalisation fundamentally entails being centred in the ways of the West, which have now been defined as universal when they are in fact merely Western. In globalectics, the surface has no one centre; any point is equally a centre with a significance of its own (Wa Thiong'o 2012). Globalectics suggests a dialectical interface between many centres mutually enriching one another; this describes a model of humanism, power and knowledge that supports mutually affecting dialogue, or multi-logue. It embraces the phenomena of nature and nurture in a global space that is rapidly transcending that of the artificially bounded spaces defined as nations and regions. Wa Thiong'o (2012, 15) says that the global is that which humans in spaceships or on the international space station see: the dialectical is the internal dynamics that they do not see. Globalectics emerges as a dynamic embedded in wholeness, interconnectedness, equality of potentiality of parts, tension and motion. It is a way of thinking and relating to the world, particularly in the era of globalism and globalisation, that promises to transcend the monologues and crises that underpin the global village, with their Eurocentric way of thinking and colonial ways of relating.

Having many centres of knowledge, of human civilisation, of cultural expression, of managing global power and of interaction means that we might soon have ways of solving the intractable problems of humanity, using many real options that a single centre cannot offer. The world we can envisage through globalectics has many equal centres of global economic activity, forcing the whole world into serious dialogue in order to advance to greater levels of mutual happiness. It has many centres of culture instead of only one – the one that now dominates, whose tendency to produce terrible levels of violence through its movie and media industries cannot be reset by any society other than the one that controls these industries. Even if that one dominant power was benign and gracious, it would still be wrong that global culture should be centred in it, rather than in many centres.

The third concept is one I have already mentioned above, namely a dialogic conception of humanity, affirming the need for different civilisations, cultures, ways of believing or spirituality, human groups, and the earth and humans together to be in continuous, mutually affecting dialogue. We therefore need to rediscover how to enter into genuine dialogues such that the ways of living of different human groups are mutually enriched, without one way of living disappearing in the face of another. We need to aim to become better without causing some people to lose their essence and difference in order to be like others. We need to make it possible, therefore, for diversity to be strengthened for the good of all humanity. The logic of being, of knowing, of power relations must be to enrich differences while growing solidarity. Diversity is our strength as a human society; it increases options and choices. This is especially true as the globalised world runs into problems that it cannot solve without changing its foundational, hierarchised logics, such as environmental degradation, water and air pollution, deforestation, climate change, the rise of lifestyle diseases, deep levels of poverty, inequality and exploration. The growing social anger everywhere in the world, with ordinary people saying, 'here and no further!' cannot be solved until we rethink how humanity is organised and what it means to enter into genuinely diversal dialogue so as to find new ways of being and doing human.

IMPLICATIONS FOR AFRICA

Africa's condition today is a function of the modern world in which it exists and for whose service it was reinvented a few centuries ago. The invention of this modern Africa was based on what Valentin Mudimbe (1998) calls the paradigm of difference that authorised the colonial production of marginal societies, cultures and human beings. It was imagined as an Africa of cheap labour and raw materials that the makers of the modern world wanted, and indeed, Africa has become just that. It has the heaviest concentration of minerals and other natural resources in the world and it exports them mainly to the West for processing into profit-making items of trade and commerce. It was seen as an Africa of stagnation, reliant on the creativity of the West in order to survive, on the fact that the Western man wanted its resources in order to enable the expansion of Western civilisation. And thus Africa has lost all of its own motive forces of progress – knowledge, indigenous civilisations, technologies of its own and so forth – and now depends on Western artefacts to succeed.

Within this paradigm of difference, Africa was imagined as a place that would consume the knowledge that the West produced and which it needed;

hence through various forms of domination Africa today is a consumer not just of goods and services made in the West but also of knowledge, concepts, theories and philosophies from the West. Africa is said to import 95 per cent of the knowledge it uses, and exports next to nothing, because the post-colonial Africa exists after the destruction and discrediting of all its indigenous knowledges.[1] All its universities are replicas of European universities, producing and reproducing knowledge from Europe lock, stock and barrel. African students learn about the human sciences – sociology, history, politics, anthropology, linguistics, geography, theology – as made and presented by Europeans, so that their education makes it necessary for them to think of Europeans as superior. They learn natural and applied sciences – biology, engineering, physics, chemistry, astronomy, architecture and nanotechnology – as Westerners present these.

The implication of all of this is to make it seem natural that Africa and Africans cannot bring anything to the modern world, and the West can do so. It produces a humanity of unequals, in which it seems as if Africans are unequal to other humans because Africa itself is unable to become equal with the West. This is the product of a paradigm of human society that is premised on the domination of the many by the few, a hierarchy of unequals. It is the product of a decadent civilisation that promotes values and ethics of decay: racism, classism, patriarchy, homophobia, sexism, domination, exploitation.

The decolonisation of humanism on a global scale is therefore in the best interests of Africa. As the most debased part of the modern world system, it is in Africa's interest to have the logic of the will to power that keeps it under the control of the West and others replaced with the logic of the will to live – the logic of human co-existence. It is in its interest to have the mono-humanist liberal conception of the globe as a single space dominated by a single centre replaced with a globalectics in which all parts of the world have the making of centres in them. It is also in the interest of Africa to end the monologue of what the West thinks, what it has done and what it can do, and replace this with a multi-logue of civilisations and cultures bringing together their shared will to live, to make good living possible for all.

It has been Africa's dream all along to take control of its destiny and be the master of its own narrative. It has been Africa's age-old desire to live, because to live is not merely to exist but also to have dignity and meaningful lives among others and with others. It has been Africa's struggle, after all, to reclaim its membership of human society as equals with others, shouting: 'We are human beings, not victims, aid recipients, terrorists or monsters. We are humans but suffocated, dying because of the domineering presence of the imperial man; we want to breathe and become beings again.' It has been Africa's aspiration to play a part in the multifarious conversation of civilisations and cultures, contributing to the fashioning of a new world civilisation made up of the diversity of humanity.

PRACTICALLY SPEAKING: AN ALTERNATIVE HUMANISM

The question is, how do we enact this decolonial move away from the colonial mono-humanism towards alternative humanisms in practice? In making the conceptual arguments above, I am also suggesting that this enactment begins with consciousness. This means that a new mind and new consciousness are an important precondition for bringing about this alternative way of being and doing human. The colonial model of being human is also a product of thought, ideology and theory. Therefore, as we contemplate practices that would enable decolonial ways of being and doing human, we should not be creating a binary between consciousness and action, thinking and doing, and theory and practice. In making the suggestions I set out below, I also do not want to be seen to be prescribing or foreclosing the opportunities for human beings to invent their own different ways of bringing about that which they have been persuaded is worth doing.

The first practical consideration is to embrace in earnest and in practice the ways of being long provided for in indigenous paradigms of being, such as *ubuntu*. This implies starting new forms of dialogues among humans, ones that are horizontal rather than vertical; conversations that are designed to revive mutual recognition and interdependence among humans as well as to rekindle the spirit of commonality and mutuality (Ogude 2019). Dialogue in the form that might be called multilogue, in the sense that it comes from all directions, is crucial for the revival of indigenous ways of being and doing human. This spells an end to vertical dialogues that engender inequality, domination and subordination of some by others.

The second practice is mutual recognition of the humanity of others (Cornell and Van Marle 2005). This entails being and doing human as a process of restoring, enriching and reinforcing the humanity of others, through our speech, the ways we relate to others, and the design of human systems and institutions. It makes it a duty for the new human to make humans of others, in order to earn their own humanity. This refers to human relationships at familial, communal, and national and international levels. It is about the ethics of mutual recognition, put into practice in how people relate to one another. It is also about infusing in one another, including in children, the value of mutual recognition. It discourages thoughts, spoken words, gestures and actions that diminish the humanity of others, the practices of putting others down.

The third practice is communalism, understood principally as a way of living, of co-existing and working with others. It requires conscious efforts to function in ways that build communities and communal practices instead of perpetuating esoteric individualism that breaks human bonds. Human activities are designed to enrich rights, responsibilities and benefits for communities of human beings rather than just for individuals, thereby strengthening the community and communal bonds enough to support endeavours that will make themselves and others more human. These endeavours may relate to developmental, security, political and intellectual goals. A communalist approach to achieving these goals breaks the bonds of patriarchy, enabling the full energies of men and women to be released for the common good. Gender roles become dynamic rather than rigidly tied to assumptions about the biological features of human beings (Ngunjiri 2016). Decolonising gender becomes a reality that delivers men from complicity with colonial systems of power, to the detriment of women (Lugones 2010).

The fourth practice involves endeavouring to achieve human excellence with humaneness. As James Ogude puts it, the aim of *ubuntu*, as one name for a variety of ways of being and doing human in indigenous thought, 'is to urge that, when deliberating within oneself or intervening between communities, one ought to bring out the best characteristics, such as the careful use of reason, especially in matters that require recognizing the humanity of others' (Ogude 2019, 5). Excelling in everything human requires conscious efforts to be an excellent human being, as the basis for being an excellent worker, leader, manager and so on. Excellence in sociality of personhood, as Kwasi Wiredu (2009) puts it, is a basic condition for excelling in every occupation and role in society. This differs from the ethics of excessive individualism that engenders the spirit of competition, the idea of succeeding at the expense of others.

The fifth consideration is that in the area of knowledge, the task of humans goes beyond knowledge production. Knowledge production as a concept likens the relationship of humans to knowledge to that of workers in a capitalist factory, where a privileged few inventors stand outside the community to invent, and the community works to carry out what has been invented. As a result, people of the South emerge as recipients of knowledge invented in the West. In this sense, knowledge comes about through what Paulin Hountondji (1997) calls extraversion, which sees the people of the South only as suppliers of raw data, and as importers of theories and methods, the insights generated by Western knowledge. This is enabled by the coloniality of being that dichotomises humans into beings in the North and non-beings in the South, for only the beings have the ability to produce knowledge. An alternative humanism engenders the culture of collective cultivation of knowledge, which mirrors the culture of communal production of food for collective self-reliance. In this way, all are beings and persons, capable of and obligated to cultivate knowledge for common and collective good; principal among their objectives is the bettering of common humanity, including overcoming threats to this humanity. There are no researchers and informants, only human beings in mutual recognition of one another as humans obligated to cultivate new knowledge, playing different but complementary roles. This implies a complete rethinking of Western research methodologies and pedagogies, in ways that Linda Tuhiwai Smith (1999) describes in detail. Smith provides a critique of Western paradigms of research and knowledge from the vantage point of an 'indigenous' Māori, and sets a new agenda for indigenous research as a contribution to the decolonisaton of ways of knowing.

CONCLUSION

The shift towards a truly diversal global dialogue, the conversation among cultures and civilisations that will enrich the diversity of the world, requires that the constitution of the human being should be renewed. This entails the liberation of humans from the coloniality of being whereby humanity came to be categorised, divided and confused through the notions of race, gender and other acquired categories that were central to the making of coloniality and its modernity. This condition explains to a great extent the dialogues of the deaf – or monologues – that characterise global conversations, both in formal negotiations and in other forms of discussion at the global level.

In these discussions, the West is speaking and others are listening, speaking back mostly in the form of mimicry, elucidation, contextualisation and application of Western ideas to their own situations. This chapter has shown that the fragmentation of humanity as a result of coloniality of being, produced through colonial humanism on a global scale, is a major stumbling block to the creation of diversal global dialogue, because it perpetuates such monologues. It prevents the coming into being of a shared humanity because it causes a portion of humanity, recognisable as the victims of genocides and an avalanche of other forms of murder, to continually have its legitimacy as full humans questioned. The vertical dialogue between those in the zone of being and the rest of us in the zone of non-being is a non-dialogue; it is a monologue designed to reinforce global coloniality and its manifestation in racism, sexism, homophobia, xenophobia and a colonial model of the world and humanism. Promoting indigenous ways of being and knowing without altering the human paradigm that suffocates anything non-Western is to slice at shadows. Critical to being and doing human is the responsibility to work towards a decolonial humanism, a shared inclusive humanity in diversal conversation with the plurality of voices that exist in the world. In doing so, we can enable an orientation towards human relations, community building and knowledge cultivation that draws from alternative traditions of being and doing human that exist in the world beyond the West.

NOTE

1 Personal communication, African Union Commission official, Addis Ababa, 22 May 2013.

REFERENCES

Acharya, Amitav. 2014. *End of American World Order*. Cambridge: Polity Press.

Bentley, Jerry. 2012. 'Europeanisation of the World or Globalization of Europe?' *Religions* 3: 441–54.

Blaut, James Morris. 1993. *The Colonial Model of the World: Geographical Diffusions and Eurocentric History*. New York, NY: Guilford.

Bull, Hedley. 1977. *The Anarchical Society*. New York, NY: Columbia University Press.

Césaire, Aimé. 1972. *Discourse on Colonialism*. Translated by Joan Pinkham. New York, NY: Monthly Review Press.

Chimni, Bhupinder S. 2006. 'Third World Approaches to International Law: A Manifesto'. *International Community Law Review* 8(3): 2–27.

Cornell, Drucilla and Van Marle, Karin. 2005. 'Exploring Ubuntu: Tentative Reflections'. *African Human Rights Law Journal* 5(2): 195–220.

Du Bois, W.E.B. [William Edward Burghardt]. [1903] 2012. *The Souls of Black Folks*. New York, NY: First Start Publishing.

Dussel, Enrique. 2008. *Twenty Theses on Politics*. Translated by George Ciccariello-Maher. Durham, NC: Duke University Press.

Fanon, Frantz. 1963. *The Wretched of the Earth*. Translated by Constance Farrington. New York, NY: Grove Press.

Goody, Jack. 2006. *The Theft of History*. Cambridge: Cambridge University Press.

Gordon, Lewis. 2007. 'Through the Hellish Zone of Nonbeing: Thinking through Fanon, Disaster and the Damned of the Earth'. *Human Architecture: Journal of the Sociology of Self-Knowledge* 5(3): 5–12.

Gordon, Lewis. 2011. 'Shifting the Geography of Reason in an Age of Disciplinary Decadence'. *Transmodernity: Journal of Peripheral Cultural Production of the Luso-Hispanic World* 1(2): 95–103.

Grosfoguel, Ramón. 2013. 'The Structure of Knowledge in Westernized Universities: Epistemic Racism/Sexism and the Four Genocides/Epistemicides of the Long 16th Century'. *Human Architecture: Journal of the Sociology of Self-Knowledge* 11(1): 73–90.

Headley, John M. 2007. *The Europeanisation of the World*. Princeton, NJ: Princeton University Press.

Hountondji, Paulin. 1997. *Endogenous Knowledge: Research Trails*. Dakar: CODESRIA Books.

JanMohamed, Abdul R. 2005. *The Death-Bound Subject: Richard Wright's Archaeology of Death*. Durham, NC: Duke University Press.

Lebron, Christopher J. 2017. *The Making of Black Lives Matter: A Brief History of an Idea*. New York, NY: Oxford University Press.

Lugones, Maria. 2010. 'Toward a Decolonial Feminism'. *Hypatia* 25(4): 743–59.

Mignolo, Walter D. and Escobar, Arturo. 2010. *Globalization and the Decolonial Option*. London: Routledge.

Mudimbe, Valentin Y. 1998. *The Invention of Africa: Gnosis, Philosophy, and the Order of Knowledge*. Bloomington, IN: Indiana University Press.

Ndlovu, Mandipa. 2017. 'Fees Must Fall: A Nuanced Observation of the University of Cape Town, 2015–2016'. *Agenda* 31(3–4): 127–37.

Ndlovu-Gatsheni, Sabelo J. 2015. 'Beyond "Clash of Civilizations" Towards "Pluriversity": Culture, Identity, and Power in Africa'. Paper presented at the Cairo International Conference on Interaction of African Cultures: Identity in African Arts and Literatures, Cairo, 1–3 June.

Ndlovu-Gatsheni, Sabelo J. 2016. *Decolonial Mandela: Peace, Justice and the Politics of Life*. New York, NY: Berghahn Books.

Ngunjiri, Faith Wambura. 2016. '"I Am Because We Are": Exploring Women's Leadership under Ubuntu Worldview'. *Advances in Developing Human Resources* 18(2): 223–42.

Nietzsche, Friedrich. [1906] 2017. *The Will to Power*. Translated by Michael A. Scarpitti and R. Kevin Hill. London: Penguin.

Ogude, James. 2019. *Ubuntu and the Reconstitution of Community*. Bloomington, IN: Indiana University Press, Kindle edition.

Patterson, Orlando. 1982. *Slavery and Social Death: A Comparative Study*. Cambridge, MA: Harvard University Press.

Quijano, Anibal. 2007. 'Coloniality and Modernity/Rationality'. *Cultural Studies* 21(2–3): 168–78.

Scott, David. 2000. 'The Re-enchantment of Humanism: Interview with Sylvia Wynter'. *Small Axe* 8: 119–207.

Sithole, Tendayi. 2016. 'Researching the African Subject in African Politics'. In *Decolonizing the University, Knowledge Systems and Disciplines in Africa*, edited by Sabelo J. Ndlovu-Gatsheni and Siphamandla Zondi, 213–34. Durham, NC: Carolina Academic Press.

Smith, Linda Tuhiwai. 1999. *Decolonizing Methodologies: Research and Indigenous Peoples*. Dunedin: Otago University Press.

Wa Thiong'o, Ngũgĩ. 2012. *Globalectics: Theory and the Politics of Knowing*. New York, NY: Columbia University Press.

Wiredu, Kwasi. 2009. 'An Oral Philosophy of Personhood: Comments on Philosophy and Orality'. *Research in African Literatures* 40(1): 8–18.

Wynter, Sylvia. 1976. 'Ethno or Socio Poetics'. In *Ethnopoetics* 2(2): 78–94.

CONTRIBUTORS

Gbenga S. Adejare is a doctoral researcher in the Department of Sociology at the University of Ibadan.

Olayinka Akanle is a research associate in the Department of Sociology at the University of Johannesburg, and a lecturer in the Department of Sociology at the University of Ibadan.

Cary Burnett is a senior lecturer in television production at Durban University of Technology (DUT). She is a practice-based academic with a PhD focusing on content and tone in South African screenwriting. She has expanded her field of practice from screenwriting and video editing to include video art.

Jojolola Fasuyi is a doctoral researcher in the Department of Sociology at the University of Ibadan.

Nokuthula Hlabangane is an associate professor in the Department of Anthropology and Archaeology at the University of South Africa, with a PhD from the University of the Witwatersrand. She has written on subjects as diverse as social, economic and epistemic justice, ethics, community and youth development, sexuality and HIV/Aids, and knowledge production from an Afrocentric purview.

Robert Maseko is a post-doctoral research fellow in the Wits Centre for Diversity Studies at the University of the Witwatersrand. His research focuses on the social conditions of black mineworkers in South Africa. His other research interests include decoloniality, decolonisation, colonialism, race and racism.

William Mpofu is a researcher in the Wits Centre for Diversity Studies at the University of the Witwatersrand. He is a founding member of the Africa Decolonial Research Network. His main research interest is decoloniality, especially the philosophy of liberation.

Morgan Ndlovu is an associate professor of Development Studies at the University of South Africa, and holds a PhD in Social Anthropology from Monash University. His research focuses are decoloniality, identity and development.

Patricia Pinky Ndlovu is a lecturer in the Department of Sociology at the University of South Africa, and a PhD candidate at the University of the Witwatersrand.

Sibonokuhle Ndlovu is a post-doctoral fellow in the Ali Mazrui Centre for Higher Education Studies at the University of Johannesburg. Her research interests are the inclusion of students with disabilities in higher learning and transformation in higher education. She also researches issues of inclusiveness in basic education, and the teaching and learning of disadvantaged learners in rural contexts.

Sabelo J. Ndlovu-Gatsheni is a research professor at the University of South Africa, and the director of scholarship in the Department of Leadership and Transformation in the Principal and Vice-Chancellor's Office. He is a historian and a leading decolonial theorist.

C.D. Samaradiwakera-Wijesundara is a lecturer in the School of Law at the University of the Witwatersrand, an associate researcher at the Centre for Applied Legal Studies, and an admitted attorney of the High Court of South Africa. She is currently a PhD candidate in the joint programme of the University of the Witwatersrand and the International Institute of Social Studies, The Hague.

Brian Sibanda is a researcher, facilitator and academic literacy co-ordinator in the Unit for Language Development, Centre for Teaching and Learning, at the University of the Free State. He is a member of the English Academy of Southern Africa and of the Africa Decolonial Research Network. His research interests focus on the decolonisation of languages and academic literacies.

Tendayi Sithole is an associate professor in the Department of Political Sciences at the University of South Africa. He is a founding member of the Africa Decolonial Research Network. He is currently completing a book project titled 'Mabogo P. More: Philosophical Anthropology in Azania'.

Melissa Steyn holds the DST-NRF South African National Research Chair in Critical Diversity Studies and is the founding director of the Centre for Diversity Studies at the University of the Witwatersrand. Her work engages intersecting hegemonic social formations and includes the publication of six (co-)edited books on race, culture, gender and sexuality. She is best known for her publications on whiteness and white identity in post-apartheid South Africa.

Siphamandla Zondi is a professor at the University of Pretoria, where he co-ordinates the Institute for Strategic and Political Affairs. He also oversees the Centre for the Study of Governance Innovation and the Centre for Mediation in Africa. Between 2004 and 2016, he worked first as the head of the Africa programme of the Institute for Global Dialogue associated with the University of South Africa, and later as the head of the institute. His intellectual interests lie in the area of Africa's international relations, as well as in theory-building in relation to decolonisation and the transformation of the modern world and its systems.

INDEX